CW01373657

Law and Opinion in Twentieth-Century
Britain and Ireland

Law and Opinion in Twentieth-Century Britain and Ireland

Edited by

W. John Morgan
Professor of Comparative Education
The University of Nottingham

and

Stephen Livingstone
Professor of Human Rights Law
The Queen's University, Belfast

palgrave
macmillan

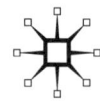

© Palgrave Macmillan Ltd. 2003

All rights reserved. No reproduction, copy or transmission of this publication may be made without written permission.

No paragraph of this publication may be reproduced, copied or transmitted save with written permission or in accordance with the provisions of the Copyright, Designs and Patents Act 1988, or under the terms of any licence permitting limited copying issued by the Copyright Licensing Agency, 90 Tottenham Court Road, London W1T 4LP.

Any person who does any unauthorised act in relation to this publication may be liable to criminal prosecution and civil claims for damages.

The authors have asserted their rights to be identified as the authors of this work in accordance with the Copyright, Designs and Patents Act 1988.

First published 2003 by
PALGRAVE MACMILLAN
Houndmills, Basingstoke, Hampshire RG21 6XS and
175 Fifth Avenue, New York, N.Y. 10010
Companies and representatives throughout the world

PALGRAVE MACMILLAN is the global academic imprint of the Palgrave Macmillan division of St. Martin's Press, LLC and of Palgrave Macmillan Ltd. Macmillan® is a registered trademark in the United States, United Kingdom and other countries. Palgrave is a registered trademark in the European Union and other countries.

ISBN 0–333–80089–3 hardback

This book is printed on paper suitable for recycling and made from fully managed and sustained forest sources.

A catalogue record for this book is available from the British Library.

Library of Congress Cataloging-in-Publication Data
Law and opinion in twentieth-century Britain and Ireland / edited by W. John Morgan & Stephen Livingstone.
    p. cm.
    Includes bibliographical references and index.
    ISBN 0–333–80089–3 (cloth)
    1. Law—Social aspects—Great Britain. 2. Public opinion—Great Britain.
    3. Sociological jurisprudence. I. Morgan, W. John. II. Livingstone, Stephen, 1961–

K376 .L355 2003
340'.115—dc21

2002192659

10 9 8 7 6 5 4 3 2 1
12 11 10 09 08 07 06 05 04 03

Printed and bound in Great Britain by
Antony Rowe Ltd, Chippenham and Eastbourne

To peace in Britain and Ireland

Contents

Acknowledgements	ix
Notes on the Contributors	x
Foreword Professor Sir Colin Campbell	xii
Introduction: Albert Venn Dicey, Lawyer, Academic and Public Intellectual *W. John Morgan and Stephen Livingstone*	1

Part I: The Citizen and the State

1 Public Opinion, Political Education and Citizenship *W. John Morgan*	9
2 The Triumph of Individualism? *Ian Forbes*	32

Part II: Public Morality and the Citizen

3 Matrimonial Property: Legal Developments and Social Trends *Lisa Glennon*	59
4 Public Opinion and the Regulation of Conception *Emily Jackson*	84

Part III: Culture and Identity

5 Language, Law and Politics *Colin H. Williams*	109
6 Ethnicity and Education *Mal Leicester*	141

Part IV: The Death of the English Constitution?

7 Europe and its Impact on the United Kingdom 165
   Daniel Wincott and Jim Buller

8 Dicey and the Celtic Nations: A Nightmare Come to Life? 194
   Stephen Livingstone

Index 217

Acknowledgements

The editors wish to thank the contributors for their patience and understanding during a project that has been several times delayed; Miss Gill Morgan and Mrs Karen Langley for their secretarial assistance; and Mrs Joyce Morgan, who prepared the index.

Notes on the Contributors

Jim Buller is a Lecturer in Politics at the University of York. His principal research interests are British public policy and the European Union. His publications include (with D. Marsh *et al.*) *Post-war British Politics in Perspective* (1999); and *National Statecraft and European Integration: the Conservative Government and the European Union, 1979–97* (2000).

Professor Sir Colin Campbell LLD, FRSA, has been an academic lawyer since 1967. He was Professor of Jurisprudence at the Queen's University, Belfast from 1974 until 1988 and has since been Vice-Chancellor of the University of Nottingham. In 2001 he was appointed Her Majesty's First Commissioner for Judicial Appointments.

Ian Forbes, FRSA, is Professor of Politics at the University of Nottingham. He is interested in the analysis of ideas and arguments within a context of social and political circumstances, rather than an analytic or rational choice framework. His current research focuses on public policy and bio-risks, such as BSE, HIV/AIDS and genetically modified organisms.

Lisa Glennon is a Lecturer in Law at Queen's University, Belfast. Her main research interest is family law and her recent publications examine the legal definition of the family in light of contemporary societal trends, the rights of same-sex couples, the viability of same-sex marriage as a strategy for reform, and the distribution of property and income on relationship breakdown. As well as being an Executive Committee member of the Socio-Legal Studies Association, Lisa is a member of the Editorial Advisory Committee of the multidisciplinary journal *Child Care in Practice* and is Northern Ireland Editor of the *Irish Journal of Family Law*. She has also acted as consultant to the Law Reform Advisory Committee for Northern Ireland.

Emily Jackson is a Senior Lecturer in Law at the London School of Economics. She taught previously at St Catherine's College, Cambridge and at Birkbeck College, London. Her principal teaching and research interests are in the field of medical law, with a particular emphasis on the regulation of new medical technologies. She is the author of *Regulating Reproduction* (2001).

Mal Leicester is Professor of Adult Learning and Teaching, the University of Nottingham and Director of EIRC (Education Inclusion Research Centre). She is also convenor of the network on migration, racism and xenophobia for the European Society for Research in the Education of Adults. Recent publications include *Lifelong Learning: Education Across the Life-span* (editor with J. Field, 2000) and articles on aspects of educational inclusion.

Stephen Livingstone is Professor of Human Rights Law, Queen's University, Belfast, Head of the School of Law and Director of the Centre for Human Rights Law. He is the author of *Prison Law* (with Tim Owen, second edition, 1999) *Re-shaping Public Power* (with John Morison, 1995) and *Civil Liberties Law* (with Noel Whitty and Therese Murphy, 2001). He is a former chairperson of the Committee on the Administration of Justice, a current member of the Equality Commission for Northern Ireland and has acted as a consultant on human rights issues for the British Council, Council of Europe, European Union and OSCE.

W. John Morgan, FRSA, is Professor of Comparative Education at the University of Nottingham and Director of the Centre for Comparative Education Research and the Commonwealth Education Documentation Centre. He is also a member of the Commonwealth Scholarship Commission for the United Kingdom. He has published extensively on the history and politics of education. His most recent book is *Post-School Education and the Transition from State Socialism* (editor with James Muckle, 2001).

Colin H. Williams is Professor in the Department of Welsh, Cardiff University and Adjunct Professor of Geography, the University of Western Ontario. His books include *Called unto Liberty: On Language and Nationalism* (1993) and *The Political Geography of the New World Order* (editor, 1993). He is a member of the Welsh Language Board and is currently writing a comparative analysis of multilingual policies in Europe and North America.

Daniel Wincott is a Senior Lecturer in Political Science and International Studies at the University of Birmingham. He was formerly Jean Monnet Lecturer in Law and Politics at the University of Warwick and has also taught at the University of Leicester. He has published widely on European integration and comparative political economy and his most recent publication is *Accountability and Legitimacy in the European Union* (editor with Anthony Arnull, 2002). From the summer of 2003 he will be a managing editor of *The Journal of Common Market Studies*.

Foreword

Dicey on law and opinion

In some ways it is remarkable that Dicey's original essays on the relationship between public opinion and the law continue to prompt serious contemporary reflection. This is probably because Dicey identified themes and questions of continuing significance, rather than that he provided fundamental insights or answers. In the original essays, and in the celebratory volumes which followed, his questions allow us to concentrate on *current* preoccupations with law and legal processes, the interface between changing opinions and cultural heritage, and the role of Parliament with special reference to issues of accountability and electability.

The context for the current volume is established by Morgan and by Forbes, both variously teasing out the tensions between ideas associated with individualism and those with collectivism. Dicey's rather patriarchal and conservative views are criticised, but frequently in ways that highlight the advances made in social scientific and philosophical understanding since then. Now our interest in sovereignty and public opinion draws us into confronting conundrums embedded in devolution and centralism (both in the UK and in Europe) and the complex challenges these raise for precious symbolic and cultural values. It is plausibly argued in this volume, by Buller and Wincott and by Livingstone, that the bigger questions involved in devolution and the European Union are still to be answered.

In considering the relationship between individuals and society, there are useful essays on the radically different agenda that now exists on gender, language and ethnicity. In Britain today there are issues of diversity that 'poor Dicey' could not have dreamt of, or rather nightmared. Dealing with matrimonial relationships and their expression through property, as Glennon shows, is massively convoluted with ever-changing versions of partnerships, home-sharing and same-sex relationships. The spectra of challenges to flow from contradictory notions of national identity and ethnicity – and the way these may be expressed in law or language – threaten most legal categories and confident social boundaries, and are considered by Williams and Leicester. We do not grasp, or even glimmer, what the fashionable notions of 'inclusion' or 'empowerment' will, or might, entail.

Relations between the sexes have been fundamentally and forever changed by the successful introduction of *in vitro* fertilisation techniques and the technologies (including cloning) that have arisen as a consequence. New questions concerning the relevance of the male of the species, the desirability or otherwise of lesbian couples having children and the difficulty of securing 'the welfare of the child, including its need to have a father' are well portrayed by Jackson. Questions here relate to the scope and tenor of regulation in a civilised society. Part of my own background involved chairing the Human Fertilisation and Embryology Authority – the first significant attempt to regulate in this area. We did not seek (or it may be we retreated from some posited) ultimate social authority. We established that protracted consultation as to what was 'acceptable' was the way forward. In a pluralistic, multi-faith, multicultural society searching for 'the right answer' is 'the wrong approach'. All that may be achieved – the most that can be achieved – is to negotiate what is not objectionable, and what is then most acceptable out of the available options. Here there are echoes of the philosophical doubts that were already familiar in the nineteenth century of Dicey.

This volume also invites us to reflect on political movements. Dicey's understanding of individualism and collectivism (and where they might lead) appears to modern eyes to be palpably simplistic and gauche. But, since his time, many groups and nationalities have embraced various ideologies and 'isms' with a certainty that was and remains frightening. Now we seem to be content to remain in retreat from the big ideologies and the arrogant 'isms'. In Britain there is widespread, if latent, support for a pragmatic commitment to 'the project' of advancing Britain's interest in a competitive world, but in a restrained and tolerant way. Certainly we are a multicultural and multi-faith society and the ways of seeking social advance are articulated within a secular framework.

As these essays suggest, it is likely that issues of gender and identity, genetic insights and scientific invention will form an important part of the agenda in defining what is meant by individual rights in democracies for the next number of decades. In Britain, finding out what the Human Rights Act will mean over the next two decades is likely to transform fundamentally our understanding of what an individual in society is, and how that person may relate to others and to wider groups. It is likely that as this process advances the 'neural framework', which dictates the relationship between individuals, regions, states and supra-national states, will be redefined as well.

This volume has been put together carefully in a way that one only appreciates on completion of all the chapters. They form a coherent set of essays. They are rich and suggestive, but not dogmatic nor definitive. They identify many of the fundamental and subversive issues which will have to be addressed in coming years. Dicey's original essays, and the volumes that followed subsequently, offer interesting social histories about debates on self and society, law and opinion, individuals and collectives. Echoes of some earlier notions remain even if the new issues we now address appear as hopelessly intractable to us now, as those early simple versions once appeared to Dicey. Argument and analysis seem to be of considerable use after all.

Sir Colin Campbell

Introduction: Albert Venn Dicey, Lawyer, Academic and Public Intellectual

W. John Morgan and Stephen Livingstone

This book takes its point of departure from Albert Venn Dicey's 1905 study *Law and Public Opinion in England During the Nineteenth Century* and the collection *Law and Opinion in England in the Twentieth Century*, edited by Morris Ginsberg in 1959. Yet who was Dicey and what relevance does he have for us in the early years of the twenty-first century? The biographical facts are fairly straightforward. Dicey was born in 1835, the son of a newspaper editor, and was brought up in a middle-class, evangelical Christian family. After studying at Balliol College, Oxford, he read for the Bar in London and practised on the Northern Circuit for a number of years. He was not a great success and struggled financially until appointed as a junior counsel to the Inland Revenue Commissioners in 1876. This was a significant disappointment to Dicey, who had always hoped for a judicial appointment.

However, at an early stage of his career as a practitioner, Dicey had also become a teacher of law; and was involved in the establishment of Law Schools at Manchester and Liverpool in the 1870s. He was elected to the Chair of Vinerian Professor of Law at the University of Oxford, the oldest professorship of English law in the world, in 1882. He was to hold this post for 27 years and, in that time, especially through his 1885 text *Introduction to the Study of the Law of the Constitution*, became the dominant figure in the defining and development of English constitutional law. In addition, Dicey's other academic writings included a major treatise on *Conflict of Laws*, which is still in use today, and the book on *Law and Public Opinion*, which began life as a series of lectures he was invited to give at Harvard Law School in 1898.

Dicey's text on constitutional law appeared at the right time. The late nineteenth century witnessed, on both sides of the Atlantic, the beginning of specialised academic teaching of law and the creation of law schools to inculcate both the principles of the law and a specific method of legal reasoning. Prior to this, lawyers had acquired their knowledge of the law on the job, relying as much on informal knowledge as on written texts. The literature that did exist comprised largely digests of cases in particular fields of law, with limited analysis of the underlying principles. When universities became seriously interested in the teaching of law, they required a different form of literature to provide the basis for students' learning. Hence the development of academic textbooks and casebooks, the latter including extracts from cases plus analysis of them – always more popular in North America than Britain – which sought to systematise particular areas of law. The late nineteenth century witnessed the first publication of textbooks in areas such as the law of contract or land, most of which have gone into several editions. Some of these textbooks are still in use today, though most have been superseded by more modern versions.

Arguably though, none has exercised so great an influence on its subject as Dicey's *Introduction to the Study of the Constitution*, though ironically this was not updated by subsequent scholars and is not in use as a student text today. Whereas later textbook writers in contract or tort have often questioned the underlying premises of the foundational texts in the field, nearly all subsequent textbooks on constitutional law in the United Kingdom still take Dicey's account as providing their organising structure. While many have criticised Dicey's arguments, they have not been able to dislodge them as providing an effective account of the underlying principles of the British constitution.

Dicey's book set out three key principles of the constitution. First, that Parliament was sovereign, in the sense that the Queen in Parliament has under the English constitution the right to make or unmake any law whatever; and that no person or body is recognised as having a right to override or set aside the legislation of Parliament. According to Dicey, therefore, England had no 'fundamental' constitutional law. Second, that the Rule of Law prevailed in England. By this he meant three things: that each had the liberty to do as they wished, except when prohibited by the law; that public officials could act only on the basis of the precise powers provided to them by the law; and that all legal disputes would be resolved by the ordinary courts of the land, even if the state was one of the parties to the dispute. Dicey contrasted the situation with that of France, where a specialised system of administrative courts existed, to deal with disputes involving the state. Third, Dicey claimed that Conventions as well as rules of law played a significant part in the English constitution. Conventions he defined as 'customs, practices, maxims or precepts that are not enforced or recognised by the courts'. However, although not enforced by the courts, some Conventions, such as that the Queen must appoint the leader of the largest party in Parliament as Prime Minister or that ministers are accountable to Parliament for the actions of their Department, were just as real and permanent as rules of law. Dicey argued that one could not understand the nature of an unwritten constitution such as that of Britain without an understanding of Conventions.

Dicey's account has come in for substantial criticism almost from the moment of publication. Critics have argued that it was wrong in fact and has become even more wrong as the years have progressed. The idea of the rule of law, for example, never sat easily with the Crown's substantial prerogative powers. Conventions like ministerial accountability proved true only until they were tested and even the sovereignty of parliament has begun to appear doubtful, especially after the United Kingdom joined the European Community. Others railed against Dicey's account as being undesirable in theory. They saw it as providing an unrealistic constitutional framework for a developing welfare state, where government, of necessity, had to have greater powers than that of the ordinary citizen. Beneath an apparently neutral account of what happened, some perceived a narrative highly favourable to the sort of mid-Victorian individualism Dicey espoused, a constitutional theory essentially hostile to socialism and state intervention.

However, despite almost a century of such criticism, Dicey's account of the constitution has not been displaced as providing the organising framework for most studies of constitutional law in the United Kingdom, and not a few studies of the politics of the constitution besides. His views have always had their defenders and have exercised an enormous influence on generations of lawyers, politicians and officials. In the absence of a written constitution his principles have offered a simple, elegant and reassuring account of what the constitution is. It has managed to straddle the empirical and normative, both claiming to describe what happened and suggesting what happened had a normative basis, that politicians and lawyers acted the way they did out of a sense of conforming to certain rules. By arguing that the key principles of the constitution can only be found in history and actions he undercut the claims of more normative accounts of constitutional theory, by suggesting these principles did have effective normative force he removed the sense of need for a more explicit constitutional framework to constrain Britain's rulers. Although, with devolution, the passing of the Human Rights Act and membership of the European Union, the constitutional landscape of the United Kingdom is now dramatically different from when Dicey wrote, his remains the map by which people continue to try to navigate.

One element of the consistent criticism of Dicey was that he sought to suggest that constitutional law could be clearly separated from politics. Whereas politics remained a matter of opinion, law could be presented as simply a question of fact. This was somewhat ironic as Dicey himself was passionately interested in political causes all his life, indeed more interested than in the legal scholarship for which he is largely remembered. His biographer saw him as a frustrated politician; who devoted many more years of his life to (largely unsuccessful) political causes than to the legal issues where his talent lay; and whose hopes of public office went unfulfilled.[1] Yet, as Stefan Collini has shown, Dicey did succeed as a public intellectual, in that he successfully placed his professional concerns 'at the heart of English politics and English history'. His work was intended to persuade opinion, his characteristic tone was pedagogic and, in comparison with other academic lawyers of the time, such as Sir Henry Maine, he was able to appeal to 'the prejudices of a wider readership'. As a result, Dicey left his mark 'on English political language in the three decades before 1914'.[2]

No issue attracted Dicey's attention as much as that of Home Rule for Ireland. Arguing strongly that Home Rule would not resolve the problem of civil conflict in Ireland but would undermine the constitutional security of the United Kingdom, Dicey launched legal and political attacks on the Liberal Home Rule proposals for over thirty years. He published three books on the issue and many other articles in journals and newspapers. Ultimately, his efforts were unsuccessful as, in the last year of his life, Ireland did leave the United Kingdom, though Dicey approved of the arrangements which allowed Northern Ireland to remain a part of it. While Ireland was his main political preoccupation Dicey also expressed considerable interest in issues of the use of referendum (of which he approved) and votes for women (of which he disapproved). He was also greatly concerned by the threat to Victorian liberalism posed by socialism and indeed *Law and Public Opinion* largely concerns the replacement of individualism by collectivism as the key animating spirit of legislation. It was a development Dicey largely opposed but also, pessimistically, considered as largely inevitable.

At the beginning of the twenty-first century the world Dicey knew has changed fundamentally. Dicey wrote at a time of British military and economic pre-eminence, though with a sense that the high point of this had already passed. His work on Home Rule was animated by a fear that this threatened the United Kingdom's standing in both spheres. No doubt he would be astonished to see how far this is now diminished and how integrated Britain is into a European political and legal order. While uncomfortable about the political implications of this he would, as an early comparative lawyer with an extensive knowledge of French public law, have welcomed the challenge of integrating different legal systems. The rise of collectivism he feared largely came to pass in the first half of the twentieth century, though arguably it has been in retreat for most of the last quarter of that century, though not as far back as is likely Dicey would have desired. Home Rule did come to pass; though not in exactly the form he feared and now has been extended to the other 'nations' of the United Kingdom. However, the connection between law and public opinion, which he stressed in the early years of the twentieth century, was maintained and strengthened throughout that century. Arguably, the influence of public opinion on law widened beyond the spheres of criminal law, labour law and public law on which Dicey largely focused, to include matters relating to the family and sexuality which might once have seemed beyond the reach of public discussion. The issue of what public opinion is relevant also broadened with immigration and the integration of the United Kingdom into a European and global order. At the dawn of the twenty-first century the relationship between law and public opinion remains as lively a one as ever and the stimulus Dicey provided to this debate may yet remain one of his most important legacies.

Who were his successors as the influential British public intellectuals of the twentieth century? Certainly the economists John Maynard Keynes and William Beveridge, both Liberals.[3] On the Left of British politics, perhaps the economic historian R. Tawney, and later the historian E. P. Thompson and the literary critic Raymond Williams?[4] On the Right, the question is more difficult to answer, although both Enoch Powell, a classicist who shared some of Dicey's concerns in his support for Irish Unionism, and Sir Keith Joseph, also a lawyer, would have a claim. Both were also Members of Parliament and held ministerial office.[5] The final decades of the twentieth century and the opening years of the twenty-first have produced no other obvious candidates, which is perhaps a commentary on the changed relationship of the academic to both intellectual and to public life. The purpose of this book is not to identify such candidates, but to examine significant themes, in an echo of Dicey and to a lesser extent of Ginsberg and his colleagues, and the relationship within them of law and opinion. These are 'The Citizen and the State' (Morgan and Forbes), 'Public Morality and the Citizen' (Glennon and Jackson), 'Culture and Identity' (Williams and

Leicester) and 'The Death of the English Constitution?' (Buller, Wincott and Livingstone). Sir Colin Campbell in his Foreword has indicated the focus of the individual chapters and we are obliged to him for doing so.

Notes

1. R. Cosgrove, *The Rule of Law: Albert Venn Dicey, Victorian Jurist*, Macmillan, London and Basingstoke, 1980.
2. S. Collini, *Public Moralists: Political thought and intellectual life in Britain 1850–1930*, Clarendon Press, Oxford, 1991, pp. 300–1.
3. R. Skidelsky, *John Maynard Keynes: A biography*, Vols. 1–3, Macmillan and Palgrave, Basingstoke and London, 1983, 1992, 2002; also J. Harris, *William Beveridge: A biography*, Clarendon Press, Oxford, 1977.
4. R. Terrill, *R. H. Tawney and His Times: Socialism as fellowship*, Deutsch, London, 1974; S. Woodhams, *History in the Making: Raymond Williams, Edward Thompson and radical intellectuals 1936–1956*, Merlin Press, London, 2001; W. J. Morgan and P. Preston (eds.), *Raymond Williams: Politics, education, letters*, Macmillan, London and Basingstoke, and St. Martin's Press, New York, 1993.
5. R. Cockett, *Thinking the Unthinkable: Think-tanks and the economic counter-revolution, 1931–1983*, Fontana Press, London, 1995. Powell was Minister of Health and Joseph was Secretary of State for Education.

Part I
The Citizen and the State

1
Public Opinion, Political Education and Citizenship

W. John Morgan

Introduction

As D. G. Boyce reminded us in his excellent short analysis of 'Public opinion and the historians',[1] A. V. Dicey's volume *Lectures on the Relation between Law and Public Opinion in England During the Nineteenth Century* is one of the better known accounts of the relationship between public opinion and public policy in British intellectual history.[2] Dicey's intention, Boyce said, was 'to bring the growth of English law during a hundred years into connexion with the course of English thought'. His analysis focused on three periods during the century. The first, between 1800 and 1830, was described as that of Old Toryism, when legislation was determined by an essentially complacent political order, self-confident after the victories in the wars against France. The second was that dominated by the rise of individualism, manifested in the political thought of Jeremy Bentham. The legislation passed during this period was essentially *laissez-faire* in intent and outcome, clearing the way for individual initiative, enterprise and the expression of personal freedom. The third and final period, between 1865 and 1900, Dicey described as one of collectivism. By this he meant a growth in direct intervention by the state in public affairs and the life of the individual citizen. He regarded this period as one influenced by 'the school of opinion often termed (and generally by more or less hostile critics) Socialism, which favours the intervention of the State, even at some sacrifice of individual freedom, for the purpose of conferring benefit upon the mass of the people'. Dicey added to this definition, identifying the types of state action he had in mind and commenting on his examples.[3] His definition and list covered practically all legislation attempting social reform introduced during the final quarter of the nineteenth century.

The originality of such reforms lay, as T. H. Marshall has commented, in that they diverged from the earlier view that the state should be concerned only with the destitute and helpless and that any action on their behalf should not affect the ordinary life of the public. As Marshall emphasised, Dicey was correct in saying that such state intervention was what most people considered as 'socialism', except, of course, 'for the real socialists who meant much more by it'.[4] But he was wrong to argue that the term was used chiefly pejoratively by hostile critics of socialism. Dicey considered the reforms of the Liberal government of 1885 to be moving, undesirably, towards a state-dominated socialism. But civic politicians such as Joseph Chamberlain responded that: 'every kindly act of legislation by which the community has sought to discharge it responsibilities and obligations to the poor, is socialism; but none the worse for that'.[5]

As Marshall points out, although Chamberlain's thinking may have been confused, the motive was clear: 'It had become necessary to assert a belief in the responsibility of government for the welfare of the people and to deny to the "official" Socialists any monopoly of good intentions, by borrowing their name and rendering it innocuous'.[6]

This interpretation, although it has since been questioned and revised by historians, nevertheless had a significant influence on general perceptions of British political life and of the development of public policy during the nineteenth century. On the other hand, as Boyce says, Dicey's methodological approach has received severe criticism, especially from political scientists. Fundamentally, he did not offer a clear definition of what he meant by the term 'public opinion', and his language was often vague and general. He regarded Benthamism as 'the pre-dominant opinion of the time' and said that 'in England the beliefs and sentiments which, during the nineteenth century, have governed the development of the law have, in strictness, been public opinion, for they have been the wishes and ideas as to legislation held by the people of England, or to speak with more precision, by the majority of the citizens who have at a given moment taken an effective part in public life'.[7] This suggested that public opinion was, in Dicey's opinion, that of a select few, of an educated elite. Indeed, he advised his readers to consider the specific influence on legislation of thinkers such as Bentham, Dickens, Harriet Martineau and John Stuart Mill.

This is not, in itself, bad advice, but it is not necessarily a guide to public opinion, unless narrowly defined. It is in contradiction to an earlier comment when he suggested that English public opinion does not, 'as in some foreign countries, mean merely the convictions held by a small number of men or even a single individual'.[8] He quoted Sir Robert Peel, who spoke of 'the tone of England, of the great compound of folly, weakness, prejudice, wrong feeling, right feeling, obstinacy, and newspaper paragraphs which is called public opinion'.[9] Given such lack of precision, it is hardly surprising, as Boyce observes, that later generations with their emphasis on the collection and interpretation of data, on the detailed content analysis of newspapers and the careful definition of concepts used in political science, have neglected Dicey. Boyce's recommendation, for historians at least, was to give up any general consideration of what is understood by public opinion and instead, by going directly to the sources, try to assess what public opinion might have been on any particular issue. This is the approach followed by the chapters in this volume.

An accumulation of such case studies might, of course, enable us to discern longer-term and more general political trends that have had their effect on public policy and legislation. It may enable us to trace the development of an ideological climate, of the political education of both elite and mass opinion away from an orthodoxy of public policy and towards the acceptance of something significantly, even radically, different. By 'ideological climate' is meant the prevalent intellectual atmosphere within which political events are shaped. It is distinct from those ideas which, whatever their intrinsic merits or the enthusiasm with which they are argued, do not have such influence.[10] This gives the term more precision than the definition of public opinion offered Sir Robert Peel quoted above.[11]

Public opinion and political education

The political education of the peoples of Britain and Ireland, as elsewhere for that matter, cannot be understood without reference to history, which defines the problems with which they have had to deal as societies. The history of British culture is not without examples, either of distinguished attempts at political philosophy amounting, it is claimed, to a tradition, or efforts, usually on clear-cut ideological lines, to develop a politically conscious population or section of it, capable of translating political philosophy into practice. As far as the former are concerned, one need only remind that the British are, after all, the compatriots of thinkers and, sometimes, activists as outstanding and as politically diverse as Gerrard Winstanley, Thomas Hobbes, John Locke, Edmund Burke, Tom Paine, David Hume and John Stuart Mill. This was, essentially, Dicey's point. In the twentieth century, it may be true that such figures were fewer and perhaps less remarkable, though liberals such as Hobhouse, social democrats such as Tawney and conservatives such as Oakeshott were still significant, as were Raymond Williams and perhaps even Enoch Powell for later in the century. As for social and political movements, there have been times, notably in the seventeenth century and between about 1750 and 1850, when the British people have engaged in political activity and debate with quite intense radicalism.

During the Edwardian period, a number of issues became the subject of bitter political contention and debate, including Ireland, trade unionism, feminism and the political status of women, and the powers of the House of Lords: a familiar list. Towards mid-century, the experiences of the interwar years, of mass unemployment, of extreme political ideologies and, later, of the so-called 'People's War' of 1939–45, brought about a level of popular political consciousness and participation which resulted in the election in 1945 of the first majority Labour government. It was this government that finally established the principle of one person, one vote at British parliamentary elections through The Representation of the People Act of 1949. This abolished the parliamentary seats reserved hitherto for the universities, which allowed graduates the opportunity of a double vote and the privilege of double representation. Yet, despite these examples, the notion persists that the British are scornful of theory, ignorant of political concepts and processes and, in comparison with their European neighbours, generally indifferent to politics. Indeed, a quasi-official report, published during Margaret Thatcher's first period as prime minister, implied that the citizens of the United Kingdom were politically illiterate to the point 'where the democratic machinery is put at risk'.[12] This was an alarming observation on the children of the 'Mother of Parliaments'. It was suggested that the prime purpose of political education in the context of adult education was to enable the British population 'to move from a representative democracy to a participatory democracy'.[13] Echoing the opinion of the important, but neglected Russell Report,[14] that adult education is a particularly suitable vehicle for social and political education, such statements rested on two fundamental assumptions. The first is that both knowledge of and participation in public affairs are limited in Britain and, second, that the purpose of an adult political education is, essentially, to achieve a combination of consciousness, empowerment and emancipation. They may be compared with the need for the education of public opinion, emphasised by Hermann Mannheim and by Ben Roberts in their respective contributions to the volume on *Law and Opinion in England in the 20th Century*.[15] Mannheim made the point that governments often 'take refuge behind what it proclaims to be public opinion without making any attempt to find out what the state of public opinion really was on the points at issue',[16] let alone attempt to educate or inform it. Yet this was the duty of government, but also of civic associations independently of the state.

This ideology, radical in intent, in fact has a long pedigree in Britain, although ignored by Dicey. It exists alongside, and usually in contention with, more conservative notions of education for citizenship. It may certainly be seen as a late challenge to the political socialisation of children during the years of compulsory education and training; in Britain, schooling extends from the age of five to sixteen. To a variable and certainly imprecise degree this experience affects political attitudes later in life. It is accepted that, as a central feature of practice, the state has not attempted to control political education either formally or explicitly until very recently. This is because the British have had state enforcement of education historically, but not in fact state-controlled education. It is an important distinction. In other words, the state has made education legally compulsory for its citizens between certain ages but, until the recent introduction of a National Curriculum, has not attempted to set down in precise terms what those citizens should learn. The British experience, it is pointed out, has been different from that of others where the state has either laid down centralised curricula or has promoted, for its own purposes, either the study of certain subjects or their proscription. France is an example of the former and the Federal Republic of Germany of the latter (to some extent mitigated by being a federal system). In both, the role of the state in education has been more explicit than in Britain. In Germany in particular, for reasons of recent history, political education has been developed as a distinct, overt and generously financed programme. Its purpose is to develop democratic values and to instil a sense of commitment to a common citizenship that will be reflected later in national public opinion.

In Britain, on the other hand, the role of the state has, until recently, been indirect, setting out a legal framework and ensuring common standards through the work of HM Inspectors. This has certainly been true of what has passed for formal political education. Indeed, it is only in the last twenty years that serious attempts have been made to introduce it into the school curriculum. Even so, what has been advocated and practised is the teaching of the discipline of political science or government as a subject, as a body of information or set of procedures or techniques. This essentially academic approach, though valuable in itself, is incomplete in that it rests on a misconception, both of the nature of political education and of the way in which it can be made effective for the overwhelming majority of citizens, of whatever age. This consists in seeing political education solely as a curriculum product that can be packaged and delivered and not also as a process that can be grasped and applied both intuitively and intellectually.

Democratic political education and civil society

Certainly, the understanding or explanation of political activity such that participation becomes both possible and meaningful is the fundamental objective of political education. Political activity should, especially in a highly developed country such as Britain, be interpreted broadly. It means essentially the manner by which common affairs are conducted, by people brought together by chance or choice, e.g. born into a nation, having acquired legal citizenship by due process or simply enrolled as a member of a club or association. The British state is the overarching institution, but beneath are to be found innumerable associations, clubs, networks, parties, trade unions, religious groups, and so on: the fabric of civil society. Each of these has its formal or informal connections to the state. Dennis Lloyd, in his contribution to *Law and Opinion in England in the 20th Century*, focused on the problem of the place of associations within the state. He argued that while 'individual freedom is of little worth if it does not include the right to associate together for common purposes not prohibited by law', there was also the necessity consider how 'the individual or a minority might be protected against the oppressive action of its own association'.[17]

The membership of such associations overlaps at innumerable points, uniting ultimately in the status of subject of the Crown and citizen of the United Kingdom of Great Britain and Northern Ireland. In addition, there is the political relationship to the state of those without such status, such as resident foreign citizens and others, such as refugees and asylum seekers. The Marxist view of the state, of course, is to consider it the supreme instrument of class power, granting ideological approval and even formal status to those groups that reinforce its own legitimacy. The conduct of each association's affairs, whether state, political party or local sports club, is then a political activity in which every member has both rights and obligations. Politics in this sense is a universal activity, while the knowledge and techniques that make it possible and effective must be learned. Whether this is done formally or informally, it is a necessary task if the group, at whatever level it may be operating, to maintain itself and function adequately in the pursuit of its objectives.

Again, such a definition of political activity and political education, or better political learning, assumes the negotiated possibility of both continuity and change. If this breaks down, then civil war, dissolution or resignation will follow. Democratic political education should, consequently, aim to provide both knowledge and the capacity for negotiation, decision and action. Finally, it should be remembered that political education should not be regarded as an optional extra, bolted on to the political process; this is one of the problems with the formal curriculum approach. Political education and political learning should be integrated with the political activity of a democratic civil society and offer the possibility of an informed practice.

D. W. Brogan analysed this definition of political education in his influential Weil Lectures, at the University of North Carolina in 1959. Identifying the traditional character of British citizenship, he referred to the thousands of societies of all types, which bring together millions of individuals for their own particular common purpose. It should be noted that this tradition of civil society pre-dates the coming of universal suffrage and built towards it. The peasant or the town worker 'who joined a Methodist meeting or a radical society' might have had, as yet, no voice in choosing the members of the House of Commons, but was, nevertheless, learning and passing on what had been understood of the nature of citizenship. Over the centuries, the British won the right, and in Brogan's opinion, retain the duty to create their own 'bodies politic'.[18]

It is not suggested, of course, that such an education in politics is confined to Britain. It in fact lies at the heart of an authentic political education, appropriate to the members of a democratic state and civil society. If such civil associations were to be suppressed, as they were during the twentieth century in Nazi Germany, Fascist Italy, Stalinist Russia and Imperial Japan, or simply fall into disuse through public cynicism, indifference or neglect, then political activity would cease also. A polarisation would eventually be reached with individuals acting less and less as social and political beings and government reduced steadily to direction by a remote, bureaucratic and even totalitarian state. Although Britain and Ireland are far from this condition, any move towards widening the range of possibilities for citizens to organise and provide for themselves is to be welcomed.

This is not, however, to move blindly in the direction of complete *laissez-faire*. In complex industrial societies, whatever the pattern of economic ownership, there are many needs that may be best or even only met through collective public action, though the mechanism for this may be devolved to the most appropriate local levels. The emphasis remains on reconciling the individual with the social, rather than on the statist. The point is that the encouragement of independent activity by groups of citizens, as well as individuals, increases both their appetite for active citizenship and their capacity for monitoring, questioning and regulating the professional activities of the state. The distinction between the broad political learning appropriate to the citizen and the more narrowly focused, professional and vocational training for government was well made by Michael Oakeshott. The former may well bring meaning to the current slogans of 'empowerment', 'participatory democracy' and 'lifelong learning'. As Oakeshott observes: 'if political activity is impossible without a certain kind of knowledge and a certain kind of education, then this knowledge and education are not mere appendages to the activity but are part of the activity itself and must be incorporated in our understanding of it'. This means, he goes on to say, 'knowledge as profound as we can make it, of our tradition of political behaviour'. Other knowledge, such as that of other societies and other systems, is certainly desirable, by way of comparison, but without our own local knowledge, based on history and experience 'we cannot make use of whatever else we may have learned'.[19]

Political education and the practice of citizenship

During the twentieth century there were many examples of the relationship between political education and civil society on the one hand, and the practice of citizenship on the other. Each of them influenced or changed the legislative behaviour of the state to some extent, usually progressively, occasionally not. A few are considered here by way of example. A classic instance in the First World War was the Union of Democratic Control (UDC), formed in September 1914, with the purpose of campaigning against 'secret diplomacy', which it held responsible for the war, and its replacement by the democratic control of foreign policy by a politically educated electorate. It also made specific policy recommendations.[20] The UDC attracted a large membership, not least from among academics and other intellectuals, though the majority of the British academic community remained militantly patriotic. The UDC accepted institutional as well as individual members and the former ranged over a broad social spectrum, including trade union branches, religious groups, co-operative societies and women's organisations. Through its programme of lectures, discussion circles and publications, the UDC achieved a considerable public influence. In the circumstances of the war, it was perhaps inevitable that the state authorities came to regard it as seditious, though its methods were educative and persuasive, rather than coercive, and its political aim unequivocally in support of parliamentary democracy. Many of its members were later to be active in support of the League of Nations; indeed, the novelist E. M. Forster went so far as to credit one member of the UDC, the Cambridge classicist Lowes Dickinson, as the original inspiration for the scheme.[21] The UDC is interesting, both in itself and as an important example of the independent political education of the British public, in government and in international affairs. It was faced, of course, with the constant dilemma of political education, the tension between propaganda for a specific political purpose and a genuine attempt to educate and to learn about complex issues and policy alternatives.

This distinction was made by the Fabian socialist, G. D. H. Cole, in an article on trade unionism and education published in the Workers' Educational Association *Yearbook* of 1918. In his opinion, propaganda was an attempt to bring others to one's own point of view; education, on the other hand, was an attempt to equip others with the means of making up their own minds. 'Both,' he said, 'are legitimate forms of activity; the point is that they are different.'[22] Cole was also a member of the Fabian Society, itself a classic example of an organised attempt to promote both objectives.[23] A further example, initiated by the state and a product of the social and political aftermath of the First World War, is the celebrated 1919 Report on Adult Education, commissioned by the Ministry of Reconstruction. Its terms of reference were 'to consider the provision for and possibilities of Adult Education (other than technical and vocational) in Great Britain and to make recommendations'.[24] The 409 pages of the Report provide an invaluable source of information about the history of adult social and political education in Britain. Amongst its authors were key figures in the liberal and social democratic movement for adult education, such as Albert Mansbridge, founder of the Workers' Educational Association, the historian R. H. Tawney and the Protestant minister the Rev. Basil A. Yeaxlee. The report defined adult education as a means to personal development, social service and 'the attainment of new standards of citizenship and a better social order'.[25] It went as far as to claim that 'in the great majority of cases, the dynamic character of adult education is due to its social motive'.[26] In the postwar years, the main agency for this concept of adult education as an experiment in democratic education was to be the Workers' Educational Association, often in partnership with the extramural studies departments of the universities. Founded in 1903, it prided itself that it was non-sectarian and non-party political, apparently unsullied by the dirty waters of ideology. During the first half of the century at least, it was challenged by an openly ideological political adult education movement that regarded the WEA as at best naïve and at worst hypocritical. This was the Plebs' League or National Council of Labour Colleges (NCLC), which was Marxist in inspiration and had its origins in a strike by worker students at Ruskin College, Oxford, in 1909.[27] The NCLC, anticipating Antonio Gramsci, considered so called 'neutral' liberal adult education and also state educational provision to be part the cultural and political hegemony of the ruling class. They advocated instead workers' education that was autonomous and based on a class analysis of economy and society. The NCLC was not, however, a wing of a political party, 'the Modern Prince' advocated by Gramsci, and it made little progress.[28] It was the programme and approach of the WEA that was to prevail in British workers' education, especially in the years after the Second World War. The NCLC dwindled away and by 1965 it had disappeared.

Although it should not be exaggerated, the majority spending their recreational hours watching films, dancing, watching or playing sport, listening to the radio or down the pub, much as people today, the interwar years were receptive to popular political education. This was provided by visiting lecturers and discussion circles, through the novelty of cheap editions of books and pamphlets, radio programmes such as the *Brains Trust* and through the various events provided by each of the political parties. This rich combination of popular cultural recreation and informal education, so misunderstood and patronised by the earnest advocates of 'lifelong learning', has recently been described in fascinating detail by the American historian Jonathan Rose in his recent book on *The Intellectual Life of the British Working Classes*.[29] The Left Book Club, for instance, was an attempt by the socialist publisher Victor Gollancz to influence the reading public politically.[30] Launched in May 1936, it was a social and political phenomenon of the 1930s and 1940s with a varied membership of workers, intellectuals, the formally educated and the autodidacts. By the time it closed, in October 1948, it had published a total of 257 books and specially commissioned pamphlets, with the final volume *The Meaning of Marxism*[31] written by the ubiquitous G. D. H. Cole. The Club established a network of discussion groups based on its peak membership of over 50,000 and provided them with a surprisingly varied list of publications, including history, philosophy, the arts and popular science, as well as the more obvious current affairs titles. In addition to *Left News*, the widely read Club newsletter, public lectures were organised and associated activities proliferated. These included the Specialist Groups for health workers, teachers and others, the Theatre

Guild, the Summer Schools (a popular and relaxing form of 'political education' during the interwar years across the ideological spectrum), language courses (German and Russian especially), film-van tours and similar activities. Altogether a considerable programme, though the Club may be criticised for its occasional naïveté and rather more frequent prejudice, most notably in its rejection of the manuscript of *Homage to Catalonia*,[32] George Orwell's attack on Stalinist tactics during the Spanish Civil War. Nevertheless, it was influential and may be compared with similar attempts, usually by the progressive middle classes, to politically educate a mass democracy. Other examples of the period were the documentary film movement led by John Grierson and the commercial venture in paperback publishing of Penguin Books pioneered by Allen Lane.[33]

It should be remembered that secondary education was still the exception rather than the rule and that many young people especially, even if not committed ideologically, welcomed such cheap and informal opportunities to add to their knowledge and to their personal confidence. This was demonstrated during the years of the Second World War. There was a massive expansion of education for the Armed Forces, both technical and general, after 1940, with the national conscription providing a kind of part-time adult education and secondary school for those who wished to participate (and for those who didn't!) By the winter of 1943–44, more than 110,000 courses were in progress. These included a compulsory course in citizenship, whose curriculum was laid down in a monthly pamphlet *The British Way and Purpose*. To this was added the work of the Army Bureau of Current Affairs (ABCA) which carried in its 1943 *Handbook* the ideal of Oliver Cromwell about the citizen soldier who 'knows what he fights for and loves what he knows'.[34] Such programmes came in for severe criticism, not least from the prime minister, Winston Churchill, because of their apparent left-wing bias. Yet the war years had called upon the British population to fight and, mindful of the easy slogans of the First World War, it was anxious to know why it should do so. A mass democracy had emerged in Britain, in which the state and public institutions generally, played an increasing role. Yet, the population was still largely without secondary education and the need for political education was very great. *The Times* recognised this in an editorial as early as 1942. Approving the fact that the official publications of the ABCA were 'necessarily cautious, detailed and objective documents', it expressed the hope that 'the ABCA habit may develop in the demobilized soldiers a social consciousness, as may make them a shrewder electorate than their fathers were'.[35]

The postwar welfare state and inclusive citizenship

A persistent theme since the publication of the 1919 *Report* has been the low rate of participation both in education and in popular governance by the poorly educated and economically and socially excluded sections of the population. It remains very much part of the rhetoric of New Labour. If all citizens are equal, they should have equal opportunities and incentive for participatory activity in society; they should recognise themselves as stakeholders. Yet the practice of citizenship has been distorted in the twentieth century by the persistence of significant inequalities in economic welfare and in educational opportunity. Given that significant sectors of society are disadvantaged in these ways, the question is whether the state should find administrative ways and means to compensate? The argument that it should was presented most forcefully in the long debates about employment policy and about social welfare generally, personified by the intellectual leadership of the political liberals John Maynard Keynes and of William Beveridge. The inclusive motives of the latter are made clear by this quotation from his *Report*: 'The aim of the Plan for Social Security is to abolish want by ensuring that every citizen willing to serve according to his powers has at all times an income sufficient to meet his responsibilities'.[36] The *Report* certainly captured the mood of the times, his biographer commenting: 'It is difficult to claim that he made any inherently original contribution to subsequent social policy. But, nevertheless, it was Beveridge who interpreted the mainstream of public opinion and who transformed an inchoate mass of popular feeling into a blueprint for social reform'.[37]

The historian and social democrat R. H. Tawney was another important spokesman for citizenship and participation, chiefly through equality in education. In 1924 he set out the Labour Party's political objective of 'Secondary education for all', with his ideas best represented in *Equality*,[38] published in 1931. The 1944 Education Act, which introduced secondary education for all in a tripartite system of grammar schools, technical schools and modern schools, is however better known as the Butler Act, after the Secretary of State for Education and Science, and prominent Conservative, R. A. Butler. Significantly, the Act left the 'public' or independent schools untouched and outside the system. This alone says something of the consensus of public opinion on such issues that had been reached by that date. The expectation was that a more literate, technically competent, politically aware and publicly spirited electorate would emerge as part of a 'silent, social revolution'.[39] Yet it has been argued that the education system continued to be stratified along class lines and that the 1944 Act only 'restructured the old apparatus on sound bureaucratic principles, derived from Balfour's original statute in 1902'.[40] It is also argued that, although 'something approaching a common, examinable core was inserted into the curriculum', largely through the patient efforts of the schools inspectorate',[41] any successful attempt at educational induction into citizenship was frustrated by the weight of inertia and a lack of resources.

The relationship of the postwar welfare state to the idea and practice of citizenship in Britain was analysed in 1949 by the sociologist T. H. Marshall, in 'Citizenship and Social Class', the first of a series of lectures dedicated to his namesake, the Cambridge economist Alfred Marshall.[42] In this and later works, he focused attention on the tension between civil and political citizenship on the one hand, and what he called social citizenship on the other. He argued that the welfare state was essentially restorative of social and community rights that had been lost through the urbanisation and proletarianisation that had accompanied the industrial revolution. The development of public systems of education was, he believed, a key factor in the creation of a modern and inclusive citizenship:

> Fundamentally it should be regarded, not as a right of the child to go to school, but as the right of the adult citizen to have been educated...the growth of public elementary education during the nineteenth century was the first decisive step on the road to the re-establishment of the social rights of citizenship in the twentieth.[43]

The historical validity of Marshall's analysis has been challenged, not least by feminism, which argues that he ignored its claim that patriarchy was as important as class in maintaining patterns of inequality and power within British society. Certainly, Marshall emphasised a class analysis and his advocacy of the inclusive rights of social citizenship led him to state unequivocally that 'in the twentieth century, citizenship and the capitalist system have been at war',[44] for citizenship is predicated upon the principle of equality, capitalism on inequality. This means that, in a capitalist democracy, the state has a permanent dilemma of decision, with policies of taxation, expenditure and wealth distribution attempting to resolve these competing claims. This it managed to do, but with increasing difficulty, with a postwar consensus on full employment and public provision of health care, social security and education that finally broke down with the election of the Thatcher government in 1979. The conflicting pressures led to growing economic instability and public dissatisfaction with both public policy and with the economy, resulting in the industrial conflict of the 1970s and 1980s with its culmination in the bitter miners' strike of 1984–85. This led to the re-emergence of individualism and of private solutions to social problems, considered in the following chapter. This gained momentum with the revival of neoliberal economic and social policies during the political administrations of Margaret Thatcher and of John Major during the 1980s and early 1990s and now challenged again by the 'Third Way' agenda of New Labour.

According to Richard Cockett[45] the intellectual origins of this neoliberal economic and social counter-revolution may be found as early as 1931 and later asserted, against the tide of opinion, by Friedrich von Hayek in *The Road to Serfdom*[46] published in 1944. This was renewed in Britain by a consistent campaign of political and economic education and propagandist persuasion, led by neoliberal 'think tanks', such as the Institute of Economic Affairs and the Adam Smith Institute. To some extent, these were more sophisticated, right-wing versions of the Left Book Club, but focusing their attention on a political and business elite, whose influence would percolate down to the population at large. There is little doubt that the core of their intellectual message remains deeply embedded in public policy-making and practice; though the counter-revolution was far from complete when the Labour Party, reconstructed as a social democratic party 'of the third way', finally recovered office in 1997. The reasons for its election may be ascribed partly to the hubris that became characteristic of the Thatcher years in government, but also to an uneasy feeling on the part of the British electorate that inequality and individual reward was accompanied increasingly by unfairness and greed. While it may be argued that the macroeconomic policy prescriptions of J. M. Keynes are now outdated intellectually, the neoliberal capitalist state has, alongside its successes, economically marginalised significant numbers of citizens, such that they no longer participate in the democratic process and are growing ever cynical about it. This is inherently unstable and dangerous and has led to the electoral reaction in favour of New Labour and its claimed 'Third Way',[47] as well as to as yet inchoate general protests against 'capitalism' and 'globalization'.

Citizenship, then, is more than a legal status, crucial though that is. It is also an obligation and a voluntary commitment. For individuals to make this step from the passive to the active, they need to believe that they share with other citizens, interests and values derived from a common experience and anticipation that these should be maintained and developed. This calls for an understanding of what is meant by the term 'political community' and one sufficiently strong to hold within it voluntarily, not only individual citizens, but also the many diverse associations and their members that constitute 'civil society'. This requires the development of civic capacities that will sustain such a community and enable its members to protect both their collective and individual interests. It also means, as shown in the next chapter, an attempt to reconcile the dual positions occupied by the individual in society, identified by the American legal philosopher John Rawls as 'that of equal citizenship and that defined by his place in the distribution of income and wealth'.[48]

Citizenship, identity and political community

Let us take some further examples from the final decades of the twentieth century. These are provided by the devolution of government within the United Kingdom simultaneous with the possibilities of a federal Europe, by immigration and the debate about refugees and asylum-seekers. The political options in fact reinforce one another in their effect on the cohesion of the British state and of the criteria for and meaning of citizenship within it. They are examples of 'identity politics' that have become more prominent in the postcolonial period of the past three decades, accompanied by the erosion of the postwar consensus over economic policy and the welfare state. These are issues to be considered again in later chapters. Consequences that should be noted here are a perceived loss of confidence in traditional definitions and practice of citizenship, a decline in public interest and participation in politics and public life, even of the informal kind, together with uncertainty about common future directions. This has led to a renewed call for 'active citizens', of which the present official enthusiasm for 'lifelong learning' is a part, together with a renewed emphasis on political education for citizenship within the formal curricula of schools and colleges. It is worth noting that this is both a European and a British phenomenon. Indeed, as the chapters in Parts III and IV show, contemporary understanding of what it is to be both British and European has become a matter of both cultural and legal debate.

Tony Blair has pledged that New Labour will modernise British politics and encourage an active definition of citizenship. He has attempted to do this through decentralising power, opening up government to accountability and through the enhancement of individual rights. The programme is well known; it includes a Scottish parliament and elected assemblies in Wales and Northern Ireland, an elected mayor and a new strategic authority for London and plans for further devolution to the regions of England. The aim is to give these nations and regions greater power over their own affairs, but still within the framework of the United Kingdom. The prime minister's constitutional programme also includes new rights for citizens with the incorporation into United Kingdom law of the European Commission on Human Rights, a Freedom of Information Act and the promise of a referendum on reform of the Houses of Parliament, especially the House of Lords. The steps towards the realisation of these constitutional changes were taken with the referenda in Scotland and in Wales on what were essentially 'Home Rule' questions. The result in Scotland was unequivocal, 'the settled will of the Scottish people' being declared at 74.3 per cent to 25.7 per cent of the vote in favour of a Scottish parliament and by 63.55 to 36.5 per cent in favour of that parliament having tax varying powers. The result in Wales, by contrast, was achieved by the narrowest of margins, with 50.35 per cent of the vote in favour of a national assembly and 49.7 per cent against.

The British state established a citizenship of the legal type. The passage of time saw the development of common institutions, of pressure for a common religious settlement, for a common language and for the acceptance of a common interpretation of history. The experience of empire reinforced this. The effect was the subordination of the peripheral nations, with the eventual aim of absorbing them, legally and culturally, in a British nation-state, but where British was effectively synonymous with English. The English historian A. J. P. Taylor claimed the term 'England' was once all-embracing, meaning 'indiscriminately England and Wales, Great Britain, the United Kingdom and even the British Empire'.[49] He went on to complain that: 'Whatever word we use lands us in a tangle'.[50]

This may be compared with the remark of the Welsh literary critic Raymond Williams, recalling that, between the wars, his parents and neighbours did not consider themselves 'British': 'the term was not used much,' he said, 'except by people one distrusted. "British" was hardly ever used without "Empire" following and for that nobody had any use at all, including the small farmers.'[51] The process of a political, legal and cultural creation of a British state was never quite accomplished. In the twentieth century, its political dominance and cultural superiority was challenged by a militant Irish nationalism, a conflict that remains unresolved, by the end of the British Empire and, in the final decade, by a resurgence of Scottish and Welsh identity politics.

The results of the devolution referenda should be seen in this context. First, the question whether the Scots require a parliament and the Welsh a national assembly 'for the better governance of their own affairs' recognises the sense of national identity that persists in both countries. It also implies that someone else has been looking after those affairs hitherto and not necessarily in the interests of the Scottish and Welsh people, a feeling that hardened during the eighteen years of Tory government at Westminster. The Scots were more than ready to respond with a referendum result that asserted their wish for a distinct political as well as cultural and historical identity, though whether this will move them on to full independence remains to be seen. The Welsh electorate was more cautious and is indeed divided. Wales effectively lost its political independence with the defeat of the revolt of Owain Glyndwr in 1415. The Scots, on the other hand, negotiated an Act of Union with England in 1707 and retained many of the institutional features of statehood, such as a separate legal system, national religious institutions and a distinctive educational structure, including universities of distinction. These historical factors contribute to a greater national awareness and self-confidence among the Scots, which were reflected in their development of the devolution debate and in the decisiveness of their vote. The remarkable thing about Wales is that a national identity, with a distinct language and culture, should survive the twentieth century at all, when one considers the pressures and indeed organised campaigns against it. The referendum result reflected this tension, showing Wales to be politically and culturally divided, with a tiny majority only in favour of an Assembly and the expression of national political identity that it represents. Nevertheless, the result was a remarkable turnaround from the vote in the 1979 referendum, when there was a majority of four to one against devolution. The challenge in Wales now is for the new national assembly to provide the focus for unity that its name implies and, as for the Scottish parliament, to do so within the context of a wider British citizenship and the prospect of a federal European Union.

In the past, those who argued for Scottish and Welsh devolution were dismissed as 'separatists'. Now there is growing pressure for Scotland and Wales to identify themselves as distinct and autonomous members of the European Union; one hears similar calls from elsewhere in Europe, such as Catalonia and Lombardy. 'A Voice In Europe!' was a powerful slogan for the 'Vote Yes!' campaigns in both countries. This was an important change in public perception and opinion and one that followed a sustained period of popular political education and debate about the issues. Tony Blair has said that, with devolution, the Labour Party honoured its electoral pledge to cut the 'democratic deficit' and gave Scotland and Wales 'exciting new roles within the United Kingdom'. But has the process of devolution come to an end, or will the twenty-first century see the constitutional relationship of the peoples of the British Isles (including both parts if Ireland) continue to be realigned? In which case, how will the voice of the English people be expressed? Although it now appears to be forgotten, a similar situation was experienced once before, though aggravated by the tensions of war. In April 1918, under the pressure of severe military setbacks in Europe and the need to extend military conscription to Ireland, the prime minister, David Lloyd George, a Welsh-speaking Welshman, gave serious consideration to a 'federal' solution. England, Ireland, Scotland and Wales would each have been given 'home rule' parliaments, with a 'federal' parliament at Westminster to be responsible for the common and imperial concerns of the United Kingdom. Born in extremity, rapidly changing circumstances saw the policy quickly abandoned by the end of 1918. Over ninety years later, the Republic of Ireland is a prosperous constituent member of the European Union, the problem of the 'Six Counties' of Ulster remains unresolved, and Scotland and Wales are experimenting with their newly acquired 'home rule'. The most imaginative way to reform the House of Lords, though not yet considered, might be that it be designated the United Kingdom's 'federal' parliament. In such a way, the tensions between citizenship and national identity that have persisted in Britain and Ireland throughout the twentieth century might be resolved, at least partially. This is not only a matter of the constitutional destiny of the 'Six Counties' of Ulster. It is often forgotten that there are over a million people of Irish birth or descent resident in Britain, comprising the largest single ethnic minority group.[52]

Again, what of those other ethnic minorities, chiefly immigrants from the former empire, who also have British citizenship? Almost all migration is economically conditioned one way or another. European Union policies encourage the free movement of the citizens of member states within its borders. However, movement of peoples across those borders has, in recent years especially, become a matter of extreme political controversy and contention. This is aggravated by political and economic instability in central and eastern Europe, by the significant increase in the numbers of asylum-seekers from all parts of the globe, and the consequent rise in racial and ethnic tension and xenophobia, affecting also migrant populations considered as already settled. The history of immigration to Britain is well known. The period after 1950 saw continued migration from Europe as a consequence of war, for example through the European Volunteer Workers programme.[53] This was accompanied, paradoxically, by the emigration of skilled and semi-skilled British workers to the 'white' dominions, especially Australia and New Zealand, under assisted passage schemes.

The postwar period was, however, dominated by a new type of international labour migration. This consisted primarily of people from countries of the New Commonwealth – those former colonies and dependent territories that elected to remain in the Commonwealth after independence, such as the West Indies and the countries of the Indian subcontinent. Patterns of migration and recruitment were similar to those of several other European countries during the 1950s and 1960s. Initially, male individuals came alone and found work in sectors where jobs were plentiful, although pay and conditions were usually poor. Wives and families soon followed and the 'immigrant' communities quickly established themselves, primarily in London and in the industrial towns and cities of the Midlands and the North of England, such as Birmingham, Leicester, Leeds, Bradford and Manchester. However, the position of the New Commonwealth immigrants was unusual in comparison with migrant workers recruited under the European Volunteer Worker scheme or with those recruited to other European countries, such as Turkish *gastarbeiter* in Germany. They were entitled to British citizenship, could vote and remain indefinitely in the country. The majority of ethnic minority children and young people in Britain today were born in the country and will remain. This development stimulated debate over questions of race, identity and citizenship. As early as 1962, the British government began to take measures to restrict entry, with the Commonwealth Immigration Act and subsequent legislation made citizenship increasingly difficult to obtain. The majority of arrivals since the early 1970s were either relatives of British citizens or refugees, including Ugandan Asians, Chileans and Vietnamese.[54]

The new century has seen a significant increase in the number of refugees and asylum seekers. This has led to a revival of public debate and to the development of government initiatives to cope with what is popularly seen as a problem rather than an opportunity, not only in Britain, but throughout the European Union. The British experience of immigration and of the integration of migrant workers through both legislation and the application of policy, especially in the field of race and community relations and in education more broadly, is of great significance. These are deep and potentially dangerous waters which, in the early years of the twenty-first century, have become increasingly turbulent. In short, fundamental questions of citizenship and identity remain to be answered.

Conclusion

The final decade of the twentieth century saw a marked revival of interest in the concepts of citizenship and of civil society. This was stimulated by the deepening inequalities brought about by the *laissez-faire* economic and social policies that dominated British politics in the 1980s and 1990s. These were aggravated by the simultaneous failure of state socialism to provide a viable alternative. The significant moment internationally was the fall of the Berlin Wall in 1989 and the rapid collapse of the bureaucratic state socialist systems that lay behind it. In Britain, as in other Western capitalist democracies, this process compelled the local socialist parties to a long overdue reassessment of their ideology. Its immediate fruit was the identification of 'the Third Way', in which the concepts of civil society and active citizenship would play a significant part.[55] The fact that they were already deeply rooted in British society was perhaps overlooked. Yet their fresh encouragement was important and this was to form the theme of the *Report of the Commission on Citizenship* established by the Speaker of the House of Commons, the Rt Hon. Bernard Weatherill, MP, in December 1988.[56]

In his Foreword, the Speaker identified the two major achievements of the *Report*. First, that the National Curriculum should include the formal teaching of the meaning of citizenship. This has now been done. Second, in establishing the importance of giving young people, at the beginning of their adult lives, 'the experience of working with others to tackle and solve real problems in their own local environment...a crucial element in the process of learning to be a good citizen'. The precepts of citizenship had to be applied throughout 'the public institutions of our society and to the great range of voluntary bodies and independent associations, and above all, to individual citizens of all ages'.[57] As Roger Scruton says elsewhere, 'citizenship is a cultural achievement, which is not everywhere and at every time the same, and which is not likely to reproduce itself without effort and will'.[58] The obligations of citizenship are bound by the historically given reality into which a citizen is born. This, in turn, gives rise to the questions of citizenship and cultural identity referred to above. Again, the reason why membership of the franchise age is established constitutionally is because citizens are admitted to membership having completed a process of cultural preparation. Citizenship is the essential means to political debate and to the reconciliation of opinion democratically so that society may function. Maintaining it successfully when globalization and a postmodern attitude to culture are increasingly set against cultural tradition, local knowledge and the need for roots will be perhaps the key social and educational challenge of the twenty-first century.

Notes

1 D. G. Boyce, 'Public opinion and the historians', *History*, Vol. 63, No. 208, June 1978, pp. 214–28.
2 A. V. Dicey, *Lectures on the Relation between Law and Public Opinion in England during the Nineteenth Century*, Macmillan, London, 1905.
3 Boyce, pp. 214–15.
4 T. H. Marshall, *Social Policy*, Hutchinson, London, 1975, p. 36.
5 Ibid.
6 Ibid.
7 Ibid., p. 215.
8 Ibid.
9 Ibid.
10 W. J. Morgan, 'Political education and full employment', in W. J. Morgan (ed.), *The Rise and Fall of Full Employment*, Institute of Modern Cultural Studies, Nottingham, 1994, pp. 5–24.
11 Ibid.
12 Advisory Council for Adult and Continuing Education, *Political Education for Adults* National Institute of Adult and Continuing Education, Leicester, 1983, p. 37.
13 Ibid.
14 HMSO, A*dult Education: A plan for development*, Report by a Committee of Inquiry appointed by the Secretary of State for Education and Science under the Chairmanship of Sir Lionel Russell, London, 1973.
15 M. Ginsberg (ed.), *Law and Opinion in England in the Twentieth Century*, Stevens and Sons, London, 1959.
16 Mannheim, ibid., p. 277.
17 D. Lloyd, 'The law of associations', in M. Ginsberg (ed.) *Law and Opinion in England in the 20th Century*, Stevens and Sons Ltd, London, 1959.
18 D. W. Brogan, *Citizenship Today: England, France, the United States*, University of North Carolina Press, Chapel Hill, North Carolina, 1960, pp. 14–15. See also B. J. Hake and W. J. Morgan (eds) *Adult Education, Public Information and Ideology: British-Dutch perspectives on theory, history and practice*, Department of Adult Education, University of Nottingham, 1989, pp. 76–89.
19 M. Oakeshott, 'Political education', an Inaugural Lecture published in M. Oakeshott, *Rationalism in Politics and Other Essays*, Methuen, London, 1962, pp. 113 and 128.
20 G. H. Hardy, *Bertrand Russell and Trinity: A college controversy of the last war*, printed for the author at the University Press, Cambridge, 1942, p. 10.
21 T. B. Howarth, *Cambridge between Two Wars*, Collins, London, p. 163.
22 G. D. H. Cole, 'Trade unionism and education', *Workers' Educational Association Yearbook, 1918*, reprinted by the Department of Adult Education, University of Nottingham, Nottingham, p. 72.

23 P. Pugh, *Educate, Agitate and Organize: 100 years of Fabian socialism*, Methuen, London and New York.
24 HMSO, *Final and interim reports of the adult education committee of the Ministry of Re-construction, 1918–1919*, London, reprinted by the Department of Adult Education, the University of Nottingham, Nottingham, 1980, p. 53.
25 Ibid., p. 168.
26 Ibid.
27 W. J. Morgan, 'The burning question of workers' education: Ruskin College and the Plebs' League', *Educational Research and Perspectives*, Vol. 15, No. 2 (1988) pp. 38–48; see also S. Macintyre, *A Proletarian Science: Marxism in Britain 1917–1933*, Cambridge University Press, Cambridge, 1980.
28 W. J. Morgan, 'The pedagogical politics of Antonio Gramsci: pessimism of the intellect, optimism of the will', *The International Journal of Lifelong Education*, Vol. 6, No. 4 (1987), pp. 295–308.
29 J. Rose, *The Intellectual Life of the British Working Classes*, Yale University Press, New Haven and London, 2001.
30 J. Lewis, *The Left Book Club: An historical record*, Gollancz, London, 1970.
31 G. D. H. Cole, *The Meaning of Marxism*, The Left Book Club, Gollancz, 1948.
32 G. Orwell, *Homage to Catalonia*, Penguin Books, Harmondsworth, 1976.
33 See, for instance, J. Pearson, *Penguins March On: Books for the forces during World War II*, Penguin Collectors Society, London, 1996.
34 Quoted in P. Addison, *The Road to 1945: British politics and the Second World War*, Quartet Books, London, 1977, p. 148; See also A. Calder, *The People's War: Britain 1939–1945*, Panther Books, London, 1969.
35 Addison, p. 150.
36 Cmd. 6404, *Social Insurance and Allied Services*, London, HMSO, 1942, quoted in D. B. Heater, *Citizenship: The civic ideal in world history, politics and education*, Longman, London and New York, 1990, p. 100.
37 J. Harris, *William Beveridge: A biography*, The Clarendon Press, Oxford, 1977, p. 449.
38 R. H. Tawney, *Equality*, Unwin Books, London, 1964.
39 G. A. N. Lowndes, *The Silent Social Revolution: An account of the expansion of public education in England and Wales*, Oxford University Press, London, 1969.
40 K. Middlemass, *Politics in an Industrial Society: The experience of the British system since 1911*, André Deutsch, London, 1979, p. 350.
41 Ibid.
42 T. H. Marshall, 'Citizenship and social class', *Class, Citizenship and Social Development: Essays by T. H. Marshall*, Doubleday, New York, 1964, pp. 65–122. It is interesting to note that 'citizenship' does not appear in the index to the volume on *Law and Opinion in England in the 20th Century*, ed. Morris Ginsberg, *Law and Opinion*. The concept is however implicit throughout the book.
43 Ibid.
44 Ibid.
45 R. Cockett, *Thinking the Unthinkable: Think tanks and the economic counter-revolution 1931–1983*, Fontana Press, London, 1995.
46 F. A. Hayek, *The Road to Serfdom*, Routledge and Sons, London, 1944.
47 A. Giddens, *The Third Way: The renewal of social democracy*, Polity Press, Cambridge, 1999.

48 J. Rawls, *A Theory of Justice*, Oxford University Press, London, 1973, p. 96, quoted in Heater, p. 101.
49 A. J. P. Taylor, *English History 1914–1945*, Pelican Books, Harmondsworth, 1970, p. 21.
50 Ibid.
51 R. Williams, *Politics and Letters: Interviews with New Left Review*, New Left Books, London, 1979, p. 26.
52 See, for instance, K. O' Connor, *The Irish in Britain*, Torc Books, Dublin, 1974.
53 See J. A. Tannahill, *European Volunteer Workers in Britain*, Manchester University Press, Manchester, 1958; also D. Kay and R. Miles, *Refugees or Migrant Workers? European volunteer workers in Britain, 1945–1951*, Routledge, London and New York, 1993.
54 F. Milburn and W. J. Morgan, 'Adult education for ethnic minorities', *European Manual of Continuing Education*, Luchterhand Verlag, Neuwied, Section 50, 30, 140, 1996, pp. 1–7.
55 Giddens, *Third Way*.
56 Commission on Citizenship, *Encouraging Citizenship*, HMSO, London, 1990.
57 Ibid., p. vi.
58 R. Scruton, *A Society of Strangers: Education for citizenship in the post-modern world*, The Institute of United States Studies, University of London, 1997, p. 13.

2
The Triumph of Individualism?[1]

Ian Forbes

Introduction

If he were writing today, Dicey would not be alone in deciding that, despite his fears of 100 years ago, individualism is thoroughly in the ascendant once more. This would give him great pleasure, given that a dramatic conflict between individualism and collectivism lies at the core of his account of nineteenth-century law in England, and animates his predictions at the beginning of the twentieth century. While individualism appears to have retained its vitality, relevance and currency, collectivism by contrast now conjures up images and debates from the past, replete with outmoded approaches and discredited political experiments.

Dicey's preoccupation with this conflict, and his prognosis, are treated politely but not altogether seriously in the first major review of his seminal work which was published at about the halfway mark of the twentieth century.[2] In the main, Ginsberg and his contributors focused on their own philosophical or political preoccupations, or presented evidence in relation to a particular area of society. The message seemed clear: the debate had moved on, and the idea of a battle between the forces of collectivism and individualism in law had ceased to be of overriding intellectual interest. It is not too surprising, then, to find that most contemporary debates on the law and public opinion contain minimal reference to what Dicey regarded as the central issue, at least in the terms that he used.

It would be a mistake, however, to think that his concerns were entirely spurious, an historical curiosity and of no relevance. Dicey's fears about the growth of the state, restrictions on the choices and freedoms of individuals, and the preference for state intervention to address political and social problems are still a commonplace for those occupying a significant section of the political spectrum. Moreover, the nature of the challenges and dilemmas facing law-makers has changed more in scale than in substance, while the range of mechanisms for dealing with them has remained quite stable.

The central question is, then, did collectivism become predominant, only to fail in its own terms, or was it ultimately overwhelmed by the stronger strain of individualism? In addressing these questions, this chapter will critically review Dicey's account of social and legal reality, and consider the mid-century evaluation of his approach contained in the Ginsberg collection. This will be followed by an account of the last half of the twentieth century, employing the terms of debate that are articulated in the previous two volumes. The intention will be to assess the evidence for the view that collectivism has lost its credibility in law and opinion, leaving individualism triumphant. Like Dicey, I will divide the time into distinct periods. This periodisation will be used to chart large-scale ideological shifts in political history and highlight continuities and discontinuities in law-making. Finally, the evidence for the connection between law and opinion will be examined, in order to provide a perspective on the claim that public opinion has an impact on fundamental aspects of law-making.

Dicey's political opinions

Although most famous for his legal work, Dicey was fundamentally a political character, ever the aspirant to high public office as a Tory. Hence, his prognosis for the twentieth century is nothing short of alarmist:

> Unless he be a person of astoundingly sanguine temperament it would be difficult for him not to perceive that the combination of socialistic and democratic legislation threatens the gravest danger to the country.[3]

In contemporary parlance, this means that all but the politically comatose should have realised that collectivism would supplant individualism, potentially wreaking havoc in an England that was at the time characterised by immense economic and military power and enviable domestic stability. It is an almost formulaic warning, sounded by a succession of Tory politicians, with varying degrees of rhetorical panache and political impact. Yet it is interesting to find that Dicey is not in the final analysis too pessimistic, since he harbours the conservative belief that his conception of individualism is so ingrained in the English character that common sense will prevail, and both modify and restrict the collectivist impulse of the age.

If we take this view at face value, there is much to applaud here. At the end of the nineteenth century, Dicey employed an historically informed awareness of the inevitability of change in society and appreciated the nature and strength of emerging intellectual and social forces. Having taken the pulse of the (English) nation, and combined this with insights about developments in law, he concluded that there was a trend towards law that reflects 'the socialist virtues' and predicted that this trend would continue and become more marked in the twentieth century. As we will see, however, Dicey's account demonstrates that a capacity for fine legal judgement does not have any necessary connection with acute or well-founded political assessment.

The main problem with Dicey's thesis arises from the various meanings that are ascribed to the key terms, and the attempt to compare two very different social and political phenomena. Individualism, in his hands, is at once a peculiarly English tradition with an historical pedigree stretching back to the 'Middles Ages', amounting to a part of the national character. It is also, in relation to nineteenth-century lawmaking, associated with 'Benthamism' (i.e. Benthamite utilitarianism or liberalism).[4] Despite this association, individualism is not articulated as a theoretical approach to enduring questions about the nature of politics. Rather, it is used to express certain political values and beliefs. In this respect, Dicey is indebted to Burke. Individualism is a nationally derived expression and instantiation of English political nature. It is not presented as an ideological construct, but a gathering together of self-evidently right principles of political understanding and conduct. Most prominent among these values are the beliefs that 'laissez-faire is in most cases, or even in many cases, a principle of sound legislation', and that 'governmental guidance or interference' necessarily limits the freedom of the individual.

By contrast, collectivism has economic and social characteristics. It is variously 'a sentiment', 'a school of opinion' and 'a doctrine' – in stark contrast to the 'definite [legal] creed' that is Benthamism.[5] Collectivism, he noted, was quite a new term, in authoritative use only since 1880. Although Dicey acknowledges that collectivism technically refers to 'the socialist theory of the collective ownership of all the means of production', he prefers a much looser definition.[6] For the purposes of his analysis, collectivism is merely 'an antithesis to individualism in the field of legislation'. This was his point of reference. He would interchange it occasionally with socialism, which was in his view 'the more popular and current expression'.[7] For our purposes, it is important to note that for Dicey collectivism will always have a negative frame of reference. It denotes an absence of, a contradiction to, and a departure from individualism in legislation. Crucially, that individualism is – while collectivism can never be – a part of the English tradition or character.

For the political theorist, then, Dicey's work is of historical interest, but there is very little of substance to discuss. At the outset, assertion takes the place of argument, and there is no evidence of development of key ideas or a hint of critical reflection. Nevertheless, it has been said that Dicey 'explained both the law and the ideas that shaped it in the language of politics'.[8] This should not be taken to mean that he produced a political analysis of the development of nineteenth-century law. Instead of a systematic approach to political evidence, Dicey gives us the view of a political actor who has at his disposal considerable interpretative skills in relation to the law, but just one blunt ideological instrument to interpret complex social and political developments. In consequence, he expects to and duly does find that 'the main current of legislative opinion from the beginning of the twentieth century has run vehemently towards collectivism'.[9]

The Ginsberg variations

When Morris Ginsberg sets out to review the situation some fifty years later, he presents a less emotive account of the age and enlists the help of social scientists to subject Dicey's claims to critical analysis. In place of a worrying trend towards collectivism, Ginsberg sees a challenging paradox that takes us an important step on from Rousseau's perception of the need to build collective political power on the strength of the natural equality of each individual. Ginsberg observes that, 'while the liberty of the individual was won through collective power, collective power also threatened individual liberty'.[10] This suggests an implicit endorsement of Dicey's judgement, but it foregrounds a much more political account of what Ernest Gallie had only recently identified as a constant battle over the meanings of political concepts that will always remain essentially contested rather than agreed upon and settled.[11] In these terms, Ginsberg points out that Dicey's concern with the freedom of the individual and state intervention is best understood as 'political individualism'. This form of individualism foregrounds certain values and can provide something of a description, but little in the way of an explanation of political reality or contribute to a research agenda. It helps us to locate Dicey on a political spectrum. In so doing, it highlights his orientation to the issue of law and public opinion, but at the same time it diminishes his claim to understand what he claims to be observing. In addition to considering the conflict at the level of ideology, Ginsberg incorporates an account of power, an element that is implicit but not analysed in Dicey's account. The power dimension draws attention to the role not just of ideas and opinion, but of structures, groups, and social and economic forces in the formulation of law. This political battle was attracting new terms – collectivism was, by the 1950s, also known as state socialism, and sometimes as totalitarianism. Individualism, too, was in some flux, with terms like 'social liberal', 'liberal socialist' and 'utilitarian socialist' indicating a complex political spectrum with a more nuanced recognition of the contemporary manifestations of enduring political dilemmas and antinomies.[12] Other writers contribute to this critical review of the law and society by attacking the representation of collectivism as the antithesis of individualism. This is done from a number of perspectives. Kahn-Freund notes Dicey's tendency to confuse the growth of union power with interventionary state power and criticises the one-dimensionality of the *laissez-faire* doctrine. His overall conclusions about the lack of collectivist law probably hold even today. Robustly, Titmuss rejects the crudity of the representation of the clash between equality and freedom, challenges Dicey's grasp of 'the tone of England', notes the paucity of his understanding of health as a political and social policy issue, and suggests that the real question was between 'different forms of collectivism, different degrees of freedom; open or concealed power'. Roberts draws attention to the possibility of '*laissez-faire* collectivism' and questions the inevitability of a total loss of liberty accompanying all collective means of dealing with social problems.[13] For political writing of an extremely high order, however, nothing beats Tawney's bracing chapter extolling the virtues of socialism.

The collectivist polity

Above all, the Ginsberg collection suggests that politics is about power and ideas. This is a common theme in the 1950s. Daniel Bell pronounced 'the end of ideology', when the demonstrable internal harmony of society indicated that the fundamental political questions had been decided, leaving room only for improvements at the margin.[14] Looking back, Hobsbawm refers to this time as 'The Golden Years' and 'The Golden Age', by virtue of stability, sustained economic growth and a successfully reformed and managed capitalist system.[15] There is a general development in the capitalist West towards states that combine affluence and welfare. In complete contrast to Dicey's association of political and economic success with individualism, the golden age is regarded as the product of collectivism. Britain, at this time, is thus regarded very positively as a collectivist polity.

In Samuel Beer's classic account of postwar politics, political culture is 'one of the main variables of a political system and a major factor in explaining the political behaviour of individuals, groups, and parties'.[16] In his understanding of politics as a struggle for power, the nature of party government and approaches to representation are essential variables, contributing to the political formation that typifies an era.[17] By the 1950s, Beer argues, British politics was dominated by collectivism. He describes collectivist politics as a new type of political behaviour, adding some form to Dicey's view that collectivism was an emerging feature of early twentieth-century politics, at least in relation to economic development.

Like Dicey, Beer highlights the connection between socialism and collectivism, which he sees as a complex and systematic approach to policy that 'diverges not only from *laissez-faire*, but also from the piecemeal intervention of Radical reform'.[18] Collectivism is characterised by 'government intervention with the economic and social system as a whole'.[19] This orientation goes well beyond a style of law-making, or the use of state intervention in relation to the interests of certain groups. Curiously, for something so closely associated with socialism, policies with redistributive intent are not central to this form of collectivism. This is government intervention that consists in 'comprehensive and continuous planning and administration'.[20] It is this political form of collectivism that came to dominate the post-war political formation. What is remarkable is that it was maintained by both Conservative and Labour parties, despite the considerable ideological distance between them. Beer notes:

> British Tories are in some degree Collectivists, not only in certain aims of policy, but also in certain methods of political action. In both respects, they have more in common with Socialists than with their contemporaries in the Liberal Party. Old traditions of strong government, paternalism, and the organic have made easier the massive reassertion of state power that has taken place in recent decades, often under Conservative auspices.[21]

Fifty years after Dicey's dire warning, the British political system was once again very stable, with all the parties accepting the constitutional framework, the legal structures and the conventions of government. Moreover, both the Labour Party and the Conservative Party recognised the need to operate as party governments, so ending the freedom of members of Parliament to vote in any way they pleased.

But what is most interesting is the extent to which they agree on how political power is to be organised within this legal and constitutional framework. This agreement sets both Tory and Socialist Democracy apart from nineteenth century political individualism and constitutes a common theory of politics in the Collectivist era. This theory is not confined to the closets of political philosophers, but pervades the political culture of twentieth-century Britain and functions powerfully as an operative ideal in daily political life.[22]

The prevailing theory of politics came to be characterised after the event as the postwar consensus. Its features included a tacit agreement about the nature of government, the tasks of government and the techniques of government. The collectivist polity, run by a party government in a two-party system, took responsibility for macroeconomic management of the mixed economy using Keynesian demand management. It sought to achieve full employment, provide universal and free benefits for all in need, recognise the right of trade unions to be consulted about government policy, and attempted to reduce inequalities of wealth, income and region. In practice, this meant sustained economic growth to deliver these aims, as well as the development of the welfare state, progressive taxation, and intervention in the economy – through nationalisation of the commanding heights of the economy and the creation of the National Economic Development Council. Also, the collective polity was typified by a tripartite approach to political management 'accept the great organized producer groups of a modern industrial society and attribute to them an important role in government and administration' knew governments of both persuasions.[23]

This ushered in the age of corporatist governance, when the representatives of labour and industry and commerce alike were given formal and informal means to pursue group interests at the highest levels of government. Governance, then, involved the development of an effective means of consultation, policy development and implementation that included these group interests. This was the high point of the collectivist polity. Tripartite or corporatist politics was successful as an avenue for the expression of organised interests. It could complement the electoral means of representation by giving voice to different viewpoints, benefit from powerful interest groups being able to check on the actions of public authorities, and give citizens greater opportunity to participate in the political process. Where this form of politics was adopted, Williamson argues, the state becomes 'a structure of domination, which seeks to maintain a particular socio-economic order'.[24]

This period saw a number of legislative innovations, but they took place against a background of law-making relations that is nevertheless consistent with a liberal framework of justice. Individual rights in relation to the state and in contract continued to be privileged. Producer groups gained some rights, but many of these extended freedoms to bargain outwith the purview of the state. The collectivist polity, contrary to superficial expectation, did not create a significant body of law that instantiated collective rights. The two interesting exceptions from this time are still in force. They are the Sex Discrimination Act of 1975 and the Race Relations Act of 1976. These exceptions, however, are not such a violation of the rule as may be supposed, for three reasons. First, the Acts are the culmination of the application of long-standing liberal-individualist ideas of fundamental equality in relation to women and men and to ethnic minorities. Second, the legislation indicates not only that significant social change has taken place, but also that law-making is responsive to changing social reality rather than relying on traditional views of 'England' or established legislative procedure. Third, these Acts are unique in that they focus on individuals *qua* individuals and individuals as members of specified groups, through the inclusion of provisions against direct and indirect discrimination. In this final sense, collectivist law augments individualist law. In no sense does it supplant it.

These are the Acts that most closely conform to Dicey's account of collectivist legislation, 'which should increase the force of each man's social and sympathetic feelings, and should intensify his sense of the responsibility of society or the State for the happiness and welfare of each citizen'.[25] These sentiments, and these Acts, remain as relevant today, and the basic assumptions employed in this legislation have since been embedded in a wide range of legislative measures in the intervening years. An example of law that incorporates the creation of group rights includes all subsequent Acts covering education, local government and employment. Nevertheless, the only new law of this kind is the Disability Discrimination Act of 1996, this time passed by a Conservative government.

Notwithstanding these important exceptions (resulting from the changing nature of society far more than a preference for legislative approaches), the collectivist tendency in law-making is minimal. It is minimal because the political culture changes and the political process undertakes as its core business a series of collectivist responsibilities. These responsibilities are not so much legislated for as they are argued over between and within parties and government, under the aegis of a corporatist ethos and practice.

If corporatism was the high point of the British collectivist polity, then it was also its last gasp. Endogenous weaknesses stemming from long-term industrial decline were exacerbated by the effects of the ending of the gold standard and the shock of the oil price of the early 1970s. What appeared as terminal strain was placed on a system of political settlement that relied on increases in productivity and taxation to meet competing demands from the major interest groups. It quickly came the conventional wisdom that corporatist Britain was no longer capable of effectively mediating political demands. This sense of failure further undermined the legitimacy of the system of governance. 'Stagflation' – the unheard of combination of high unemployment and high inflation – plus a balance of payments crisis led to the need for support (and some control over economic policy) by the International Monetary Fund. These experiences provided powerful evidence that state intervention in the workings of the economy had become counterproductive, if not practically unfeasible. Further, trades unions – the embodiment of collectivism and the home of socialism – were regarded by some as too powerful, too partial and too unaccountable.

For Vernon Bogdanor, 'the central themes were ungovernability and overload', revealing a deepening crisis of authority.[26] To the surprise of Beer and most other observers, Britain was no longer regarded as a model democratic government, and was quickly dubbed the 'sick man' of Europe. It was then subject to severe criticism as a failing political system by a wide range of domestic and foreign observers.[27] For those wedded to the analysis of political culture, the development of 'pluralistic stagnation' was associated with a new populism and the decline of civic culture. The broad cultural revolution that took place in all western industrial societies signalled the end of deference and an assault on traditionalism in Britain, bringing about attitudinal changes that were to impact heavily on the collectivist polity, just when it was struggling to mobilise consent and maintain legitimacy.

Was this the failure of collectivism? It was not, since collectivism was not an organised movement, with clear links between political orientation, law and practical outcome. Multiple factors had a role to play, including especially global and regional developments that cannot be pressed into the service of one interpretative schema. Cultural changes, and their effects, were magnified by the fundamental problems with the British economy, the loss of sovereign control in relation to foreign currency movements, and the lack of consensus about what to do about it. A further variable must include the impact of international economic institutions and the development of the European Common Market. This range of factors makes it highly unlikely that something as amorphous as a given political culture will prevail, much less one ideology.[28] It is, however, fair to observe that a transition to another political era was taking place, one in which collectivism was identified as the major problem and individualism promoted as the ideal solution.

Politics before policy

The problems that beset governments in the 1970s cruelly exposed some long-standing structural and systemic weaknesses. Long-term economic decline, external shocks to the economy and increasing social demands were severely testing systems of governance that embodied little room for manoeuvre, experienced decreasing influence over key actors and had their ability to control outcomes drastically reduced. Collectivist ideas were too readily associated with political failures, thereby further reducing confidence in the mechanisms of governance and undermining the legitimacy of government. Governments were aware of these difficulties, and were beginning to adapt their strategies to take account of the new circumstances. For some, such movement was too little, too late and too timid. Into the breach stepped Margaret Thatcher, carrying with her some sturdy if crude ideological baggage culled mainly from the thought of Friedrich Hayek.[29] The following contrast between individualism and collectivism, from his *Road to Serfdom*, has clear echoes of Dicey's view and is central to her political position:

> The various kinds of collectivism, communism, fascism, etc., differ among themselves in the nature of the goal toward which they want to direct the efforts of society. But they all differ from liberalism and individualism in wanting to organize the whole of society and all its resources for this unitary end and in refusing to recognize autonomous spheres in which the ends of the individual are supreme.[30]

As Leader of the Opposition until 1979, she departed from adherence to the principal elements of the postwar consensus. An overtly political agenda was deemed more appropriate than the corporate political process: conviction replaced consensus. The Conservatives came to and stayed in power for eighteen years, on the basis of a 'radical' programme dedicated to 'rolling back the frontiers of the state' and creating a 'popular capitalism' and an 'enterprise culture'. When she became prime minister, Thatcher inherited a structurally weak economy that was nevertheless still producing a reasonably healthy rate of growth, but a state that lacked authority. As Bogdanor argues, she soon re-established authority, if at some cost to the democratic underpinning of its legitimacy.[31] The collectivist polity was, at least ideologically, at an end. It had exhausted itself, shown itself to be inadequate as a method of government, and had lost the support of the people. Individualism, held at bay for too long by a coalition of interests that gave trades unions far too great a role in the polity, was about to be consciously reasserted.

For a number of commentators, the British reaction to the problems of governance at the end of the golden age was both excessive and ill conceived. Graham and Prosser, for example, regarded the neoliberal agenda adopted by successive Conservative governments as having constitutional significance, involving the 'redrawing the boundaries between public and private spheres and changing the principles on which public bodies should act'.[32] Similarly, Bogdanor detected policies 'designed to topple the bastions of social democracy – not only the trades unions, but also local government, the education system, the National Health Service, and even the professions themselves', thus bringing the constitution 'back into the centre of British politics'.[33]

In relative terms, examples of overtly 'individualist' legislation were more prominent under the Conservative governments of Thatcher and John Major, although many of these were controversial. The key examples relate to legislation associated with a general preference for deregulation and for privatisation. Both orientations stem from the ideological preference for minimising the role of the state, in the belief that individual choice and entrepreneurial endeavour were values in themselves, and that these features of human motivation had become far too constrained after decades of state control and intervention.

Deregulation, it should be noted, is now associated with significant failures, for example the mis-selling of pensions and the outbreak of BSE in cattle. In both cases, the economic and political costs have been huge and have had long-term negative consequences. These cases have also revealed the danger of relying on the market to mediate and manage complex policy areas, and have led to a renewal of interest in mechanisms of control and regulation that are backed up by the authority of the state, as well as international institutions.

Privatisation also has a mixed record. Originally, this approach enjoyed considerable success. The sale of council houses had the dual effect of minimising the role of the (local) state and enhancing the autonomy of the individuals who came into possession of property that had been built and owned by state agencies. Increasing home ownership was regarded as emblematic of an increase in individual freedom, as an important indicator of a change in the nature of British society. Subsequently, privatisation was applied to other areas. The sale of state enterprises and utilities served a number of purposes, each of which was consistent with the individualist underpinning of the government's neoliberal approach to policy. First, it divested the government of ownership and control of important areas of the economy, while reducing substantially the public sector borrowing requirement. Second, it was consistent with the view that governments were ill suited to the task of managing businesses. Third, it promised to break up large monopolies and reap the benefits of increased competition. Fourth, it expressed a great confidence that previously state-owned enterprises would be more successful in the market environment. The disciplines of the market would improve efficiency and performance, while the market offered opportunities for investment and growth that were denied under state control. Finally, the sale was intended to increase the stake of ordinary individuals in the economy, through individual shareholding.

This was presented as a political and practical rolling back of the collectivist actions of postwar Labour governments. In this sense, it became a key part of the hegemonic project of Thatcherism. Privatisation was intended to play its part in the Conservatives' search for long-term electoral advantage. In a revealing interview early in her premiership, Thatcher said: 'Economics are the method; the object is to change the soul.'[34] Patrick Dunleavy puts this point another way. Through its privatisation policy, the Thatcher government 'used state finance in an unprecedented way to push through "preference-shaping" changes that tended to build their support base and erode the opposition's vote'.[35]

There are some problems of detail with even the successful privatisations, such as the undervaluing of state assets and the tendency for shares in these new companies to migrate rapidly away from individual ownership into pension fund ownership. More significant problems have arisen when privatisation has been inappropriately chosen as the solution. It is now clear that the privatisation of the railway system has not solved any of the technical problems of achieving a high-standard and integrated transport system. Nor has it solved the problem of how to fund that system, or the effect of long-term and chronic under-investment.

Such privatisation remains a problem for government, and has necessitated the creation of a new and powerful regulatory framework, ironically increasing the powers of the state by creating, according to Michael Moran, 'a corporatist structure which is evolving into a system of bureaucratic control' to ensure that collective interests are served.[36]

The return to political individualism under the neoliberalism of the Thatcher and Major years is, ultimately, a matter for judgement on the values they espoused as well as the actual performance. We have seen that the strong critique of collectivism was accompanied by an equally strong account of an apparently coherent and feasible alternative. The Conservative government espoused a consistent ideological position, and Dicey's summary of individualism could fairly be applied to the intent of the Conservative Party in government, and in opposition. Like the nineteenth-century Liberals:

> They have also assumed, and surely not without reason, that if a man's real interest be well understood, the true welfare of each citizen means the true welfare of the state. Hence Liberals have promoted, during the time when their influence was dominant, legislation which should increase each citizen's liberty, energy and independence; which should teach him his true interest, and which should intensify his sense of his own individual responsibility for the results... of his own personal conduct.[37]

From a liberal perspective, such use of government power has as its ideal the improvement of individuals and therefore human society. In Conservative hands, the ostensibly normative mantra of liberty and true interest is in the service of the more venal use of power to shape voting preferences. It is also associated with the determination of Thatcher and her allies to be proved right about the conscious rejection of the collectivist polity, and the transforming effect that her individualist policies were having on the electorate. In 1987, when the Conservatives won their third general election in a row, individualism was deemed by supposedly informed opinion to be thoroughly triumphant. Indeed, 'all commentators and politicians agreed that the Thatcher revolution had transformed the values of the British people', such that they had become 'more materialistic' as a result of policies that 'enabled more and more people to discover that unrestrained individualism was right for their character'.[38]

John Rentoul, in *Me and Mine*, dissects the political claims associated with Thatcher's use of power against a collectivism that was, as with

Dicey, synonymous with socialism. He points out that the enthusiasm for this thesis was remarkable, given that the political debate was conducted 'in a sort of evidence-free zone'.[39] Rentoul turned to the *British Social Attitudes* surveys and *British Election Studies*, both of which provide a wealth of in-depth and long-term data using reliable methods and techniques, and some individual interviews. He found the evidence quite striking. It pointed categorically to the failure of Thatcher's ideological and practical attempts to wean the people away forever from collectivism.

> With all the advantages of holding power, economic growth and social change in her favour, she has failed to increase the Conservative percentage of the vote at two successive general elections. And she has failed to shift the electorate from its collectivist values.[40]

Furthermore, he predicted a 'reaffirmation of collectivism', where 'public service is an elevated motive, and where efficiency is pursued as much for collective benefit and collective pride as for individual gain'.[41] Ten years later, these broad findings about values are confirmed in the 14th report on *British Social Attitudes*. As the editors note, the Conservatives 'failed' in their attempt at 'winning over the hearts and minds of the electorate as well as collecting their votes'.[42] If we accept that the Conservative governments were indeed a test of the supremacy of individualism over collectivism, then the case for individualism was far from proven by 1987, and seems in total collapse after eighteen years in power.

What this evidence does show, however, is that governments can be elected and re-elected, even though their ideological stance and policies are at marked variance with the electorate. This finding has implications for the quite stunning electoral successes of the Labour Party in 1997 and 2001.

Evidence before policy

The end of the Conservative era of government, when it finally came in 1997, was cataclysmic. The government went to the country with the economy in a stable and healthy state. Yet the Labour Party was returned to power with a huge majority of 179 seats, having pledged to preserve the spending plans of the previous government for the first two years and not to increase income tax. In short, the Labour Party consciously had repositioned itself in an attempt to claim enough centre ground support to win. This meant jettisoning much of the overtly ideological rhetoric that created negative associations with the failed governments of the 1970s. The removal of Clause 4 from the constitution of the Labour Party – with its commitment to the redistribution of wealth and power – was both emblematic and indicative of a conscious distancing of the party from the perceived failings of its collectivist past. There were good reasons for such a shift to different ground. The Labour Party was attempting to differentiate itself not only from the failures of socialism and collectivism, but also from the failures of neoliberalism and individualism. Furthermore, the Labour Party was reacting to a general reduction of trust in government. As Andrew Gamble has observed, 'the lines of argument have shifted but they have shifted for all parties and all ideologies, and the crisis of belief is general'.[43] As well as the breakdown of voter loyalty and the decline of class politics, parties also had to face the material impact of the rise of globalisation, an end to national economies and a shift to post-industrialism, if they were to be credible.[44]

The decline of mass politics is a general phenomenon with significant implications for politics and law-making. Manifestly, the grand narratives of inequality and equality are much less attractive to peoples and policy-makers alike. This loss of faith, or suspicion about the certainties offered by ideologies, has had a profound effect on the possibilities for party political action. In Britain, it means that political parties are no longer able to rely on a specific social identity, such as the labour movement, to secure electoral support. Its offsetting moment has seen the emergence of new ideologies, particularly feminism and environmentalism in their many forms, and identity politics. These have successfully garnered strength and support, and contributed to a shift towards a micro-politics of protest and single-issue politics. The end of the monolithic party structure and the fragmentation of political action are manifest in the creation of 'New Labour', the promulgation of the 'Third Way' and the very conduct of the first term of the Labour government under Tony Blair.[45] While in Opposition, the Labour Party had plenty of time to develop detailed policies that focused on particular problems. While it nurtured the electorate's belief that the Labour Party was more likely to protect and develop public services, it was careful not to identify its policies with the old ideological frameworks. It sought instead technical and evidence-based justifications for issue-based and outcome-oriented policies that were intended to convey competence and preparedness for government.

Thus the climate of opinion for those interested in evidence was altered dramatically in 1997 with the election of the Labour government.

Since coming to office, it has been keen to take advantage of social science research findings. This had led to two key changes. First, the government has supported moves to incorporate a social science perspective in all elements of research funding. This embraces the European Union's massive Framework Programme for research and development, as well as the government's own Foresight Programme. Second, it has accepted that social science can contribute to better government, most notably in a speech by the Secretary of State for Education and Employment, David Blunkett.[46] Social scientists have responded with a willingness to share expertise, methods and knowledge, not just with politicians and policy-makers, but with natural scientists. Rather than being ideologically informed, the government has claimed that its policies are based on the best available evidence. Consensus was replaced by conviction, which in turn was rejected in favour of evidence.

This particular party political response is now associated with near identical and back-to-back electoral victories, an historic occurrence in 100 years of Labour Party politics. In terms of governance we have seen a move away from grand narratives to a pragmatic politics of scaled down ambitions and policy-led change in place of efforts to bring about structural transformation of an unequal society. This is evident in the kinds of political claims that are made. The commitment is to equality of opportunity, not equality of outcome. 'We are working to make Britain better,' Prime Minister Blair has written, 'step by step.'[47] While this is a perfectly good intention, it conveys no vision. Instead, it is an invitation for each individual, cause group and lobby to define and demand the 'step' that must be taken to make Britain better. However, when the government weighs up these demands and chooses which will be met – and when and how – some criteria must be employed to discriminate between them. In the absence of an overarching vision and schema, such an approach risks either government overload redolent of the 1970s or, much worse, an uncritical transmission into policy of the systematic advantages that accrue to the wealthy and powerful in society under a reactive policy-making regime. Not just evidence, but also who is presenting it, must be a part of the policy-making equation. In other words, it is not at all clear whether the rejection of the old ideological compasses has yet been offset by the new 'output driven' political methods being used to chart progress to a 'better Britain'.[48]

On any account, this is a long way from the connection that Dicey drew between opinion and law-making in the early 1900s. If evidence replaces opinion, does this fundamentally change the character of law making? Evidence-based policy-making raises many questions, not least of which concerns the nature of social science research. Social science – like politics – also entertained within it the divide between individualism and collectivism for a large part of the twentieth century. On the central issue of social inequality, individualist social science favoured the view those private efforts, motivated by self-interest and enabled by innate entrepreneurship, could only bring progress with minimal state interference. Collectivist social scientific analysis, however, argued that inequality had structural causes that were best addressed by state intervention. For much of the twentieth century, social science methodology offered a choice between methodological individualism and methodological collectivism and by association an affinity with one or other of the contending political parties. ('Value-free' approaches implausibly proceeded as if content, methodology and findings were scientific and therefore somehow non-political.) However, as the social sciences have matured, the best research is increasingly less characterised by a sharp division between these nodal points.

Such developments have helped establish the independence of social science research from party and ideological perspective, despite some political attacks from governments of both left and right. Prime Minister Wilson, for example, once ordered a review of the entire Social Science Research Council expenditure on the basis of one inaccurate press report of research into mini-skirts.[49] Some fifteen years later, Thatcher famously claimed that 'there was no such thing as society', backing up her robust view on the very possibility of social science with a severe reduction in the research funding base in the early 1980s. Equally unwisely, then Education Secretary Blunkett responded in a similar fashion to press coverage of research findings not to his liking in 1999. He publicly called for a review of the funding of social science research. Not only was the research commissioned by the respected and wholly independent Joseph Rowntree Foundation, the quality of the research had already been praised by the government's own Social Exclusion Unit.[50]

While it may be accepted that the use of evidence is better than unblinking adherence to an ideology, scientists and social scientists alike are concerned about the quality of the evidence that can be obtained, and about the appropriateness of the evidence used to support a policy stance or decision.[51] In this respect, the political parties have a case to answer. Underlying the emphasis on evidence-based policy and the easy political rhetoric of the Third Way is a serious attempt to escape from the rigidities of the construction of the left/right divide in contemporary politics that prevailed throughout the twentieth century.

It took some time for the Labour Party to realise that it was more damaged than assisted by this crude dichotomisation, but once it did, it has fought hard to free itself of the collectivist label. Its re-election suggests that it has been successful, but there are questions about the extent to which the Labour government is deluding itself about its electoral appeal. The defeat of a weak, poorly led and divided opposition party on a near-record low turnout hardly establishes that the government is in tune with the majority. It may be that the electoral system has once again delivered a government with a value orientation that is still at variance with the population. The available evidence is that, in relation to the macro-policies on inequality, on support for public services and on taxation, the party has decided in its internal wisdom not to reflect public opinion. In 1997, there was already a gap between publicly expressed preferences and the priorities of the incoming government.

> For instance, most people, increasingly concerned about reducing inequality, insistently want to see more public spending on services such as health and education even if it means higher taxes – a policy that the new government is very unlikely to adopt, at least in the short term.[52]

The 16th report on *British Social Attitudes* (subtitled 'Who Shares New Labour Values?'), confirms the findings of earlier reports, particularly in relation to sympathy for higher public spending, as well as a general resistance on the part of the public readily to relinquish their core values.[53] In the light of the survey evidence, the 2001 election campaign, and its subsequent enthusiasm for private financing of public services, it is fair to ask whether the Labour government would ever adopt such a policy. At the same time, the campaign was notable for the degree of frustration at the lack of decisive action to reverse the decline in public services, even from people who would eventually return the government to power.

The world after 11 September 2001

It is tempting, given the dramatic nature of the events on 11 September 2001, to conclude that a recognisably new period in world history has begun. There is very little evidence to support this idea. There has been no change in the structure of world or national politics, while there is also continuity in the way that the processes of political power are played out. Nevertheless, this event has brought about a number of interesting reactions in relation to public opinion and law-making, and the connection to individualism and collectivism.

At one level, the attacks on the US illustrate the continuing clash of two incommensurable world-views. It was not a clash of individualism versus collectivism understood as a kind of in-house debate taking place within western civilisation. Rather, the clash is between the rich, powerful and secular states dominated by market values and political individualism and a non-western religious movement that foregrounds a set of radically conservative cultural values and a political agenda that is hostile to all forms of individualism and western imperialism. Both are totalising world-views: each has different means of promoting its interests. The battle between these two forces has been going on for some time (at least since the nineteenth century), and will continue well into the twenty-first.

At the symbolic level, the events can be read in a number of ways. A few determined individuals showed how vulnerable the centres of political, military and corporate power in the United States could be. The actions of a handful of would-be Davids against the Goliath produced shocking results, but not a knockout blow to a nation supposedly enfeebled by rampant individualism. Indeed the actions against institutions that were deemed so representative of American power, prestige and perfidy did not trigger a moral collapse. Instead, public sector workers dominated the initial response to the attack on the World Trade Center. Most prominent among these were the firefighters, who reacted immediately to the human catastrophe that unfolded and just as quickly engulfed many of them. The involvement and death of so many civilians and the role played by public servants transformed the political impact of the attack. It became a reminder of the central and irreplaceable role of public services in modern societies. The role of government, at local and national levels, was also highlighted positively, after a long period of challenges over the size of, and need for, government. These reactions are more consistent with a collectivist understanding of politics.

It is surely contrary to the expectations of those who planned and carried out the attacks that the governments of the US and Britain have been strengthened in the short term, with the leaders of both countries enjoying unprecedented levels of public approval. Moreover, there is some evidence of a reverse in the steady decline in attendance at places of Christian worship in the UK.

However, the impact on law-making in the US and Britain may tell a different story. Both countries have taken action that could not be more antagonistic to the liberal individualist tradition. New anti-terrorism laws, measures and practices have been introduced, curtailing the freedoms of ordinary citizens through an extension of the unaccountable powers of the state. There is no triumph here for individualism, but of the state perceived not as a collectivity, but as a threatened entity.

Conclusion

Has individualism triumphed? My concluding answer requires reflection on how it is that such a question can still be posed, followed by an interpretation of my sketch of the last fifty years. Two aspects of Dicey's account of public opinion and law-making are relevant. They animate the discussion, yet they pose problems throughout, almost entirely because Dicey's work has been so influential. This is unfortunate, because this influence has its malign aspects, in that he has become an authority in areas in which he has little or no competence and dubious methodological grounds, where any exist at all, for his claims. Specifically, his political individualism is shallow, and his account of the connection between law-making and public opinion fanciful.

His account of individualism and collectivism imbues the former with entirely good qualities and the latter with strictly dangerous tendencies. It is necessary therefore to distinguish between a judgement on Dicey's political hopes and fears (these are predictable and should be regarded as of no great consequence) and an evaluation of the extent to which individualistic characteristics predominate over collectivist features of law in society. Furthermore, his view of the relation between public opinion and law-making needs critical scrutiny. An examination of the nature of law in the last fifty years does reveal some contrasting examples of law, but this has had minimal impact on the liberal-institutionalist legal framework. This remains firmly in place, and shapes law-making accordingly. Moreover, that framework is maintained by a strong state.

> Public opinion continues to resist the rhetoric of both right and left about the near-universal virtues or dangers of state involvement, choosing instead to discriminate between policy areas in which the state should or should not intervene. Thus, there is on the one hand near-unanimity ... that the state should maintain or increase its spending on health and pensions, but considerable diffidence about the state's proper role in the regulation of business or industry.[54]

This brings us to Dicey's idealist assumption of the existence of a prevailing political culture that is decisive in the direction of both opinion and law-making.[55] He concludes his most Burkean chapter, and the whole book, with the claim that:

> Each kind of opinion entertained by men at a given era is governed by that whole body of beliefs, convictions, sentiments or assumptions, which, for want of a better name, we call the spirit of an age.[56]

There are two important claims embedded in this conservative view of history: human nature and public opinion. First, Dicey rejects a Benthamite account of a rationally knowable world, privileging instead a Burkean sense of an English tradition and culture that is not reducible to measurement or calculation. In this society, habits, custom and prejudice, not reason, animate individuals. Just as common law represents a form of collective rationality, modified over long historical time and according to circumstances, these patterns of behaviour stem from Burke's notion of habit as 'the collected reason of ages'.[57] The 'spirit of an age' is a version of the implicit knowledge of a traditional society embedded within and arising out of 'moral feeling and character',[58] that prejudice and practical wisdom memorably characterised by Burke as 'the bank and capital of nations and ages'. Dicey then attributes causal effect to that inaccessible spirit of the age, implying also that there is just one public opinion for the lawmaker to consider, namely that which connects to the underlying sentiments of the population. In effect, Dicey does not need actually to find out what public opinion is, since he already knows what it should reflect.

At this point, it is worth acknowledging that the last fifty years will always be divided into two great 'eras', namely the postwar consensus and Thatcherite conviction politics. Politicians and political scientists alike have defined these eras as political cultures defined by collectivism and individualism. Such commentators will imbue these eras with differing 'spirits of the age'. If Dicey is right, this is all we would need to know. Changes in public opinion would flow from the spirit of the particular age into public opinion and hence the law and individualism has triumphed to such an extent that a Labour government is studious in its avoidance of the taint of collectivism.

However, political cultures work better as colourful descriptions of a time rather than explanations of power and the complex of social forces and tendencies at play. Hence, an accurate account of the last fifty years must also consider how the dominance of Keynesian demand management gave way to neoliberal economic policy in the wake of changes to the local as well as the global economy (both of which have individualist as well as collectivist features in practice). As the longitudinal findings show in uncompromising detail, apparently obvious changes in the political culture, even when allied with deliberate attempts to shift values through a range of government policies will not be sufficient to shift the most important social attitudes. Moreover, such descriptions often ignore the structural and exogenous forces that contribute to political change within any one society.

Ultimately, a significant variation on Dicey's individualist theme is required. It appears that the majority of the members of the public do want greater individual freedom where they regard it as relevant. They will pursue their individual interest, they will develop individual responsibility, and they believe that this will contribute to the social good. However, they can also recognise that there are collective goods and responsibilities, and will perceive it as part of their duty to demand that the state act accordingly, even if it may involve some loss of individual freedom. Problems arise when the state is reluctant to accept its collectivist responsibilities, and when citizens are not adequately prepared and enabled to generate the benefits of collective action. Under these conditions, trust in the political process will decline. Fundamentally, it will be a reflection of the failure of a political process to respond to a stable set of political values held by the public but not, apparently, taken seriously by political elites. We may have left behind the era of conviction politics, but we will only move forward if law making can develop to the point where it reflects what the public appears to have known for some time – that individualism and collectivism are co-requisites for a just, equal society and a well-run polity. That would be a triumph.

Notes and References

1 My thanks to Andy Denham and Alison Edgley for their assistance with this chapter.
2 M. Ginsberg (ed.), *Law and Opinion in England in the 20th Century*, Stevens and Sons, London, 1959.
3 A. V. Dicey, *Lectures on the Relation between Law and Public Opinion in England during the 19th Century*, second edition, Macmillan, London, 1963, p. xc.
4 Ibid., pp. xci, xciii, 63–4.
5 Ibid., pp. 63–4, 67.
6 Ibid., pp. 64, 259.

54 Ian Forbes

7   Ibid., p. 64, note 1.
8   R. Titmuss, 'Health', in Ginsberg (ed.), p. 301.
9   Dicey, p. liiii.
10 Ginsberg (ed.), pp. 4–5.
11 E. Gallie, 'Essentially contested concepts', *Proceedings of the Aristotelian Society*, 56, 1956, pp. 167–98.
12 Ibid., pp. 14, 16.
13 See O. Kahn-Freund, 'Labour law', R. Titmuss, 'Health', and B. C. Roberts, 'Industrial relations', in Ginsberg (ed.), pp. 221, 300, 313, 366.
14 D. Bell, *The End of Ideology*, Westview Press, Glencoe, 1960.
15 E. Hobsbawm, *Age of Extremes*, Michael Joseph, London, 1994, pp. 257ff.
16 S. Beer, *Modern British Politics*, Faber and Faber, London, 1965, p. x.
17 Ibid., p. x.
18 Ibid., p. 80.
19 Ibid., p. 80.
20 Ibid., p. 81.
21 Ibid., p. 69.
22 Ibid., p. 70.
23 Ibid., p. 70.
24 P. J. Williamson, *Corporatism in Perspective*, Sage, London, 1989, p. 216.
25 Dicey, p. 301.
26 V. Bogdanor, 'The constitution', in D. Kavanagh and A. Seldon (eds.), *The Thatcher Effect*, Oxford University Press, Oxford, 1989, p. 133.
27 S. Beer, *Britain against Itself*, Faber and Faber, London, 1982, p. xiii.
28 A. Gamble, 'Ideas and interests in British economic policy', in M. Kandiah and A. Seldon (eds), *Ideas and Think Tanks in Contemporary Britain, Volume 2*, Frank Cass, London, 1996, pp. 1–21.
29 A. Denham and M. Garnett, 'Think tanks, British politics and "the climate of opinion"', in D. Stone, A. Denham and M. Garnett (eds.), *Think Tanks across Nations*, Manchester University Press, Manchester, 1998, p. 33.
30 F. Hayek, *Road to Serfdom*, Routledge and Kegan Paul, London, 1944, p. 56.
31 Bogdanor, p. 133.
32 C. Graham and T. Prosser, 'Conclusion', in C. Graham and T. Prosser (eds.), *Waiving the Rules: the Constitution under Thatcherism*, Open University Press, Milton Keynes, 1988, p. 174.
33 Bogdanor, p. 137.
34 *Sunday Times*, 3 May 1981.
35 P. Dunleavy, 'Electoral representation and accountability', in I. Holliday, A. Gamble and G. Parry (eds.), *Fundamentals in British Politics*, Macmillan, Basingstoke, 1999, pp. 224–5.
36 M. Moran, 'Politics and law in financial regulation', in Graham and Prosser (eds.), p. 72.
37 Dicey, p. 300.
38 John Rentoul, *Me and Mine*, Unwin Hyman, London, 1989, pp. xi, 1, 6.
39 Ibid., p. 24.
40 Ibid., p. 158.
41 Ibid., p. 170.
42 R. Jowell, J. Curtice, A. Park, L. Brook, K. Thompson and C. Bryson (eds.), *British Social Attitudes the 14th report*, Ashgate/SCPR, London, 1997, p. i.

43 Andrew Gamble, 'Conclusion: Politics 2000', in P. Dunleavy, A. Gamble, I. Holliday and G. Peele (eds.), *Developments in British Politics 5*, Macmillan, Basingstoke, 1997, p. 363.
44 Stuart Thompson, *The Social Democratic Dilemma: Ideology, governance and globalisation*, Macmillan, Basingstoke, 2000.
45 Anthony Giddens, *The Third Way*, Polity, Cambridge, 1998.
46 David Blunkett, 'Influence or irrelevance: can social science improve government?', ESRC Lecture Speech 2 February 2000, Economic and Social Research Council/Department or Education and Employment.
47 Tony Blair, 'Foreword', in G. Kelly (ed.), *Is New Labour Working?* Fabian Pamphlet 590, Fabian Society, London, 1999, p. 1.
48 Michael Temple, 'New Labour's Third Way: pragmatism and governance', *British Journal of Politics and International Relations*, Vol. 2, No. 3, October 2000, p. 313.
49 *The Guardian*, 1 January, 2000.
50 *The Observer*, 21 November, 1999.
51 Douglas Black, 'The limitations of evidence', *Perspectives in Biology and Medicine*, 42(1), Autumn 1998, pp. 1–7.
52 Jowell et al., p. xiv. What is even more striking about these findings is that they establish that there is no substantive difference in the pattern of beliefs between the generations born before Margaret Thatcher came to power, and those brought up entirely under Conservative rule.
53 R. Jowell, J. Curtice, A. Park and K. Thompson (eds), *British Social Attitudes the 16th report*, Ashgate, London, 1999, chs 1 and 10.
54 R. Jowell, J. Curtice, A. Park, L. Brook, K. Thompson and C. Bryson (eds), *British – and European – Social Attitudes the 15th report*, Ashgate/SCPR, London, 1998, p. 52.
55 Dicey, p. 465.
56 Ibid.
57 E. Burke, *Reflections on the Revolution in France* (ed. C. C. O'Brien), Penguin, Harmondsworth, 1968, pp. 101, 193.
58 Dicey, p. 465.

Part II
Public Morality and the Citizen

3
Matrimonial Property: Legal Developments and Social Trends

*Lisa Glennon**

Introduction

Family law confers legal rights and duties upon 'family' members, which may, at times, conflict with the exercise of their individual rights.[1] A tension between competing rights can be seen in the context of matrimonial property law, a focus of Lecture XI in Dicey's *Law and Opinion in England during the 19th Century*. The tension in this context has generally been between the property rights of individuals and the extent to which these rights are affected by marriage. Such questions are not simply of historical interest, however, as the legal regulation of matrimonial property has yet to be resolved satisfactorily. In the twenty-first century there is an added dimension. Revolutionary changes in family formation means that marriage can no longer be said to be the social norm. The question, therefore, is no longer confined to 'How does marriage affect individual property rights?' What must also be asked is 'How does cohabitation and family membership generally, affect the property rights of the individuals involved in the familial relationship?' This chapter considers how the courts and the legislature respectively have struggled in determining the ownership of (quasi)-matrimonial property and how their responses have been informed by contemporary societal trends.

In his work, Dicey used the development of matrimonial property law in the nineteenth century to illustrate how judge-made law can determine the 'course and character of parliamentary legislation'.[2] Dicey reflected upon the common law doctrine of unity which meant that upon marriage a husband and wife became one person,[3] a corollary of which was that upon marriage a wife's property was assigned to her husband and she lost the right of control and enjoyment of it.[4] The

59

introduction of reforming statutes, commencing in 1870 and culminating in the Married Woman's Property Act 1882, enshrined the doctrine of separate property, which meant that a married woman could hold property independently of her husband. It is clear, however, that this conceptual idea was not revolutionary when enshrined in the legislation as the Courts of Equity for centuries had been developing equitable principles to enable a married woman to hold her own property, thus mitigating the hardship of the common law doctrine of unity.[5] They had done this by the development of marriage settlements, whereby the property of a woman about to enter marriage could be transferred to a trustee for her separate use.

One of the most interesting themes from Dicey's work regarding the evolution of matrimonial property law is the relationship between legislation and existing judge-made law. Several aspects of Dicey's assessment are pertinent. First, Dicey argues that, not only did the judge-made law of the Court of Equity mould the substantive content of the legislation in the latter half of the nineteenth century, it also delayed its enactment as the hardship of the common law had been mitigated for women with property to settle upon marriage, thus postponing the required impetus for reform.[6] Second, it is clear that legislative reform was required, as the principles developed by judge-made law were uneven in their application. As the use of marriage settlements was of real benefit only to a limited number of women of a certain wealth and class, the common law system and the developments of equity coexisted, which led to 'an unforeseen inequality between the position of the rich and the position of the poor'.[7] It was only when the legislature intervened that all married women, under the doctrine of separate property, became entitled to hold and dispose of their own property at will. Finally, the impetus for legislative intervention is also instructive. Dicey reasons that change in public opinion, particularly in relation to the role of women in society and an increase in the number of working women, meant that the wrong caused by the common law doctrine of unity was 'far more visible to the public in 1870 than in 1832'.[8] The search for gender-based equality has been a consistent theme in the relationship between matrimonial property law and public opinion and it has remained a concern to the present day.[9]

The purpose of this chapter is to consider the main reforms in matrimonial property regulation in the context of relationship breakdown in the latter half of the twentieth century. The focus is on the contextual response of both the courts and the legislature. As family formation changed, the institution of marriage altered in line with formal equality reform[10] and the role of women changed both inside and outside the home.

Division of property on relationship breakdown

Any discussion of the evolution of matrimonial property law must begin with the doctrine of separate property. The historical intervention of equity in devising ways to enable a wife to hold her own property, put on a legislative footing in the late nineteenth century, has resulted in the legacy of individualism upon which the doctrine of separate property is based.[11] As Dicey noted, the separate property regime was introduced in the late nineteenth century in order to achieve formal equality between men and women. Ensuring that each was legally entitled to hold and dispose of their own property at will during marriage was considered necessary to achieve this end. Concerns about gender-based equality have, however, continued to pervade the evolution of matrimonial property law in the twentieth century, as it became clear that the formal equality notion inherent in the separate property regime did not lead to substantive equality between the sexes.[12] With the prevailing male breadwinner model of family economics, the fact that legal ownership of the matrimonial home was usually vested in the husband meant that the separate property regime was working against those whom it was designed to protect.[13] This was essentially because the separate property doctrine precluded the circumstances of family life from having any bearing on the parties' respective property rights. If a wife did not legally own the matrimonial home along with her husband, then neither the fact of marriage, nor the circumstances of family life, gave her an interest in it. The courts and the legislature in Dicey's era had struggled to ensure equality of treatment between men and women. In the latter half of the twentieth century, by contrast, their struggle has been to mitigate the hardship of the separate property regime as the main issue became 'whether and how to give to each spouse a share in the acquests of the other'.[14]

In the 1970s, legislation was passed, which gave the court a wide discretion to transfer property between spouses on divorce. Prior to this the only mechanism at the court's disposal to give a spouse an interest in the matrimonial home was the law of trusts, the principles of which apply in the determination of all property disputes and not just those between spouses. Just as the Courts of Equity 'reacted' to the problems caused by the doctrine of unity prior to nineteenth-century legislative reform, the judiciary in the latter half of the twentieth century were faced with resolving property disputes on divorce without the aid of legislative intervention as evolving postwar social conditions gradually highlighted the 'unfairness' of the separate property regime. Increasing separation and divorce rates brought the resolution of marital property disputes to the attention of the courts,[15] while the increase in owner-occupation,[16] and the rise in the value of properties meant that, upon spousal separation, 'the real question in issue between the parties... referr[ed] to the division of what may be regarded as a windfall for both or either'.[17] Without legislation the judiciary were forced to apply principles which were of general application. The net result was an era of judicial tension between an orthodox application of trust law regardless of the circumstances of domestic life and manipulation of the principles in order to maximise the property sharing of the spouses.

Reflecting briefly on the principles of property law, it is important to note that two species of property ownership coexist. Legal ownership of land is determined by the name(s) appearing on the title deeds, while the law of trusts determines equitable ownership. In basic terms an express trust of land must be evidenced in writing while implied trusts (resulting and constructive trusts) are imposed by law in order to protect the non-legal owner from the inequitable conduct of the legal owner. The operation of trust law means that a wife whose name does not appear on the title deeds (a non-legal owner of the property) may be entitled to proportionate ownership on the basis of equitable principles and the imposition of either a resulting or constructive trust in her favour. Direct financial contributions to the purchase price of the property, which is conveyed into the name of the other, will give rise to a resulting trust and will entitle the contributor to a share in the property proportionate to the amount of the contribution. It is the extent to which indirect financial contributions (such as contributions to the family's general expenses) and domestic labour entitles the non-legal owner to an equitable interest in the property which led to conflicting judicial principles in the latter half of the twentieth century.

The constructive trust provides a certain amount of leeway to take contributions, other than direct financial contributions to the purchase price, into account. In basic terms, a constructive trust will be imposed in a contributor's favour where there was a common intention between the parties to share the equitable interest which was subsequently relied upon by the non-legal owner to his or her detriment, known as the common intention constructive trust. The seminal decisions in the development of this doctrine are *Pettitt* v *Pettitt*[18] and *Gissing* v *Gissing*,[19] although, in the words of Youdan, the House of Lords was much clearer in the principles it rejected in these cases than in the principles it propounded.[20] Both before and after these decisions, in which the House of Lords emphasised the need for an orthodox application of established principles, members of the Court of Appeal, particularly Lord Denning, attempted to use trust principles to increase the property sharing of the spouses.

'Straining' equitable principles to achieve fairness

One consistent theme in the twentieth-century debate on family property is the attempt to achieve fairness between the parties. In terms of the judicial development of equitable principles, this can be seen as the primary objective underlying Lord Denning's ideology. While the orthodox application of trust principles focuses on financial contributions to the acquisition of the property or an agreement between the spouses to share ownership, Lord Denning attempted to use traditional principles to achieve a fair outcome. He did this by introducing a discretionary approach through his interpretation of section 17 of the Married Woman's Property Act 1882 and the development of the 'family assets' doctrine.

Section 17 of the Married Woman's Property Act 1882 states that '[I]n any question between husband and wife as to the title to or possession of property, either party ... may apply [to the court] ... and the judge ... may make such order with respect to the property ... as he thinks fit.' Lord Denning regarded this section as giving the court discretion to determine the parties' property rights, transcending all legal or equitable rights, in accordance with the notion of fairness.[21] In the exercise of this discretion His Lordship developed the 'family assets' doctrine which meant that the parties' acquisition of family assets by their *joint efforts*[22] during the marriage enabled the court to attribute to them the intention that they were to share the product of their efforts jointly.[23]

The House of Lords subsequently ruled, however, that section 17 was procedural only. While the court could *declare* the parties' respective proprietary interests on the basis of ordinary trust principles, it could not re-distribute them.[24] The lack of clarity in the principles to be applied when dealing with indirect contributions, however, gave Lord Denning the opportunity to reconceptualise his discretion in subsequent Court of Appeal decisions.[25] Indeed, in several post-*Gissing* cases Lord Denning once again adopted his discretionary approach through the development of the 'new model constructive trust', which was imposed by law whenever justice and good conscience required it.[26] In line with His Lordship's earlier approach, circumstances where the property was acquired by the parties' joint efforts for their joint use[27] justified the imposition of the trust, regardless of whether the parties had either an express or implied agreement regarding the equitable ownership.[28] In deliberately avoiding the difficulties in applying the referability test (the requirement that the claimant's contributions be clearly linked to the acquisition of the property), Lord Denning preferred the holistic approach to family expenditure. This asked whether the non-legal owner had made a substantial contribution, direct or indirect, to the acquisition of the house or repayment of the mortgage or loan.[29]

While other jurisdictions have accepted a similar ideology of the constructive trust in the development of family property law,[30] it has not been accepted in English law. The manipulation of orthodox principles to achieve a 'fair outcome' survived until a differently constituted Court of Appeal reasserted the traditional application of property principles.[31] In 1990, when the House of Lords had the opportunity to consider the contextual operation of trust principles, it diminished the relevance of indirect contributions in establishing an equitable interest.[32] The net result of the case law is that indirect contributions by themselves do not justify an ownership right in the property unless supported by evidence of an agreement, arrangement or understanding that such an interest would be conferred upon the non-legal owner.

It is generally accepted, therefore, that strict property law principles are inadequate to resolve (quasi-)matrimonial property disputes.[33] Indeed, more recent decisions reveal that the courts are still struggling with rationalising the parties' indirect contributions within the remit of established principles.[34] Lord Denning's attempts to deal with the issue by the development of a flexible judicial approach failed and legislation was ultimately required. Indeed, it has been suggested that this legislation gave the courts the power which Lord Denning 'had sought to assume in the context of adjusting property rights when he was presiding over the Court of Appeal'.[35] The legislation, which was enacted, governs both financial and capital distribution on divorce and it is this to which we now turn. It is worth noting initially, however, that the legislation only applies on divorce. The property disputes of spouses during their marriage; unmarried cohabitants[36] and other homesharers are still determined by the law of trusts.

Property division on divorce

On divorce, two questions usually arise: how should matrimonial property be divided and should one spouse continue to support the other?[37] Prior to 1970, these questions were decided separately. As we have seen, ownership of matrimonial property depended on the application of trust principles, while maintenance on divorce was 'inextricably linked with the concept of divorce as a relief for wrongdoing'.[38] When divorce was first introduced into the civil courts in England in 1857[39] it was based upon the doctrine of matrimonial offence, which meant that the provision of maintenance on divorce was to ensure that a husband who divorced his 'innocent wife' discharged his marital obligations towards her. The Divorce Reform Act 1969, however, removed fault as the conceptual basis for divorce and provided the impetus for the Matrimonial Proceedings and Property Act 1970. The removal of fault as the governing factor in the availability of divorce led to the removal of fault as the basis of post-divorce financial arrangements. The 1970 Act gave the court power to order one spouse to make 'financial provision' for the other through periodical payments, lump-sum payments or a property adjustment order. Indeed, the property adjustment order was one of the main innovations of the Act as it gave the court the power to redistribute matrimonial property and other assets on divorce.[40] This was a significant development, which has been judicially stated as introducing the remedy of *'equitable distribution'* of matrimonial property reflecting *'social change and compelling social need'*.[41] It had become quite clear that the doctrinal limitations of strict property law principles precluded the court from either resolving the financial consequences arising from the relationship through property distribution or from giving a spouse a share in the property, on the basis of non-financial contributions to the welfare of the family. The introduction of the property adjustment order meant that the court could redistribute property ownership on divorce unfettered by the restrictions inherent in trust law.

The principles are now embodied in the Matrimonial Causes Act 1973. In deciding whether, and how, to exercise their powers, section 25(1) of the 1973 Act provides that it is the duty of the court to have regard to all the circumstances of the case, first consideration being given to the welfare of any child of the family. Section 25(2) contains a further list of factors for the court to have regard and includes the parties' present and future earning capacity; the present and future financial needs and obligations of the parties; the age of the parties and the duration of the marriage and the contribution which each of the parties has made or is likely to make in the foreseeable future to the welfare of the family, including any contribution by looking after the home or caring for the family.[42] It is worth noting that the introduction of the court's power to rearrange the parties' financial and capital assets on divorce through periodical payments, lump-sum payments or a property adjustment order allowed the court to fuse together the issues of spousal support and property division.[43] Indeed, the power to redistribute property ownership is one tool at the court's disposal to implement the parties' post-divorce obligations and, in deciding whether to make such an order, the claimant's contribution to the welfare of the family is one factor for consideration. Although only one factor listed in the statutory criteria, however, this was an important inclusion considering the limitations of the law of trusts. As we have seen, inequality between the sexes rendered the principles of trust law open to critique, primarily because the court could not effectively take account of non-financial contributions when resolving property disputes. Once 'contributions to the welfare of the family' became a legitimate factor for consideration, however, was the property adjustment order used to achieve substantive equality between the sexes?[44]

One must take account of the social conditions in the latter half of the twentieth century as the search for gender-based equality has been affected by the changing socio-economic position of women. The practice of the working woman using her earnings on general family expenditure rather than on property acquisition highlighted the unfairness of the separate property regime. However, this practice, along with the male breadwinner model of family economics, is less prevalent today.[45] This means that if the property adjustment order is simply used as a remedial device, the extent of its application may be called into question as the harshness of the separate property regime has been tempered by external socio-economic factors. This social context adds another dimension to the contemporary resolution of the 'family property question'. It is against this backdrop that we must discern the policy of capital distribution on divorce, whether it is exercised to give property rights by virtue of the marriage itself; to satisfy the claimant's needs and equalise the economic consequences of the marriage or to give property rights on the basis of contributions, widely defined.

The policy of the legislation

The legislation, when first enacted in 1971, stated that the court's power to make financial and capital distribution on divorce should, as far as possible, be exercised in such a way as to place the parties in the financial position in which they would have been in had the marriage not broken down and had each properly discharged his or her financial obligations and responsibilities towards the other.[46] This principle, which was based on the notion of keeping alive the financial obligations of an otherwise dissolved marriage, was criticised as being inconsistent with the modern law of divorce[47] and proved unworkable in practice. Its removal came in 1984[48] and provisions were introduced which instructed the court to give first consideration to the welfare of any children and to consider the appropriateness of a 'cleanbreak'.[49] However, neither the clean break ideal nor the children's welfare principle are overriding objectives and the statutory factors listed for the court's consideration when deciding whether to make an order are not listed in a hierarchical fashion. With no overriding objective, therefore, it was left to the judiciary to interpret the statutory criteria. In *Piglowski* v *Piglowski*[50] Lord Hoffman said that the guidelines informing the application of the judicial discretion were derived from the values about family life which it considers would be widely accepted in the community. One consistent theme is that post-divorce settlements should achieve a 'generally accepted standard of fairness'.[51] In low-income cases, circumstances, to a large extent, dictate the outcome as the assessment of the parties' needs will 'lean heavily in favour of the children and the parent with whom they live'.[52] Indeed, it is hard to get away from the fact that where resources are limited the housing and income needs of the parties and their children take priority. It is only really in higher-income cases where 'it becomes necessary to consider the ultimate limits of the court's discretionary powers'.[53] In other words, where judicial 'policy' becomes more visible.

From the mid-1970s, Ormrod LJ, in a series of so-called 'big-money' cases,[54] took the concept of the parties' 'needs',[55] equated this with their 'reasonable requirements' and elevated this to a position where it became determinative in the making of an order on divorce.[56] Judicial practice, then, placed the claimant's contributions as one factor for consideration when determining the 'reasonableness' of their requirements which meant that

> those contributions became subservient to a subjective assessment of 'desert', rather than a free-standing assessment of the value they may have added to the family's wealth.[57]

Reflecting on whether the legislation remedied the defects of trust law, this judicial interpretation is relevant. Rather than widening the type of contributions which gave a non-legal owner an entitlement to share in the family's financial and capital assets, the court's power to order 'financial provision' on divorce was implemented to satisfy the claimant's dependency and prospective needs. Such a remedial interpretation of the legislation called into question the justification for such orders in light of the contemporary socio-economic position of women, which has already been highlighted. Significantly, it also had an impact on the value placed on non-financial contributions. One of the main criticisms of trust law was the fact that non-financial contributions did not, by themselves, give rise to an ownership right in the property. The subsequent 'needs-based' interpretation of the legislation, however, similarly distinguished the value of domestic labour and the value of a claimant's work outside the home. For example, cases reveal an increase in the claimant's share beyond her 'reasonable requirements' on the basis of contributions, which had a clear economic value, such as participation in her husband's business enterprise. In *Preston* v *Preston*[58] Ormrod LJ stated that the claimant's work in the family business would greatly enhance her contribution to the welfare of the family and may result in a substantial increase in her award on the basis that 'she [had] "earned" her share in the total assets'.[59] The 'needs-based' approach, therefore, undermines the value of non-financial contributions in their own right and, ultimately, affects the nature of the property adjustment order itself. Indeed, the integration of property transference within the general ambit of support law makes the justification for such transfers bound up with notions of dependency and support rather than redistributive ownership on the basis of entitlement.

The move to entitlement?

The House of Lords decision in *White* v *White*[60] could, however, mark a re-conceptualisation of the principles based upon the notion of entitlement. One clear aspect of the decision is the realignment of the statutory criteria where 'needs', in the guise of 'reasonable requirements' is removed as the determinative factor. While this is relevant for the policy of future 'big-money' cases, aspects of the judgement may be relevant for post-divorce disputes generally, particularly the recognition of the value of domestic labour. The leading judgement of Lord Nicholls stressed that in order to achieve a fair outcome on divorce there is no place for gender-based discrimination. In other words, if each party contributed equally to the family, there should be no bias in favour of the money-earner and against the homemaker and the child-carer.[61] This assimilation of financial and non-financial contributions is important. It suggests a movement away from the provision of domestic labour merely being seen as giving rise to the claimant's future needs, upon which the post-divorce settlement is constructed. Instead, such contributions render the claimant entitled to share in the family's assets on divorce. Following from this, to ensure that domestic contributions are not undervalued, it was stated that judges in future cases should check their tentative views against the yardstick of equal division of assets on divorce.[62] This does not mean, however, that equality of division is a presumption or even a starting point in future cases. The fact that Parliament did not introduce a fractional approach to the division of assets on divorce meant, for Lord Nicholls, that any greater judicial imposition of fixed legal rights would go beyond the correct judicial function. It was stated, however, that there must be good articulated reasons for departing from equal division. As His Lordship did not develop this point beyond the context of the case it is likely that much discursive and legal debate will attempt to discern what those reasons might be.[63]

To what extent, however, does this decision suggest the beginning of an approach where 'contributions to the welfare of the family' give the contributor entitlement to a proportionate distribution of the capital assets on divorce? Certainly, the decision does suggest a movement away from 'needs' and towards entitlement. The principle to draw from *White*, however, is not the principle of equal division of assets on divorce, but the affirmation that post-divorce financial provision should be determined on the basis of fairness, an ideal which led to the assimilation of financial and non-financial contributions. However, that entitlement is based on the retrospective judicial assessment of the parties' contributions may give rise to difficulty in cases where the facts do not display such clear evidence of a wife's integration of domestic and business roles. The contextual assessment in *White* involved a couple whose thirty-year marriage constituted both a marital and business partnership where the wife's overall contributions could clearly be quantified as economically valuable in building up the family's assets.[64]

What value will be placed upon non-financial contributions in future cases where the parties did not build up substantial assets from scratch? As the principle of equality of division is a yardstick and not a presumption, or even a starting point, there is room for judicial confusion surrounding the respective weight to attach to the differing contributions to the family. Take a case where one spouse's non-financial contributions to the welfare of the family, perhaps as a parent with primary responsibility for child-care, is not simultaneous with a husband building up a burgeoning business. Cases where there is no obvious causal connection between one spouse's non-financial contributions and the acquisition of the family's assets may not be adequately resolved by the *White* principles. Lord Nicholls discussed the issue of property acquired outside the marriage, which His Lordship stated was generally unavailable to the claimant unless it was required to satisfy her needs. It may be that situations where there is a tenuous link between domestic labour and the acquisition of the family's capital assets may be similarly regarded, and we return to the situation where financial and property division is limited to satisfying the claimant's needs. However, the claimant's contributions to the welfare of the family in such cases may be no less valuable and may, in economic terms, be viewed as important to the retention of existing property and assets.[65] While the policy has moved from the narrow conception of satisfying the claimant's needs (although in low-income cases this may still be the dominant factor) and the notion of entitlement has emerged, there may be some difficulties surrounding the future application of the principles.[66]

Resolving the 'family property question': from the law of trusts to legislative reform

The division of matrimonial property has obviously been an important legal question in the latter half of the twentieth century. As we have seen the judiciary's reaction to the 'family property question' preceded legislative reform as the gender-based disparity in economic contributions to the acquisition of property gradually highlighted the unfairness of the separate property doctrine. Neither judge-made principles nor subsequent legislative reform, however, have resolved this issue. Trust principles had to operate within doctrinal constraints, while the post-reform years, until recently, witnessed familial contributions merely influencing the 'reasonableness of a claimant's requirements'.

If one reflects on the theme identified by Dicey, that is, the relationship between early, judge-made principles and subsequent legislation, the inadequacies of the orthodox application of trust law highlighted the need for legislative reform[67] and helped to influence the reform debate. According to Glendon, the impetus for reform in 1970 was based on the failure of the separate property regime to take account of need and dependency on relationship breakdown.[68] Tied in with this, however, was the under-valuation of domestic labour, as judicial principles did not succeed in getting a wife a proprietary interest in the matrimonial home on the basis of non-financial contributions. In his analysis of the mischief Parliament intended to remedy in 1970, Lord Denning referred to an earlier Law Commission Report, which stated that the legislative inclusion of 'contributions to the welfare of the family' was particularly important to the adjustment of property between spouses.[69] The Report went on to say that this inclusion should meet the complaint that contributions which 'wives make towards the acquisition of the family assets by performing domestic chores' is ignored in the determination of their rights.[70]

This illustrates the intended connection between ownership of matrimonial property and the parties' respective contributions, where for the first time non-financial contributions were relevant. The fact that Lord Denning, in the early case of *Wachtel* v *Wachtel*,[71] stated that the division of the family's capital assets on divorce should not be affected by the prospect of the wife's remarriage as 'she has earned it by her contribution in looking after the home and caring for the family', suggests that early judicial interpretation of the legislation based capital distribution on entitlement due to the claimant's contributions, widely defined. Subsequent judicial practice, however, did not adequately separate the issues of property division and spousal support and this was compounded by the elevation of 'needs' as the guiding factor. The fusion of these issues meant that capital assets were distributed on the basis of 'need' in order to satisfy the claimant's post-divorce dependency. As a result, the underlying tension became that of female dependency versus self-sufficiency, an argument, which some feminists say, cannot be resolved without being open to critique.[72]

Capital distribution on the basis of entitlement would, however, side step the dependency/self-sufficiency question.[73] Indeed, the judicial attempts to redistribute the parties' property prior to legislative intervention avoided this debate. One reason for this may be the timing of the decisions in an era when the improved socio-economic status of women may not have been developed to such an extent as to render post-divorce dependency unjustifiable, while it is also the case that the more controversial point at this time was the inappropriate use of trust principles to increase property sharing. It is worth noting, however, that the jurisprudence of Lord Denning was not constructed on the basis of dependency but on the basis of entitlement, albeit exercised through unauthorised judicial discretion.

What is clear, however, is that neither the principles of Lord Denning nor subsequent legislation gave the non-owning spouse an automatic right to share matrimonial property by virtue of the marriage itself. While the approach of Lord Denning looked beyond direct financial contributions to the acquisition of specific property, contributions which entitled a non-legal owner to a proportionate share of the property had to be substantial and in money or money's worth.[74] While the court may have been 'giving effect to the partnership aspects of matrimony',[75] it was the combined economic efforts of spouses which gave rise to an equitable interest in the property.[76] In remedying the inadequacies of trust law, however, the legislature opted for a broad judicial discretion to redistribute property on divorce as opposed to a system of automatic co-ownership by virtue of the marriage. While marital status is the prerequisite for accessing this adjustive regime on divorce, the application of the court's powers is based on other contextual factors.[77] Unlike the position in some other jurisdictions, therefore, a spouse has never had an automatic right to ownership of matrimonial property either during or after the marriage.

The viability of such a 'status-based' approach today depends on the legitimacy of conferring rights by virtue of the marriage itself. Statistics reveal, however, that marriage rates continue to decline while cohabitation rates increase[78] and commentators note that the legal status of marriage has lost significance.[79] One could speculate, therefore, that the conferment of property rights on the basis of the marriage itself might be an unlikely prospect. Indeed, any future development of the law must take account of the increasing diversity of family formation. The obvious drawback of the present adjustive regime on divorce is its exclusive application to married couples who are divorcing. The system does, however, have elements of a functional approach to capital distribution (in other words, distribution which is based on contextual factors) although the potential benefits of this have been hampered by the judicially imposed policy of satisfying the claimant's needs. The decision of *White* may signify the emergence of the notion of entitlement but much depends on future judicial interpretation. The fact remains, however, that the regime is unavailable to resolve the property disputes of unmarried cohabitants and other home-sharers, which means that it can only ever provide part of the solution to the contemporary 'family property question'.

An alternative mode of entitlement

By way of comparison it is interesting to note the recent proposals of the Northern Ireland Law Reform Advisory Committee in relation to matrimonial property.[80] The proposals seek to remedy the unfairness of strict property law principles both for spouses during marriage, where the adjustive regime has no application and for unmarried cohabitants where there is no legal mechanism for the court to determine property rights outside traditional principles. As the main criticism of ordinary property law principles is the under-valuation of domestic labour and other non-financial contributions, one can say that the policy of the proposals is to remedy the gender inequality in heterosexual relationships.[81]

The Committee recommends statutory co-ownership of the matrimonial home, and other property, of spouses and qualifying cohabitants in order to give effect to the presumed intention of the parties that such property is to be co-owned.[82] This intention, it was said, could be presumed in marriage, where the relationship was intended to be permanent, but could only be presumed between unmarried cohabitants in a quasi-spousal relationship.[83] The mode of entitlement is thus based on the status of certain identified relationships which are assumed to display a sufficient degree of permanence and stability, married couples and heterosexual unmarried cohabitants whose relationship, on the basis of objective factors, most closely resembles marriage.[84]

We have already seen that the public policy concern of achieving substantive gender-based equality is evident in the development of matrimonial property law. When it comes to legislative inclusion, however, the competing public policy concern of keeping within accepted familial parameters is also apparent, as statutory inclusion may be seen as giving legitimacy to certain relationships. Indeed, the original remit of the Northern Irish proposals provides an illustration of the relationship between public opinion and legislative development. Initially the Committee intended to restrict the proposals to married couples as it was 'reluctant to engage in matters which might be regarded as involving controversial policy decisions. It felt that there was certain sensitivity in the community about placing cohabitants on the same level as married couples'.[85] It was only because other legislative provisions recognise unmarried cohabitants[86] that the Committee felt able to justify the inclusion of cohabitants in this instance.

This illustrates how pragmatic policy reasons influence law reform and, in the context of family law, can render the process slow and gradual.[87] Indeed, Neave has commented that substantive reform of capital distribution on relationship breakdown may be better focused on heterosexual relationships, as, for pragmatic reasons, it may be difficult to achieve simultaneous reform for same-sex couples.[88] Neave has also suggested that for policy reasons, the gender-inequality in hetero-normative structures may further justify the exclusive focus on heterosexual relationships.[89] Similar reasoning can be found in the Committee's proposals and coupled with the fact that it is unlikely that wider recommendations would receive the requisite political support for enactment, it is unsurprising that qualifying cohabitants are restricted to those who satisfy the 'marriage model' of family form. In a similar vein, Willmott has stated that:

[If] the recommendations of a body proposing law reform are received by the general public with widespread reservation or even hostility, it is unlikely, perhaps correctly so, that those recommendations will receive the political support necessary for their carriage into legislation.[90]

If the Committee's proposals do become law this will mark a significant change in direction for Northern Ireland. While the English Law Commission, referring to public support for joint ownership of matrimonial property,[91] has previously recommended statutory co-ownership of the matrimonial home, such proposals have never been enacted. The fact that the adjustive regime on divorce came into operation and that legislation gave the courts the power to reallocate spouses' property upon death[92] meant that the impetus for the introduction of co-ownership or a community property regime was lost.[93] Hale's view is that while the Law Commission's support for co-ownership of the matrimonial home in the early 1970s may have 'caught the same tide of public opinion' which led to other legislative enactments such as the Sex Discrimination Act 1975,[94]

continued examination and reform of the discretionary remedies on marital and family breakdown is more likely to bear fruit than attempts to introduce new rules of substantive law...[95]

Indeed, the Northern Irish proposals must be viewed against the backdrop of contemporary trends in family law. The diminution of the legal status of marriage has already been noted and it is particularly interesting that commentators acknowledge an increase in the policy of individualism, defined by Eekelaar as the absence of distinctive family obligations.[96] Indeed, Lewis states that the dilemma at the end of the twentieth century is how far adult family members should be treated as independent individuals?[97] The impetus for the growth of individualism may derive from externally related forces such as increased female participation in the labour market, which could be said to reduce the need for remedial legislation facilitating ongoing dependency. The breakdown of the male breadwinner model of family economics and the increasing diversity of family formation and responsibility for domestic labour, could, in fact, diminish the justification for the Committee's proposals. Indeed, constructing a system of fixed legal rights in order to remedy the gender imbalance caused by the economic, social and biological reality of women's lives is problematic if such considerations provide the sole means of identifying which relationships should come under the statutory scheme as of right.[98] The inherent conflict of these proposals with the notion of individualism lies in the imposition of a fixed set of rights on certain relationships due to their status and regardless of their character. It can be questioned whether the assumptions made by the Committee reflects the substance of all (quasi)-spousal relationships today and, in the words of Zuckerman '[In] order to justify automatic joint ownership one [has] to show that it reflects widespread and uniform social conventions...'.[99] A preferable model would seek to remedy, amongst other things, gender-based inequality within a functional system which does not make assumptions about the dynamic of certain relationships solely by reference to their (quasi)-marital status.

Conclusion

Otto Kahn-Freund said in 1971:

> [W]e are living through times of revolutionary changes in society. It is these changes much more than anything that has happened inside the law which has caused the upheaval in matrimonial property law...[100]

The search for substantive equality between the sexes has pervaded the development of matrimonial property law and it continues to be an influential force. However, the diversity of contemporary society dictates that gender-based inequality can no longer be the sole factor influencing policy and that the status of certain relationships cannot be the sole indicator of an intention to share property. Indeed, for these reasons, the reform proposals in Northern Ireland are open to critique.

The English Law Commission is currently looking at the property rights of 'homesharers', largely as a result of the dissatisfaction with the continued operation of orthodox trust principles to resolve the property disputes of unmarried cohabitants.[101] However, as we have seen, the legislation governing the property distribution of spouses on divorce can also be criticised. Indeed, the adjustive regime on divorce has been under scrutiny in recent years.[102] The present review, therefore, could be used as an opportunity to re-consider capital distribution generally.[103] It is submitted that one option for reform is to start with the recognition that post-relationship entitlement to property division and income can be viewed as conceptually different. Indeed, a recent empirical study by the National Centre for Social Research found that people viewed entitlement to assets and income in different ways. Except in relation to provision for children, income was not regarded as 'joint' following separation, while in relation to the family home 'non-financial contributions (the running of the home, and caring for children) appeared to play a key role in a sense of entitlement'.[104]

Non-financial contributions and domestic labour can be viewed on two levels, both of which can be built into a broad functional regime, which is accessible to all regardless of marital status or sexual orientation. While such contributions play a part in the acquisition and retention of capital assets, they may also have a detrimental affect on a person's economic prospects. This could be recognised in a functional regime, which provides for an entitlement-based distribution of capital assets coupled with the possibility of rehabilitative financial provision.[105] While it is beyond the scope of this paper to consider the details of such a regime, learning from previous failures on the part of the judiciary to assess contributions on a case-by-case basis, statutory presumptions would be required. In other words, certain functional aspects of the relationship would entitle the contributor to proportionate ownership of the parties' capital assets. Eekelaar, for example, suggests that after the accommodation needs of the children and the parties are met, all property[106] should be subject to the presumption of equal sharing if the parties have lived together for a certain period and if they have brought up at least one child during that period.[107] This model, according to Eekelaar, would not exclude property division in cases not involving children, although in such cases direct contributions may be required.[108] This is one example of how a functional approach could determine property division in the context of domestic disputes.[109] One of the benefits of such an approach is its inclusiveness. Furthermore, the difficulties in obtaining the necessary public and political support for proposals which seemingly give legal status to non-marital relationships may be avoided by a regime which does not actually identify relationships for inclusion, but which gives rights to the 'functional family'.[110] Of course, difficult questions would arise, for example, identifying the assets available for distribution[111] and the contextual factors triggering the presumption of joint ownership. Eekelaar's model, cited as an example, focuses on the joint upbringing of children and suggests that, in the absence of this, direct contributions may become more relevant. This raises the question, however, of whether 'there is a legitimate role of homemaker when there are no children?'[112] As capital distribution would be based on entitlement, a further question would arise as to whether a spouse could claim ownership rights during marriage. Indeed, in relation to present law, connotations of dependency may arise because the property adjustment order is only available on divorce and the claimant is, therefore, getting something that she was not entitled to during marriage. These are just some of the questions which would arise if such an approach were to be taken by policy-makers.

Finally, certain parallels may be drawn between the evolution of matrimonial property law in Dicey's era and in the twentieth century. Dicey charted the link between law and opinion in the struggle for gender-based equality in this area. Social change was the catalyst for reform and prompted the judiciary to 'react' prior to legislative intervention in the nineteenth century. Similar trends can be seen in the twentieth century as the changing socio-economic position of women and diversity in family formation has had an impact on the legal response to the 'family property question'. While the law has been struggling to find a solution, societal trends have altered the nature of the question and the law remains open to critique. To meet the needs of contemporary society, however, consolidating the debate surrounding the property rights of spouses, unmarried cohabitants and other homesharers could lead to the development of a functional approach where capital distribution is based on entitlement and rehabilitative financial support is available if required. Such an approach, which combines a rights-based focus with a remedial element, may provide the best opportunity to avoid making assumptions about the substance of certain relationships and resolve individual family law problems by giving rights and remedies to those who deserve/need them. It is doubtful whether such an approach is immediately forthcoming, but merely tinkering with the present law will not provide a comprehensive twenty-first-century solution to the 'family property question'.

Notes

* I would like to thank Claire Archbold for commenting on an earlier draft. Any errors or omissions remain my responsibility.
1 In his essay on 'Social Responsibility', Ginsberg makes reference to the notion of legal rights which are assigned to persons and which have been extended to apply to 'other entities', such as families. The tension between individualism and the notion that the consequences of family membership dictates the

extent and enjoyment of individual rights is reflected in the general statement of Ginsberg that 'rights founded on one set of relations might conflict with rights founded on other relations and that this involve[s] a balancing of claims in the interests of greater freedom on the whole'. M. Ginsberg, 'The growth of social responsibility', in M. Ginsberg (ed.), *Law and Opinion Ain England in the 20th Century*, Stevens & Sons Ltd, London, 1959, pp. 5–6.

2 A. V. Dicey, *Lectures on the Relation between Law and Opinion in England during the 19th Century*, Macmillan & Co Ltd, London, 1905, p. 359.

3 See Blackstone, *Commentaries on the Laws of England*, 8th edition (1824) Vol. 1, p. 149.

4 Dicey, pp. 369–73.

5 Ibid., p. 373.

6 Glendon notes that in the US, marriage settlements were not used to the same extent as they were in England which, she argues, explains the earlier enactment of the Married Women's Property Acts in that jurisdiction. M. A. Glendon, *The Transformation of Family Law; State, Law, and Family in the United States and Western Europe*, University of Chicago Press, Chicago, 1989, p. 111.

7 Dicey, p. 381.

8 Ibid., p. 383.

9 Karminski states that public opinion in the twentieth century insisted upon making spouses equal partners. Karminski, 'Family law', in Ginsberg (ed.), p. 289.

10 In short, where marriage became more akin to an economic and emotional partnership which could be dissolved in the absence of matrimonial fault.

11 At the other end of the spectrum from the separate property doctrine is the notion of community property by which property acquired by either spouse during marriage belongs to them both jointly.

12 See the Law Commission Working Paper No. 42, *Family Property Law* London, HMSO, 1971, para. 0.12.

13 A. A. S. Zuckerman, 'Ownership of the matrimonial home – common sense and reformist nonsense', *Law Quarterly Review*, 26, 1978, at 55, referring to Cretney, *Principles of Family Law*, 2nd edition (1976), p. 258.

14 Glendon, p. 124.

15 T. G. Youdan, 'Equitable transformations of family property law', in *Equity and Contemporary Legal Developments* (ed. Goldstein), Hebrew University of Jerusalem, Jerusalem, 1992, p. 528.

16 Owner-occupation increased from 29 per cent in 1951 to 45 per cent in 1964. Between 1961 and 1998 the number of owner-occupied dwellings in the United Kingdom more than doubled to 16.9 million, while the number of rented dwellings fell by a sixth. *Social Trends* No. 30, 2000, Chart 10.4.

17 *Rimmer v Rimmer* [1953] 1 QB 63 at 67 *per* Sir Raymond Evershed MR.

18 [1970] A. C. 777.

19 [1971] A. C. 886.

20 Youdan, p. 531.

21 *Hine v Hine* [1962] 3 All ER 345 at 347.

22 Where it sufficed if the non-legal owner contributed to the family's general expenses. See *Hazell v Hazell* [1972] 1 All ER 923.

23 *Rimmer v Rimmer* [1953] 1 QB 63 at 74.

24 *Pettitt* v *Pettitt* [1970] A. C. 777 and *Gissing* v *Gissing* [1971] A. C. 886.
25 H. Lesser, 'The acquisition of inter vivos matrimonial property rights in English law: a doctrinal melting pot', *University of Toronto Law Journal*, 23, 1973, 148 at 182.
26 *Hussey* v *Palmer* [1972] 1 WLR 1286. See also *Heseltine* v *Heseltine* [1971] 1 All ER 952.
27 *Cooke* v *Head* [1972] 1 WLR 518 at 520.
28 *Hazell* v *Hazell* [1972] 1 All ER 923 at 925 *per* Lord Denning M. R.
29 *Hargrave* v *Newton* [1971] 3 All ER 866.
30 Australia has developed the concept of unconscionability (*Muchinski* v *Dodds* [1985] 160 CLR 583), while Canadian jurisprudence has developed the notion of unjust enrichment (*Pettkus* v *Becker* [1980] 2 SCR 834).
31 See *Burns* v *Burns* [1984] Ch 317.
32 *Lloyds Bank* v *Rosset* [1991] 1 A. C. 107.
33 To remedy this unfairness in 1969 a Private Member's Bill, proposing a system of community property between spouses, was given a Second Reading in the House of Commons. This was subsequently withdrawn, but the Lord Chancellor stated that the new Divorce Reform Act 1969 would not be enacted until legislation dealing with the financial consequences of divorce had been introduced.
34 See *Midland Bank* v *Cooke* [1995] 2 F. L. R. 915 and *Drake* v *Whipp* [1996] 1 FLR 826.
35 Davis et al., *Simple Quarrels*, Clarendon Press, Oxford, 1994, p. 103 referring to Barrington-Baker et al., *The Matrimonial Jurisdiction of Registrars*, Social Science Research Council, London, 1977.
36 It is worth noting, however, that unmarried cohabitants do have certain legal rights. For example, they have occupation rights under the Family Law Act 1996 and the right to claim from the estate of their deceased partner under the Inheritance (Provision for Family and Dependants) Act 1975, amended by the Law Reform (Succession) Act 1995. However, their rights are not as extensive as those given to spouses and distinctions are made between heterosexual and same-sex cohabitants.
37 *White* v *White* [2000] 3 WLR 1571 at 1573 *per* Lord Nicholls.
38 Law Commission, *The Financial Consequences of Divorce: the Basic Policy: a Discussion Paper* (Law Com. No. 103) (1980) HMSO, London, para 13.
39 By the Divorce Reform Act 1857 which supplanted the jurisdiction of the ecclesiastical courts.
40 Prior to 1970 the courts had limited powers regarding the couple's capital assets on divorce. While they could determine and declare the respective property rights of the parties and had the limited power to vary ante-nuptial or post-nuptial settlements, they could not transfer property between the parties.
41 *Dart* v *Dart* [1996] 2 FLR 286 at 294.
42 See section 25(2) of the Matrimonial Causes Act 1973 for a full list of the statutory criteria, which is considered by the court when determining 'financial provision' on divorce.
43 Glendon, p. 199.
44 For a discussion of the distinction between formal equality and substantive equality in this context, see A. Diduck and H. Orton 'Equality and support for spouses', *Modern Law Review*, 57, 1994, p. 681.

80 Lisa Glennon

45 In 1971, 56 per cent of women in the United Kingdom were either in work or seeking work ('economically active'). By 1999 this had risen to 72 per cent. *Social Trends* No. 30, 2000, Chart 4.4. By contrast, the proportion of 'economically active' men has fallen from 91 per cent in 1971 to 84 per cent in 1999. Furthermore, the number of married women in work has increased and, in 1999, 75 per cent of married or cohabiting women of working age were 'economically active'. *Social Trends*, Chart 4.5. The net result is a decrease in the number of households where only the man is working from 40 per cent in the early 1980s to 26 per cent in 1996–7. *Social Trends*, Chart 4.6.
46 Known as the 'minimal loss' principle, section 5(1) of the Matrimonial Proceedings and Property Act 1970.
47 See Law Commission, *The Financial Consequences of Divorce: the Basic Policy: a Discussion Paper* (Law Com. No. 103) (1980) London, HMSO, para 24.
48 The Matrimonial and Family Proceedings Act 1984.
49 In other words, to consider whether a settlement can be constructed in such a way as to terminate post-divorce obligations as soon as possible.
50 [1999] 3All ER 632.
51 *White* v *White* [2000] 3 WLR 1571 at 1573.
52 *Dart* v *Dart* [1996] 2 FLR 286 at 303 *per* Butler-Sloss LJ. See Eekelaar, 'Some principles of financial and property adjustment on divorce' (1979) *Law Quarterly Review* 253; Jackson, Wasoff, Maclean and Dobash 'Financial support on divorce: the right mixture of rules and discretion?' (1993) 7 *International Journal of Law and the Family* 230.
53 *Preston* v *Preston* [1982] 1 All ER 41 at 47 *per* Ormrod LJ.
54 Where resources exceed the parties' needs.
55 One factor for consideration in the statutory criteria, section 25 of the Matrimonial Causes Act 1973.
56 See *O'D* v *O'D* [1975] 2 All ER 993; *Page* v *Page* (1981) 2 FLR 198; *Preston* v *Preston* [1982] 1 All ER 41.
57 Eekelaar, 'Back to Basics and Forward into the Unknown' [2001] *Family Law* 30.
58 [1982] 1 All ER 41.
59 Ibid., p. 47. See also *Page* v *Page* (1981) 2 FLR 198 at 201.
60 [2000] 3 WLR 1571.
61 Ibid., p. 1578.
62 Ibid.
63 One reason may be where property has been acquired outside the marriage; Lord Nicholls referred to this as 'inherited property'. Preferring to look at the origins of the property as opposed to its use, it was suggested that a claimant may have a weaker claim to such property, although this can be displaced if the claimant's financial needs cannot be met without recourse to it.
64 It is notable that even in this case equal division was not awarded.
65 See *Haldane* v *Haldane* [1977] AC 673 at 697 *per* Lord Simon of Glaisdale.
66 Subsequent decisions illustrate the difficulties in applying the principles of *White* in the absence of legislative direction. Indeed, cases reveal the judicial exploration of the grounds which justify the unequal division of surplus assests in 'big-money' cases. Of particular note is the Court of Appeal decision in *Cowan* v *Cowan* [2002] Fam 97 where the court made a comparative

assessment of the parties' respective contributions and held that the husband's entrepreneurial activity was a 'special contribution' which justified the unequal division of the assets. Since writing this paper, however, the Court of Appeal in *Lambert* v *Lambert* [2002] All ER(D) 208 has criticised the practice of making retrospective value judgements as to the performance of each of the parties during the marriage. Indeed, Thorpe LJ made it clear that '*it is unacceptable to place greater value on the contribution of the breadwinner than that of the homemaker as a justification for dividing the product of the breadwinner's efforts unequally between them*'. While finding that one party made a 'special contribution' remains a legitimate possibility, it appears that this will only be the case in exceptional circumstances.
67 Lord Hodson said in *Pettitt* v *Pettitt* [1970] AC 777 at 811 that 'I do not see how one can correct the imbalance which may be found to exist in property rights between husband and wife without legislation'.
68 Glendon, p. 198.
69 *Wachtel* v *Wachtel* [1973] 1 All ER 829 at 838.
70 Law Commission, '*Report on Financial Provision in Matrimonial Proceedings*' (Law Com. No. 25) (1969) London, HMSO, para 69.
71 *Wachtel* v *Wachtel* [1973] 1 All ER 829.
72 C. Smart, *The Ties that Bind: Law Marriage and the Reproduction of Patriarchal Relations*, Routledge & Kegan Paul, London, 1984.
73 Eekelaar, 'Post-divorce financial obligations', Ch. 18, in Katz, Eekelaar and Maclean (eds.) *Cross-currents: Family Law and Policy in the United States and England*, Oxford University Press, Oxford, 2000, p. 420.
74 Lesser, pp. 177–9. See, for example, *Falconer* v *Falconer* [1970] 1 WLR 1333 at 1336.
75 Zuckerman, p. 29.
76 Lesser, pp. 177–9.
77 Eekelaar argues that the policy of post-divorce obligations has little to do with the marriage itself but instead is based on '*entitlement earned by work expended on a common project*', such as parenthood. Eekelaar, 'Post-divorce financial obligations', pp. 406 and 420.
78 The total number of marriages in the United Kingdom has fallen from a peak in 1972. In 1997 there were 310,000 marriages, cited as amongst the lowest figures recorded during the twentieth century, *Social Trends* No. 30 (2000) Chart 2.6. In 1999 there were 264,000 marriages, 1.4 per cent fewer than in 1998 and 14 per cent fewer than in 1991. *Population Trends* 103, Spring 2001, pp. 83–4. By contrast, the latter half of the twentieth century has witnessed the growth in cohabitation. Statistics reveal that the proportion of all unmarried women aged 18 to 49 who were cohabiting in Great Britain increased from 11 per cent in 1979 to 29 per cent in 1998–99. *Social Trends*, p. 40. It is estimated that the number of cohabiting couples, 1.56 million in 1996, will rise to 2.93 million in 2021, which would mean more than one in five of all couples cohabiting. See J. Haskey 'Cohabitation in Great Britain: past, present and future trends – and attitudes', *Population Trends*, pp. 5–25.
79 See Eekelaar and Maclean, 'Introduction', in *Oxford Readings in Socio-Legal Studies: A reader on family law*, Eekelaar and Maclean (eds.) Oxford University Press, Oxford, 1994, pp. 1–28.

80 Law Reform Advisory Committee for Northern Ireland (LRAC) (2000) *Matrimonial Property*, Report No. 8, Belfast: The Stationery Office.
81 'In reality our recommendations would represent an enhancement of the position of women in relationships'. LRAC Final Report, para 4.13.
82 Thus extending the recommendations of an earlier English Law Commission Report on Matrimonial Property. See Law Commission, *'Family Law: Matrimonial Property'* (Law Com. No. 175) (1988) London, HMSO. It is proposed that where a spouse or qualifying cohabitant transfers property to the other, or transfers property to both, or where one purchases property or both purchase property, the equitable ownership of that property shall vest in both spouses or cohabitants as joint tenants unless the parties agree otherwise expressly in writing.
83 LRAC Final Report, paras 4.10, 4.14–4.15.
84 To qualify as cohabitants the parties must have been living together in the same household, effectively as husband and wife, for at least a total of two years within the period of three years preceding the property transaction; or have a child by the relationship and have been living together in the same household effectively as husband and wife. LRAC Final Report, para 4.15.
85 The Law Reform Advisory Committee for Northern Ireland, Eleventh Annual Report 2000, p. 7.
86 For example, the Succession (Northern Ireland) Order 1996 and the Family Homes and Domestic Violence (Northern Ireland) Order 1998.
87 While the legal recognition of unmarried heterosexual cohabitants has been piecemeal and their legal rights less extensive than spouses, there is no meaningful recognition of same-sex couples. See, however, *Fitzpatrick v Sterling Housing Association* [1999] 4 All ER 705.
88 M. Neave, 'Property disputes in de facto relationships: commentary', Ch. 7, in Cope (ed.) *Equity: Issues and Trends*, Federation Press, Sydney, 1995, p. 219.
89 Ibid., pp. 219–20.
90 L. Willmott, in ibid., p. 226.
91 In a survey carried out in 1971 it was found that, at this time, 52 per cent of couples owned their own home, and among the home owners 52 per cent had their home in joint names. It was also found that when a home was purchased in the name of one spouse in 87 per cent of cases the spouses mistakenly believed that they owned the home jointly. Office of Population Census & Surveys, Social Survey Division, Matrimonial Property, J. E. Todd and L. M. Jones, HMSO, London, 1972.
92 Inheritance (Provision for Family and Dependants) Act 1975.
93 Glendon, p. 128.
94 One of the main objectives of this Act is to ensure equality between the sexes in the public sphere.
95 B. Hale, 'Family law reform: *Wither or Whither?*' (1995) *Current Legal Problems* 217, pp. 228–9.
96 In other words, the absence of a fixed set of familial obligations based on the status of particular relationships.
97 J. Lewis, 'Family policy in the post-war period', Ch. 4 in Katz, Eekelaar and Maclean (eds.) p. 82.

Matrimonial Property 83

98 Other relationships are not totally excluded from the remit of the Northern Irish proposals, however. In the case of disputes not covered by the principle of statutory co-ownership it is proposed that the court should determine what it considers to be a just division of the equitable interests between the parties taking into account a specified list of factors. LRAC Final Report, para 5.32–5.35.
99 Zuckerman, pp. 51–2.
100 Otto Kahn-Freund, 'Matrimonial property: where do we go from here?' The Josef Unger Memorial Lecture, 1971, p. 9.
101 Harpum, 'Cohabitation consultation' (1995) *Family Law* 657. The Law Commission has now issued its long-awaited discussion paper on the property rights of those who share a home. *Sharing Homes, A Discussion Paper.* Law Com No. 278. Law Commission.
102 The Green Paper 'Supporting Families: A Consultation Document', HMSO, Home Office, 1998 proposed that having dealt with the needs of the children, housing needs of the couple and after taking into account any nuptial agreement, the court should divide the surplus to achieve a fair result, recognising that fairness will generally require the value of the assets to be divided equally between the parties.
103 The incorporation of the European Convention on Human Rights into domestic law (Human Rights Act 1998, section 2) may, in the future, call into question domestic policy on the property rights of spouses and unmarried cohabitants.
104 Arthur, Lewis, Fitzgerald and Maclean, *Settling Up: making financial arrangements after separation and divorce: Report of Interim Findings* (National Centre for Social Research, November 2000), para 3.4.
105 The aim of this is to enable the recipient to become self-sufficient. See the Law Commission, *'The Financial Consequences of Divorce: the Basic Policy: a Discussion Paper'*, HMSO, London, 1980, para. 73.
106 Possibly excluding gifts or inherited property.
107 Proportionate distribution would be on a sliding scale, 'prior to the effluxion of the set period (say 15 years) the allocation would be made in proportions other than 50–50, say 10:90 after 3 years; 20:80 after 6, 30:70 after 9, and 40:60 after 12', Eekelaar, Should section 25 be reformed? (1998) *Family Law* 469 at 472.
108 Ibid.
109 See also R. Bailey-Harris, 'Property disputes in de facto relationships: can equity still play a role?', Ch. 7 in Cope (ed.), *Equity: Issues and Trends.*
110 Willmott, p. 228, who notes the acceptance of the concept of 'domestic relationship' in the A. C. T. Domestic Relationships Act 1994.
111 Options would include the purpose test (assets which were used jointly, see Professor Otto Kahn-Freund, note 99 above) or the origins test (focused on the source of the assets).
112 P. Symes, 'Indissolubility and the clean break', *Modern Law Review*, 48, 1985, 44 at 56.

4

Public Opinion and the Regulation of Conception

Emily Jackson

Introduction

In the lifetime of Albert Venn Dicey, conception was simply a natural and largely unregulated consequence of heterosexual sexual intercourse. Of course, rules governing eligibility for marriage indirectly attempted to shape people's reproductive behaviour, and the social and moral stigma of illegitimacy meshed with illegitimate offspring's disadvantageous legal status to create a powerful, if not always effective deterrent against reproduction outside of marriage. But since facilitating conception was simply impossible, the need for legislation determining the circumstances in which positively assisting procreation might be legitimate would have been unimaginable. It was not until the 25 July 1978, following the birth of Louise Brown, the first child to have been conceived through *in vitro* fertilisation (IVF), that governments throughout the world were forced to contemplate instituting regulatory mechanisms to control the practice of artificial conception. Yet, while the precise subject matter of this chapter would, without doubt, have been beyond Dicey's comprehension, his concern about the relationship between law and public opinion undoubtedly continues to have considerable resonance for the regulation of assisted conception techniques.

The introduction of techniques that involve entirely unprecedented human intervention in the once mysterious and invisible process of conception has been accompanied by a similarly unprecedented opportunity to regulate formerly ungovernable natural processes. Unlike natural conception, the use of reproductive technologies can be controlled or restricted without 'policing the nation's bedrooms'. In this chapter I focus upon the regulation of two issues that have provoked particular public controversy in order to think about the relationship between regulation and public opinion. First, in addition to enabling clinically infertile individuals to reproduce, assisted conception techniques can also facilitate childbearing by women whose inability to conceive naturally is not the result of a physical abnormality in their reproductive organs. Because heterosexual intercourse is no longer an essential precursor of pregnancy, the question of whether single or lesbian women should have access to techniques that enable them to reproduce autonomously arises. My second example relates to a different sort of regulatory dilemma that has emerged in recent years. Following pre-implantation genetic diagnosis (PGD), a clinician is able to decide which out of a range of embryos should be transferred to a woman's uterus. Before pregnancy, therefore, it is now possible to choose between a variety of potential children. Unless PGD is to be available for every detectable genetic trait, it may be necessary to devise criteria specifying the circumstances in which embryo selection on genetic grounds is acceptable. Thus both the separation of sexual intercourse and reproduction and our novel capacity to pre-select embryos on the basis of genetic test results create new challenges for regulation. In determining the conditions under which such practices are legitimate, what role might there be for public opinion? If we do believe that regulators ought to take public attiudes to assisted conception techniques into account, how might this best be achieved? Does our parliamentary democracy offer sufficient opportunities for public scrutiny? Could judicial review enable the judges to bring their sense of public morality to bear upon questions of particular ethical complexity? Or should we foster more active participation in the regulatory process?

What is public opinion?

Before it could be taken into account, it is also of course necessary to work out what we mean by public opinion. According to Dicey, it is the predominant 'body of beliefs, convictions, sentiments, accepted principles or firmly rooted prejudices, which, taken together, make up the public opinion of (our) particular era'.[1] But while one hundred years ago there may indeed have been *one* cluster of predominant values and convictions, at the beginning of the twenty-first century public opinion seems far more fragmented. In relation to assisted conception, as with many other developments in the field of biotechnology, a disparity often appears to exist between lay perspectives and those of the scientists themselves. Furthermore, lay opinion itself may be made up of multiple and divergent perspectives. There will, for instance, commonly be differences between the attitudes of patients and their friends and relatives, and opinions held within the wider community. Because the techniques may be of direct benefit to them, people who cannot conceive without medical assistance and couples who are at risk of passing on an inherited genetic disorder may be more enthusiastic about reproductive technologies than individuals for whom conception has so far been safe, easy or unwanted. This enthusiasm may be shared by friends and family members who have witnessed the anguish associated with either involuntary childlessness or genetic disease, and are therefore able to picture the tangible benefits that may flow from new assisted conception techniques.

But while directly affected friends and family members may be trusted sources of information about the positive advantages of interfering with the reproductive process, the public obtains most of its information about reproductive technologies from the media, whose presentation of the issues raised by greater human intervention in the process of conception is frequently both alarmist and pessimistic. The fear, commonly expressed, is that greater control over the human reproductive process will have profoundly negative consequences for future generations and for society as a whole.

Of course, for some people doubts about the wisdom of interfering with the once wholly mysterious process of conception are the result of religious convictions. It is axiomatic that family bonds that flow from the randomness of love can more easily be attributed to divine providence than can kinship relations created by scientists. Yet public anxiety about new reproductive technologies extends far beyond those with specific religious objections to human beings' attempts to 'play God'. The randomness and naturalness of sexual conception are also widely assumed to have important social and evolutionary benefits. Unlike other 'unnatural' medical technologies, such as chemotherapy or kidney transplant operations, manipulating the very earliest stages of human life is believed to be inherently, and perhaps uncontrollably dangerous. For example, the possibility of women reproducing without male involvement provokes anxiety because of its potential to transform familial norms. This fear was clearly evident in the 'virgin birth' hysteria that accompanied the announcement in 1991 that women who had never had sexual intercourse were being provided with infertility treatment.[2] Similarly, the spectre of 'designer babies', created to the exact specifications of their parents, looms large over the media's representations of pre-implantation genetic diagnosis. Intolerance of imperfection, and the creation of a so-called 'genetic underclass', whose parents could not afford to screen out undesirable genetic traits, are among the various dire consequences that are assumed to lie only slightly further down the slippery slope.

The general public is often fearful about what *might* become possible in the future, whereas scientists tend to believe that until a particular procedure is technically feasible, regulation is redundant. Because the regulatory process is indeed directed towards controlling *existing* techniques, rather than speculative future developments, the public often feels that its concerns have been ignored and that the first step upon an extremely slippery slope may have already been taken. Simultaneously, scientists' belief in their own much prized objectivity and rationality can then lead them to feel exasperated at the public's technological 'illiteracy', and to assume that the solution lies in education that will automatically dispel prevalent subjective and misguided assumptions.

Yet it is this assumption that there should be 'one-way traffic' between scientists and the public which has itself been instrumental in alienating lay opinion and in exacerbating the public's perception that science, particularly in areas such as reproduction and genetics, is fundamentally uncontrollable. The failure by regulators to involve the public in dialogue about the risks and benefits produced by new technologies results in the prevailing assumption that the real risks are being suppressed because they are profoundly unacceptable. In effect, there is a danger that the public and the experts are simply talking past each other. 'Where will this lead?' is a different question to 'is this safe?' Scientists and regulators refer to their evidence base in order to answer the latter question. But because the public is concerned with *future* developments, evidence about current safety does little to dispel the fear that the former question cannot be answered satisfactorily. The fear that tampering with nature will have disastrous effects for future generations is a strong one which cannot be discounted simply on the grounds that it is based upon certain misunderstandings about reproductive technologies and genetics. Rather lay perspectives and scientific perspectives ought to engage in a process of communication so that public concerns are accommodated by regulators at the same time as members of the public who have no direct experience of reproductive technologies become better informed. Adopting Iris Marion Young's model of 'deliberative democracy', the process of democratic discussion is conceptualised not merely as a means to express and register opinions, but as a process through which preferences, interests and beliefs can be *transformed*.[3] A key purpose of regulation might therefore be to enable the various different interest groups – scientists, doctors, patients and the wider public – to communicate effectively about the risks and benefits of various reproductive technologies. This sort of participatory model of regulation may be necessary in order to avoid the impasse that arises from entrenched mutual mistrust.

Public opinion and regulation

In the United Kingdom, it took the legislature many years to decide precisely how new reproductive technologies should be regulated. The Warnock Committee was established in 1982, four years after the birth of the first baby conceived following *in vitro* fertilisation. Their report was published two years later, but it was not until 1990 that a statute based in large part upon Warnock's recommendations was enacted. This protracted delay undoubtedly benefited those who were in favour of a more liberal or facilitative regulatory framework. Between 1978 and 1990, public perception of infertility treatment had undergone a subtle transformation, from almost universal uneasiness to qualified approval.

Since embryo research is an essential precursor of infertility treatment, unsurprisingly the anti-abortion movement objects vociferously to reproductive technologies' reliance upon embryo destruction.[4] Following the publication of the Warnock Report, anti-abortion lobbying groups such as SPUC (Society for the Protection of the Unborn Child) and LIFE campaigned vigorously against its relatively liberal proposals for the regulation of embryo research and infertility treatment.[5] Initially, those opposed to Warnock's conclusions were much better organised and appeared to have both public and parliamentary opinion on their side.[6] In 1985 their efforts were very nearly successful: Enoch Powell's Unborn Children (Protection) Bill would have permitted *in vitro* fertilisation only if *every* fertilised egg was going to be transferred to the uterus of an identifiable woman. In practice, this would have prohibited most IVF treatment, and all research upon human embryos. The Bill passed its first reading on the 14 February 1985 by an overwhelming majority (238 MPs voted in favour of Powell's Bill, 66 MPs voted against it), and only failed to become law because an alliance of scientists and MPs succeeded in talking it out of time. A year later Ken Hargreaves MP reintroduced the Unborn Children (Protection) Bill, and again it was initially approved by the House of Commons, this time by 229 votes to 129, although lack of Parliamentary time meant that it had no chance of becoming law.

Between 1985 and 1990 the scientific and medical community campaigned to sway public and parliamentary opinion, largely by stressing the potential *health* benefits of embryo research. An organisation called the Progress Educational Trust was set up in November 1985 to work for increased public understanding of embryo research and the benefits of infertility treatment. The passage of a relatively liberal statute in 1990 was indubitably assisted by the fortuitous announcement that doctors and scientists working at the Hammersmith Hospital had successfully performed pre-implantation sex diagnosis in order to prevent the birth of a child suffering from a debilitating sex-linked genetic disorder.[7] Prior to the Parliamentary debates on the Human Fertilisation and Embryology Bill, Progress arranged for members of the House of Lords to be visited by families affected by genetic disease. Arrangements were also made for MPs and members of the House of Lords to visit clinics and talk to patients and clinicians.[8] Five days before the House of Commons voted on the Human Fertilisation and Embryology Bill, newspapers published a picture of Professor Robert Winston with the pregnant women who would be the first to benefit from pre-implantation sex diagnosis when their healthy children were born in a few months time.[9] That IVF could help to prevent serious disease and acute suffering undoubtedly significantly advanced the case for facilitative regulation.

However, among MPs, the media and the general public, approval of assisted conception often seems to be confined to *certain* uses of these new techniques. For example, helping an infertile, heterosexual couple to reproduce is generally perceived to be legitimate, whereas the treatment of single, lesbian or postmenopausal women continues to be much more controversial. Similarly, the use of pre-implantation genetic diagnosis to prevent the birth of a child whose life would be both short and painful is widely supported, whereas there tends to be vigorous opposition to any suggestion that the same techniques could be employed to select an embryo with certain desirable characteristics. Thus, public opinion does not appear to draw a simple distinction between artificial and natural conception; rather it distinguishes between resort to these new technologies when there is a *clinical* or therapeutic indication, and the use of identical treatments for trivial reasons, or to satisfy *social* preferences. So where new techniques can be presented as restoring or ensuring 'normal' functioning, there is much less alarm at the prospect of unnatural interference with the reproductive process. It is the possibility of using these new procedures in order to alter certain basic features of family life, namely the 'natural' connection between heterosexual intercourse and parenting, and the 'natural' randomness of genetic inheritance, that causes anxiety. As suggested earlier, this may be because the public is principally concerned with the question of where these new techniques might be leading. If assisted conception can just 'give nature a helping hand' in order to avoid certain individuals' lives being blighted by the misfortune of either clinical infertility or genetic disease, its potential to transform society itself is limited. If, on the other hand, these new techniques presage the possibility of women reproducing autonomously, or parents actively choosing their babies' attributes, their transformative potential is indeed dramatic.

Taking as examples the way in which access to infertility treatment is restricted, and the limits currently placed upon the use of pre-implantation genetic diagnosis, I explain below that public perception that a clear boundary exists between 'social' and the 'clinical' uses of assisted conception techniques has indeed been incorporated into the rules governing their provision. But far from being an example of mature democratic participation in action, I suggest that both supporters and opponents of this clinical/social distinction should be sceptical about its inclusion in the regulatory scheme. First, because power is largely delegated to medical professionals, enforcing this clinical/social boundary is in practice almost impossible. So while the regulations may appear to reflect dominant public opinion, the ease with which patients and clinicians can avoid their impact reveals that little more than lip service has been paid to public concerns. Second, I argue that the distinction itself may be evidence of a breakdown in communication between the various interest groups. The general public is anxious about reproductive technologies' potential to wreak havoc upon the health and well-being of future generations by fundamentally altering certain 'natural' facts about human reproduction. Because the transformative potential of the various technologies is as yet rather limited, scientists tend to dismiss public concerns as irrational and grounded in ignorance, and regard fear of the ubiquitous slippery slope as evidence of public misunderstanding of science. Yet dismissing public apprehension because the feared adverse outcome is not yet possible itself further aggravates public distrust.

In recent years the public's experience has been that science's capacity to accurately predict the future is profoundly fallible. Extrapolating from accidents, such as Chernobyl, and misjudgments, such as the shifts in farming practice that directly led to the BSE crisis, the public has understandably become unwilling to accept scientists' prognoses that the future should be considered risk-free. If sceptical lay perspectives are dismissed perfunctorily, the public will continue to be concerned about what is being hidden by scientists. And within this communicative deadlock, the perspectives of the patients themselves may become obscured. A dialogue in which lay anxieties about the future are taken seriously at the same time as the public becomes better informed about the risks *and benefits* associated with assisted conception might lead to a more transparent, accountable and participatory regulatory process.

Access to treatment

By enabling women whose inability to conceive is due to the absence of a male partner to reproduce, the fear is that reproductive technologies might hasten the collapse of the traditional family. Women no longer need to have had a sexual relationship with a man in order to conceive, and techniques such as cloning, and a new technique, so far attempted only in mice, which uses body cells rather than sperm to fertilise an egg, might even make it possible to dispense with the need to obtain male gametes (sperm) prior to conception. Thus one recurring public concern has been the future redundancy of men in the process of human reproduction. The media too has generally been hostile to the prospect of women reproducing autonomously. In 1978, headlines such as 'Ban These Babies' appeared in response to reports that lesbian women were reproducing with the help of donor insemination (DI).[10] And in 2001, *The Times* reported the attempts to fertilise mice ova without using sperm under the headline 'Fertility scientists try to make sperm redundant'.[11]

The Warnock Report, upon which the Human Fertilisation and Embryology Act 1990 was based, also expressed anxiety about the social consequences of women pro-creating without men, stating that: 'We believe that as a general rule it is better for children to be born into a two-parent family, with both father and mother.'[12] And six years later, when the Act was debated and passed, there was vigorous opposition among both peers and MPs to the treatment of single or lesbian women. David Wilshire MP warned, for example, that

> However clever we might become, and however much science might advance, we cannot avoid the facts of life. They are blindingly clear... To reproduce, we still need mothers and fathers.[13]

Unsurprisingly, therefore, the statute incorporates this prevailing concern about the use of assisted conception techniques to establish unconventional family units.

But unlike other countries that specify that only married or cohabiting heterosexual couples are eligible for treatment, there are no statutory prohibitions upon the treatment of single or lesbian women in the UK.

Instead, under section 13(5), before any patient may be provided with treatment, the clinic is under a duty to take account of 'the welfare of any child who may be born as a result of the treatment, (*including the need of that child for a father*)' (my emphasis).

If interpreted literally, this section makes little sense. It demands that a clinician bases her decision to attempt to bring a child into the world upon an assessment of whether it would be in that child's best interests to be conceived. Yet in other legal contexts, it has been accepted that existence must generally be judged preferable to non-existence,[14] making it difficult to imagine how a clinician could decide that a child would be benefited by not being born. So section 13(5) cannot, in fact, charge a clinician with deciding whether being conceived would promote a child's welfare, because if the alternative is not being conceived, it obviously would. Rather, section 13(5) indirectly exhorts the clinician to take into account the prospective patient's aptitude for parenthood, and specifies that single or lesbian women's parenting abilities should be subject to particular scrutiny.

Elsewhere, the statute sets up rules for the ascription of maternity and paternity following the use of assisted conception. Importantly these rules contemplate the birth of children who will have *no* legal father. Because children born to single or lesbian women treated in licensed clinics with anonymously donated sperm will be legally father*less*, clinics' duty to consider their potential child's *need for a father* translates into an oblique statutory obligation to take into account the undesirability of single or lesbian motherhood.

Why was unease about single and lesbian women's access to treatment translated into the structured exercise of medical discretion rather than a clear, prospective statutory prohibition? One argument put forward in Parliament was that a blanket ban upon the treatment of single or lesbian women might simply encourage them to organise their own self-insemination in a regulatory vacuum. The purpose of delegating decision-making authority to clinicians was therefore to ensure that an 'unsuitable' would-be parent first discussed the implications of her treatment with an authoritative infertility specialist, who would help her to appreciate that her status might be incompatible with proficient motherhood. According to the then Lord Chancellor, Lord Mackay

> through counselling and discussion with those responsible for licensed treatment, (single women) may be discouraged from having children once they have fully considered the implications of the environment into which their children would be born or its future welfare.[15]

There is a clear parallel here with some of the arguments put forward in Parliament in the debates that led to the legalisation of abortion in 1967. In 1967, a number of MPs speaking in favour of the Abortion Bill, advocated delegating the gate-keeping role to the medical profession, on the grounds that a woman who initially intended to terminate her unwanted pregnancy might be persuaded to change her mind following her consultation with a calm, rational, medical practitioner. A complete prohibition upon abortion would, according to this line of argument, miss this opportunity to bring such women within an effective framework of medical control. In a similar vein, if the formal eligibility criteria for assisted conception services appear to be inclusive and flexible, single or lesbian women will, so the argument goes, be more likely to submit themselves to medical scrutiny and thus receive credible and persuasive advice about the wisdom or otherwise of bringing a fatherless child into the world.

A further parallel with abortion law is the relative invisibility of control once it has been delegated to doctors. Clinical judgement has proved to be extraordinarily resilient to legal scrutiny, with two principal consequences. First, it is difficult for anyone whose request for treatment has been rejected to challenge a clinic's refusal to treat him or her. In a case, decided prior to the implementation of the Human Fertilisation and Embryology Act 1990, for example, Schiemann J rejected an application for judicial review of a consultant's decision to remove a woman from the waiting list for IVF treatment on the grounds of her perceived unsuitability for parenthood, arguing that

> It is not, and could not be, suggested that no reasonable consultant could have come to the decision to refuse treatment to the applicant.[16]

The Human Rights Act 1998, on the face of it, would appear to offer additional grounds for judicial review of decisions taken within NHS hospitals. Could lesbians or single women argue that section 13(5) unlawfully interferes either with their right to 'found a family' protected by Article 12, or with their right to respect for their family life, enshrined in Article 8? Challenges along these lines are of course possible, but for a number of reasons they are unlikely to be successful. First, the regulation of reproduction and family life has conventionally been treated as an area where individual nation states' margin of appreciation should be particularly wide, as witnessed by the vast differences that exist within the European Union in relation to both abortion and infertility treatment. Some European countries restrict assisted conception services to married or cohabiting heterosexual couples of reproductive age; others have virtually no restrictions upon access. Second, both the 'right to found a family' and the 'right to respect for family life' are widely believed to be negative rather than positive rights. They guarantee freedom from external constraints upon one's reproductive decision-making, or from interference with one's domestic arrangements, rather than a right to the resources and services that may be necessary in order to start a family with medical assistance. In one of the first British cases to address the interpretation of Article 12, the Court of Appeal were adamant that there could be no absolute right to found a family.[17] A further possibility would be to challenge section 13(5) on the grounds that it discriminates against people on the basis of their sexual orientation. Yet because section 13(5) has equivalent impact upon *heterosexual* single women, it might be difficult to argue that it is discriminatory within the scope of Article 14.

The second consequence of delegating decision-making to individual clinicians is that eligibility is judged on a case-by-case basis, leading to considerable variation in practice. Some clinics will only treat heterosexual couples, while other clinics' promotional material is explicitly designed to attract single and lesbian patients. The London Women's Clinic, for example, states that it has been 'welcoming single and lesbian women on to their treatment programmes [since] 1997'. Their leaflet goes on to say: '[We] understand the difficulties that single women have in trying to obtain information on the subject, and know just how hard it can be to make that first telephone call.' In theory clinics that were blatantly ignoring the injunction to consider the child's welfare, or need for a father might face withdrawal or non-renewal of their licences. But because there is no prohibition upon the treatment of single or lesbian women, in practice it would be extremely difficult for the licensing authority to decide in any particular case that a clinic had exceeded the discretion that it undoubtedly has to assist single or lesbian women to conceive. So, for example, neither the London Women's Clinic's openness about its willingness to treat single women or lesbian couples, nor its estimate that such women constitute approximately 80 per cent of its DI patients would represent grounds for licence non-renewal.

In addition, provided that they can afford to pay for their treatment, all British women are now entitled to seek treatment in any other country within the EU, some of which place practically no restrictions upon access to treatment. This is why, for example, postmenopausal British women have sometimes found it easier to obtain treatment in Italian clinics. Thus throughout the EU, rules designed to incorporate public opinion in one country can readily be avoided by affluent and determined citizens. In short, wealthy, mobile and well-informed single and lesbian women will be able to have relatively straightforward access to assisted conception services both within the UK and in certain other European countries.

So the mechanism which was designed to address public concern about reproductive technologies' potential to subvert conventional familial norms is in fact largely ineffective. Instead, because assisted reproduction is expensive and is seldom available within the National Health Service, access to assisted conception services is in practice limited more by affluence than by marital status or sexual orientation. Many health authorities do not pay for any infertility treatment at all, while others may, subject to exceptionally strict eligibility criteria and long waiting lists, fund an upper limit of three cycles of treatment per couple. Less affluent women and heterosexual couples commonly find affording infertility treatment impossible. Interestingly then, the statutory provision that was intended to incorporate public opinion about the circumstances in which infertility treatment is legitimate is in practice much less significant than discretionary funding decisions taken within the NHS.

It is not clear to what extent public opinion is relevant when allocating scarce NHS resources, although disparity between different health authorities' policies would certainly appear to indicate that there has been no coherent attempt to discover whether or not taxpayers are willing to pay for assisted conception services. Deciding upon the relative priority that fertility treatment should have within the NHS has, until recently, been left to individual health authority's managers who are not under any formal duty to take public opinion into account. The National Institute now provides some centralised control over resource allocation for Clinical Excellence (NICE) which assesses new or expensive medical treatments in order to determine whether they should be available at public expense. NICE's appraisals are based upon an assessment of a procedure's clinical and cost-effectiveness, rather than its public acceptability, and public consultation does not appear to be part of their remit. Judicial review has also proved to be a singularly ineffective mechanism for subjecting NHS funding decisions to scrutiny and public accountability. It is almost impossible to convince a judge that any particular instance of rationing within the NHS is irrational or *Wednesbury* unreasonable. In rejecting an application for judicial review of Sheffield Area Health Authority's decision to refuse to fund infertility treatment for women over 35 years old, for example, Auld J held that health authorities were entitled to make decisions on the basis of the financial resources available to them and in the circumstances Sheffield AHA's policy was neither illegal or irrational.[18]

So dominant public concerns about reproductive technologies' potential to radically transform family relationships by facilitating procreation among single or lesbian women are in theory accommodated by the regulatory regime. But the relevant statutory provision has much less practical impact upon access to treatment than the twin mechanisms of clinical discretion and setting of priorities by health service managers, neither of which has proved to be particularly responsive to public opinion. Yet while this pragmatic compromise through which lay perspectives are simultaneously both taken into account and readily ignored may have some practical advantages for both providers and patients, it is plainly not a satisfactory resolution of the issue. Especially in the light of new techniques, which may further reduce the need for male involvement in conception, there is a need for sustained debate about access to, and perhaps public funding for reproductive technologies.

Greater public involvement in decisions about whom should have access to new reproductive technologies, and whether their treatment should be provided at public expense might promote public confidence in the efficacy of regulation. It might also facilitate better-informed debate about the reasons why access to assisted conception services should be restricted. For example, there are perhaps two reasons why the general public is concerned about women reproducing autonomously. First, if this were to become the norm, rather than a minority practice, it might have a profound impact upon society. There is, however, no evidence that the number of women who want to reproduce through sexual intercourse is in decline. Assisted conception, with its associated discomfort, inconvenience and expense shows no sign of replacing natural reproduction where this is both possible and safe.

Second, the welfare of children born to single or lesbian women is commonly posited as another reason to restrict their access to treatment services. But again, this equation of children's best interests with the presence of a father figure at the moment of conception lacks any sound empirical basis. There is, for example, no proof that lesbian parents impair their children's social and emotional development. On the contrary, studies carried out by psychiatrists and psychologists consistently demonstrate 'that the sons and daughters of lesbian mothers are at no greater risk for emotional or behavioural problems in childhood or adulthood than their peers from heterosexual homes'.[19] And while there have been many studies that purport to demonstrate a link between single parenthood and impaired future life chances, they may have little relevance for children born to single women following assisted conception. The chief causes of problems experienced by children who grow up with a single mother are poverty, isolation, residential mobility and the family discord associated with parental separation.[20] Women who choose to have fertility treatment on their own will be neither poor nor young, and they will not have had single motherhood thrust upon them as a result of either an unplanned pregnancy or a relationship breakdown.

Studies repeatedly show that it is the quality of the *relationship* between a parent and child that matters, rather than that parent's marital status or sexual orientation. Better outcomes for children are associated with parental warmth, sensitivity and responsiveness. Their family's conformity or otherwise with traditional familial norms makes no difference to children's psychological development.[21] Of course, prior to infertility treatment it is not easy to judge whether an individual or couple are capable of offering a child unconditional love and a stimulating environment. But if we are really concerned to refuse treatment requests from inadequate parents, this, rather than the existence of a male partner, is what clinicians should be attempting to assess. Some public anxieties about the consequences of non-sexual reproduction may, therefore, be misplaced, but it is only by taking them seriously and engaging in debate that a dialogue about the purpose of restrictions upon access to assisted conception becomes possible. In short, decisions about access to treatment have tended to be shielded from public scrutiny that in turn leads to the prevailing assumption that regulation will not be able to prevent the feared adverse consequences. These are assumed, perhaps wrongly, to flow from allowing single or lesbian women to overcome their natural inability to conceive. In the following section, I explore a similar tendency in relation to pre-implantation genetic diagnosis.

Pre-implantation genetic diagnosis (PGD)

Towards the end of the twentieth century, it became possible to remove one or two cells from a very early human embryo without interfering with its capacity for normal development. Those cells can then be analysed and certain genetic abnormalities detected. PGD is generally used when a couple have had one affected child and/or one or more terminations of pregnancy following conventional prenatal diagnosis.

Because doctors are able to transfer only unaffected embryos to the woman's uterus, couples who are at risk of passing on a genetic disorder can avoid undergoing pre-natal diagnosis and (possibly repeated) abortion and instead start a pregnancy in the knowledge that the resulting child will not have a particular abnormality. The sex of an embryo can also be identified, thus making it possible for a couple to avoid having a child with a sex-linked recessive condition.

As the first drafts of the human genome project are completed, one of the principal issues around which public anxiety has crystallized is the possibility of increasingly routine pre-implantation genetic selection. Critics of PGD are alarmed by the possibility that parents might habitually be in a position to choose between various potential children. David King, for example, argues that in pre-implantation diagnosis:

> Parents adopt a far more pro-active, directing role, choosing their children in a way which is not so far removed from their experience as consumers, choosing amongst different products... Selecting the 'best' amongst multiple embryos sets up a new relationship between parents and children.[22]

As the number of conditions that can be diagnosed before implantation inevitably increases, so does the associated moral panic.

One particular concern is that tests will eventually be devised in order to identify, and subsequently dispose of embryos found to have the gene 'for' particular behavioural patterns or physical features. If, so the argument goes, it becomes possible to detect genes associated with height, intelligence or homosexuality, PGD could be used for reasons that many would consider to be trivial or grounded in prejudice. The fear that PGD could be employed not only to prevent disease and disability but also by prospective parents anxious to maximize their offspring's brains, beauty and conformity to conventional behavioral norms is commonplace. In one of the House of Lords' debates on the Human Fertilization and Embryology Bill, for example, the Duke of Norfolk said that it was easy to

> imagine parents who wanted a boy or a girl, or a blond child, or a blue-eyed child asking the doctor to select an embryo with these characteristics.[23]

Scare stories about screening out embryos with a predisposition to, for example, criminality, homosexuality or obesity abound,[24] in spite of the improbability that single gene markers exist for these complex personality traits. Again, the public wants to know the answer to the question 'where will this end?' whereas scientists are principally interested in 'what might be possible *now*?' As a result of this disjuncture between lay interest in the future, and expert analysis of the present, there is both consensus among scientists that there is no single gene responsible for characteristics such as intelligence, attractiveness or sexual orientation, *and* persistent public alarm about PGD's potential for misuse.

Before exploring the impact that this public anxiety has had upon the regulation of PGD, I first want to consider some of the reasons for the intensity of concern. One factor might be the tendency to use cartographic metaphors in order to describe the achievements being made by scientists working on the human genome project. If told that the human genome has been 'mapped', or that we now know the 'blueprint' for life, the lay person may understandably fail to appreciate that the functions of each gene will not be identified within the foreseeable future. In addition, the mixture or fascination and fear generated by the familiar image of the mad scientist creating humans to order clearly exercises considerable hold over the popular imagination. Repeated references to Aldous Huxley's *Brave New World* or to Mary Shelley's *Frankenstein* convey the fear that the development of artificial means of reproduction will inexorably lead to their uncontrollable abuse. Futuristic images and narratives drawn from popular culture tend to activate collective suspicion of scientists. For example, the significance of Frankenstein mythology for the public's perception of science should not be underestimated. The word Frankenstein itself, for example, has acquired a strikingly specific cultural meaning: it communicates both wonder at the extraordinary power of science, and fear of the horrifying repercussions if scientists are allowed to give their amoral curiosity free rein.[25] In the context of reproductive technologies, we can trace this ambivalence in popular representations both of 'miracle' babies bringing unbounded joy to the infertile, and of the dangers to society if 'designer' babies are produced to order.

The assumption that greater human control over procreation will inevitably lead to its future misapplication underpins much of the criticism currently levelled at PGD. Since risks tend to seem especially threatening if the feared adverse outcome is unfamiliar or unpredictable, it is probably unsurprising that a variety of fears about newly emerging risks have converged upon the uncertainties that emerge from biotechnology, and in particular from new genetic knowledge. Our unprecedented capacity to control reproductive outcomes seems to be accompanied by the fear that this new technology may itself be uncontrollable. In parallel with public concern about genetically modified food, the prospect of genetically modified babies seems to provoke similar anxiety. As a result, although global environmental contamination and individual reproductive decision-making may have little or even nothing in common, it is often suggested that the regulation of *all* new genetic technologies should be informed by the 'precautionary principle'.

In what circumstances, therefore, is pre-implantation genetic diagnosis legitimate? PGD was discussed at length in the Parliamentary debates on the Human Fertilisation and Embryology Bill, and an attempt was made to introduce an amendment which would have allowed it to be used only for genetic diseases 'which are life-threatening or severely disabling'.[26] This was rejected on the grounds that the Licensing Authority might need greater flexibility in order to accommodate the rapid pace of advances in genetic science. The statute therefore offers no guidance to clinics and PGD is regulated instead by the HFEA's licensing procedures and Code of Practice. Clinics intending to offer PGD must first obtain a license, and thereafter their license renewal will be contingent upon conformity with HFEA's guidelines. Unsurprisingly, the HFEA's policy distinguishes between the medical and social uses of PGD, and adopts a model similar to that used to control access to abortion on the grounds of foetal abnormality.[27] Hence, PGD can lawfully be carried out only to detect conditions where there is 'a substantial risk that, if the child were born, it would suffer from such physical or mental abnormalities as to be seriously handicapped'.[28] So, although it would technically be possible for PGD to be used by couples who want to choose the sex of their child, sex selection for social reasons has been prohibited by the HFEA.[29] Pre-implantation sex identification is lawful only if it is carried out in order to prevent the transfer of embryos where there is a risk that the parents will pass on a sex-linked disease. In 2000 the Mastersons, a couple with four sons whose only daughter had died, failed to persuade the HFEA that their circumstances merited pre-implantation sex selection. Mr and Mrs Masterson then took advantage of their right to be treated elsewere within the European Union, and underwent PGD in Italy, where the absence of a tight regulatory structure means that PGD for 'social' reasons is not unlawful. However, they could only afford one cycle of treatment, and since no female embryos were produced, their treatment was abandoned.

It would be possible for PGD to be employed in order to ensure that the resulting child would be a good tissue match for a relative in need of, for example, a bone marrow transplant. This has happened in the

United States and in 2000 Adam Nash was born following PGD in which an embryo was selected that was not only free from the genetic disease suffered by an older sibling, but was also a tissue match for her.[30] It is not clear what the HFEA would decide were a similar case to arise in the UK. In part the selection was done in order to prevent the birth of a child affected by Fanconi's anaemia, and this aspect of the screening procedure would have been unproblematic. For a couple to prefer an unaffected embryo, that *also* happens to be a good tissue match for their dying child, over an unaffected embryo with incompatible tissue seems readily understandable. However, a literal interpretation of the HFEA's guidance would make it difficult to justify any selection that is not directed towards avoidance of disease in the child that would be born following PGD.

Given that control over the provision of PGD has been delegated first to the regulatory agency whose job it is both to formulate policy and to police its implementation, and second to individual clinicians, what role is there for public opinion? In common with other regulatory agencies in the fields of biotechnology and genetics the HFEA are under a duty to carry out public consultation exercises in order to ensure scientific progress is contained within publicly acceptable boundaries. In practice, however, comparatively few people respond to, or even know about, the existence of these public consultation questionnaires. So while they may offer the HFEA a 'snapshot' of public opinion, they do not engage the wider public in debate. Moreover, most decisions about whether to offer PGD to a particular couple, and what course of action to adopt following positive test results are in fact made within the privacy of the doctor/patient relationship. Only where there is an especially controversial request will an individual case come before the HFEA itself. Again, we can see how the delegation of control to individual clinicians has largely shielded PGD from political and judicial scrutiny. Regulation is informed by public opinion not via the normal democratic process, but through surveys and opinion polls conducted by the regulatory agency itself. The providers of PGD are held accountable by the HFEA's licensing procedures, rather than through judicial review of their decisions. And as we have seen, wealthy patients may even be able to evade HFEA control by seeking treatment in countries, such as Italy, where the rules are less restrictive.

In a further parallel with the rules governing access to assisted conception services, the public's perception of PGD may again point to a breakdown in communication between lay and expert perspectives. Scientists tend to assume that regulation should be directed towards controlling risks that are *now* feasible, rather than addressing risks that *might* one day materialise. Yet it is precisely these latter risks that preoccupy the public. Geneticists agree that it is not going to be possible to devise tests to screen out embryos with complex personality traits within the foreseeable future. Yet given popular culture's saturation with narratives about the extraordinary and terrifying power of biotechnology, it is not surprising that the media's coverage of reproductive genetics reproduces these futuristic scenarios. It is, however, important to recognise that while media coverage may amplify public interest in PGD, the problem is not just one of inaccurate or lazy journalism. The public is not simply irrational and ignorant; instead there are some important concerns about the broader social consequences of genetic selection that must be addressed. Simply providing more information is not enough; we need to address the reasons why people are so fearful about genetic screening of early human embryos.

Why does the public assume that interference with the human genome is 'a disaster waiting to happen'? A central concern is clearly that the more nefarious uses of these new techniques are going to happen regardless of the existence of regulatory measures designed to prevent them. In recent years the 'technology=progress=good' equation has collapsed,[31] to be replaced by an image of scientists as arrogant, distant and unresponsive. The public's sense that it's opinion is ignored by scientists and policy-makers exacerbates this 'decline in deference'.[32] But rebuilding trust and confidence will only be possible if the public feel that its anxieties are taken seriously. Two-way communication about the risks and benefits that flow from PGD should be integrated into the regulatory process. Public participation should not simply be an exercise in legitimisation, in which low levels of response to consultation documents are regarded as an unfortunate, but inevitable fact of life. Rather, the connection between the public's perception that it is being ignored and its largely negative response to new genetic technologies should be acknowledged. By integrating the perspectives of patients themselves into this dialogue, the quality of debate might also be enhanced. Parents whose children's lives have been blighted or ended by serious genetic diseases and couples who are at risk of transmitting a genetic disorder are uniquely well qualified to spell out PGD's immediate health benefits. Avoiding intensive public scrutiny by delegating decision-making to individual clinicians may be easier and cheaper than ensuring that the public is equipped to take part in informed and mature debate about reproductive genetics, but it also points to a failure in participatory democracy.

Conclusion

Dicey could not have imagined the dense set of regulations that are directed towards controlling reproductive technologies. As new techniques proliferate, the law will indubitably face more novel regulatory dilemmas. But the mechanisms through which these new techniques are regulated reveal much about the complexity of the modern regulatory state. Towards the end of the twentieth century, new regulatory agencies and authorities have proliferated. No longer does law consist solely in legislation and the decisions of the higher judiciary. Particularly in relation to rapidly shifting technologies, such as reproductive genetics, legislation inevitably has an in-built obsolescence. As a result, licensing authorities, and other new regulatory bodies appear to offer a more flexible framework through which to manage the provision of services. Control over the treatment of individual patients is yet further delegated to the discretion of individual clinicians, within the privacy of the doctor/patient relationship. As I hope I have demonstrated in this chapter, this multi-layered fragmentation of decision-making authority has important consequences for democratic participation and accountability.

Medical control over assisted conception may help to depoliticise some of these complex issues, and shield individual clinicians and their patients from political scrutiny. However, it also runs the risk of alienating the general public and heightening their sense that the science and its regulation could easily spiral out of control. Low levels of public trust in scientists and their regulators result from the public's twin perceptions that science is inherently unstoppable and that the public is being kept in the dark. A better and more inclusive strategy might be to address public concerns directly, and to take seriously lay reservations about the wisdom of human interference with conception. The public is not simply suffering from a 'knowledge deficit' that could be corrected by more information. Rather, anxiety about what the future might hold is both real and understandable and should be integrated into a reflexive regulatory process within which the public can be reassured that the pace of scientific development will constantly be subjected to sustained scrutiny.

If Parliament and the courts are to have a restricted role in the ongoing development of regulations governing new assisted conception techniques, we need to be sure that alternative methods for public scrutiny and accountability are in place. New regulatory agencies must therefore have a responsibility both to foster active participation, and to ensure the provision of readily understandable information so that the public's opinion is not blighted by its lack of confidence in scientists and regulators.

Promoting negotiation between different perspectives may therefore be a principal goal of regulation. In relation to assisted conception, scientists, patients and sceptical members of the public all have points of view that may be equally valid. Balancing these various competing considerations is by no means a straightforward exercise, but it is important to recognise the equivalent legitimacy of a wide variety of opinions. A lack of transparency in the regulatory process both produces and buttresses the belief that meddling with nature is inherently and profoundly dangerous, and stifles effective communication between different interest groups.

Of course, we will have to experiment with new ways in which to actively involve the public in the regulatory process. Low response rates to consultation documents demonstrate that more active engagement with the public may be necessary. Citizens' juries, public hearings, consensus conferences, public opinion surveys, etc. may all have to be systematically evaluated. An effective model of communicative or deliberative democracy might also rely upon other public fora within which different perspectives can be expressed, debated and transformed. Jürgen Habermas' conception of an enhanced public sphere where policy dilemmas can be discussed and competing values synthesised envisages a variety of dispersed communicative networks.[33] Democratic participation is thus framed as a communicative *process* rather than a moment of decision. Putting in place arrangements to both foster reflective public debate and accommodate contesting viewpoints is unlikely to be cheap, but given the rapid pace of scientific advances in genetics and reproductive technologies, further alienation of public opinion may be inevitable unless mutual distrust is replaced by informed democratic participation.

Notes

1 A. V. Dicey, *Lectures on the Relation between Law and Public Opinion During the Nineteenth Century*, 2nd edition, Macmillan, London, 1914, pp. 19–20.
2 Marilyn Strathern, 'A question of context', in Jeanette Edwards, Sarah Franklin, Eric Hirsch, Frances Price and Marilyn Strathern (eds.), *Technologies of Procreation: Kinship in the Age of Assisted Conception*, 2nd edition, Routledge, London, 1999, pp. 9–28, p. 10.
3 Iris Marion Young, *Inclusion and Democracy*, Oxford University Press, Oxford, 2000, p. 26.
4 E. Yoxen, 'Conflicting concerns: the political context of recent embryo research policy in Great Britain', in M. McNeil, I. Varcoe and S. Yearley (eds.), *The New Reproductive Technologies*, Macmillan, Basingstoke, 1990, pp. 173–99, at pp. 184–8.
5 M. Mulkay, *The Embryo Research Debate: Science and the politics of reproduction*, Cambridge University Press, Cambridge, 1997, p. 22.

6 Ibid., p. 19.
7 A. H. Handyside E. H. Knotogianni, K. Hardy and R. M. L. Winston, 'Pregnancies from biopsied human pre-implantation embryos sexed by Y-specific DNA amplification', *Nature*, 244, 1990, pp. 768–70.
8 S. Franklin, 'Making representations: The parliamentary debate on the Human Fertilisation and Embryology Act and orphaned embryos', in Edwards et al., pp. 127–70, p. 157.
9 Mulkay, p. 41.
10 Susan Golombok, *Parenting: What really counts?*, Routledge, London, 2000, p. 47.
11 Mark Henderson and Roger Maynard, 'Fertility scientists try to make sperm redundant', *The Times*, 11 July 2001.
12 M. Warnock, *Report of the Inquiry into Human Fertilisation and Embryology*, Cm 9314, Department of Health and Social Security, London, 1984, para. 2.11.
13 HC Debates, 20 June 1990, col. 1025.
14 *McKay v Essex AHA*, 1982, AC 1166.
15 HL Debates, 6 March 1990, col. 1098.
16 *R v Ethical Committee of St Mary's Hospital (Manchester) ex parte Harriott*, 1988, 1 F. L. R. 512, at 519.
17 *R v Secretary of State for the Home Department, ex parte Mellor* (unreported) 4 April 2001.
18 *R v Sheffield AHA ex p. Seale* [1994] 25 BMLR 1.
19 Golombok, p. 56.
20 Sara McLanahan and Gary Sandefur, *Growing up with a Single Parent: What hurts, what helps*, Harvard University Press, Cambridge, Mass, 1994.
21 Golombok, p. 102.
22 D. King, 'Pre-implantation genetic diagnosis and the "new" eugenics', *Journal of Medical Ethics*, 25, 1999, pp. 176–82, p. 180.
23 H. L. Debates, 8 February 1990, col. 996.
24 For examples, see D. Thom and M. Jennings, 'Human pedigree and the "best stock": from eugenics to genetics?', in T. Marteau and M. Richards (eds.), *The Troubled Helix: Social and psychological implications of the new human genetics*, Cambridge University Press, Cambridge, 1996, pp. 211–34, p. 243.
25 See further A. Tudor, *Monsters and Mad Scientists: A cultural history of the horror movie*, Blackwell, Oxford, 1989.
26 H. L. debates, 8 February 1990, col. 1006.
27 Human Fertilisation and Embryology Authority and the Advisory Committee on Genetic Testing, *Consultation Document on Pre-implantation Genetic Diagnosis*, HFEA, London, 1999, para. 22.
28 Abortion Act 1967, s. 1(1)(d).
29 Human Fertilisation and Embryology Authority, *Public Consultation on Sex Selection*, HFEA, London, 1993.
30 R. Dobson, '"Designer baby" cures sister', *British Medical Journal*, 321, 2000, p. 1040.
31 Ian E. Taylor, 'Political risk culture: not just a communication failure', in Peter Bennett and Kenneth Calman (eds.), *Risk Communication and Public Health*, Oxford University Press, Oxford, 1999, pp. 152–69, p. 153.
32 Sheila McKechnie and Sue Davies, 'Consumers and risk', in Bennett and Calman (eds.), pp. 170–82, p. 170.
33 Jürgen Habermas, *Between Facts and Norms*, MIT Press, Cambridge, Mass., 1996, p. 360.

Part III
Culture and Identity

5
Language, Law and Politics
Colin H. Williams

Introduction

The relationship between indigenous languages and dynastic and representative politics has been an enduring feature of the history of the British Isles. Indeed, when Dicey was at the peak of his influence, language, religion and dissenting politics combined to forge Celtic assertions of separateness against the dominance of the hegemonic state. Following Irish independence, it was assumed that political divisions based upon ethnic or religious distinctiveness would yield to class-based issues and wither away. All the Celtic languages, let alone issues of mass religious dissent, have subsequently atrophied. But the political context wherein remedial strategies to revitalise Celtic identity may be implemented is being strengthened.

Would such trends have surprised Dicey? A common misconception is that the United Kingdom's constitutional settlement, particularly Welsh devolution, when granted, was done so in a vacuum. Nothing could be further from the truth if one adopts a Whig or a nationalist perspective on the history of these isles. Scottish parliamentary history up to 1707 and Irish parliamentary developments post-independence, are well understood, as are the Scottish and Irish legal systems (before and after partition). Wales, lacking both a separate parliament and legal system, has engaged its indigenous language and culture to delimit the contours of the nation. Thus, however Celtic nations are analysed, language-related issues have more purchase in Wales than elsewhere. Indeed the post-devolution settlement in Wales both recognises official bilingualism as a socio-political reality and seeks through National Assembly policies to strengthen and deepen societal and institutional bilingualism. By contrast, Northern Ireland, Scotland and Ireland have demonstrated varying degrees of support for their own indigenous languages, yet none has succeeded in convincing their residents to become functional bilingual citizens. Consequently issues of language in both law and politics remain problematic.

The defence of the Celtic languages may be characterised as a struggle for survival, recognition and equality. By the end of the twentieth century the infrastructural developments necessary to enable both Wales and Ireland, if not Scotland and Northern Ireland, to function as bilingual societies had been assembled. Yet individual and social behaviour had not taken advantage of opportunities created by language revitalisation efforts. These have revolved around greater *institutionalisation*, i.e. ensuring that the languages are represented in key strategic areas such as the law, education and public administration, together with *parallelism/normalisation*, i.e. extending the use of the languages into the optimum range of social situations, for example, the private sector, entertainment, sport and the media.

Wales

Rapid industrialisation and integration into the burgeoning state and its attendant anglicised culture during the latter part of the nineteenth century resulted in massive language shift a generation later during the period 1914–45.[1] The foundations of the language movement were laid down between c.1890 and 1914 when *Cymru Fydd*, and elements of the Liberal Party employed Celtic nationalism to secure the national recognition of Wales. During a second period, c.1921–39 dissenting intellectuals and *Plaid Cymru*, sought to anchor the fate of the language to the establishment of an independent nation-state.

Intellectuals in the language movement made culture, history and education their constant reference points. This collective search for identity was predicated on a platform of struggle, recognition and legitimacy. This was realised in social reforms and cultural initiatives, such as *Urdd Gobaith Cymru* (The Welsh League of Youth) founded in 1922, in educational reform, particularly the development of the Welsh university and college sector, in the Disestablishment of the Church of England to become the Church in Wales in 1920, in the formation of *Plaid Genedlaethol Cymru* at Pwllheli in 1925, in the Tân yn Llyn episode of 8 September 1936 when three leading Nationalists – Saunders Lewis, D. J. Williams and Lewis Valentine – set fire to buildings at the RAF bombing school in the Llyn peninsula, in the presentation of a language petition to Parliament in 1941, and in the Welsh Courts Act of

1942 which eradicated the 'language clause' in the original Act of Union of 1536 and gave limited statutory legitimacy to the use of Welsh in the courts of Wales.

In the postwar period *Plaid Cymru*, the Party of Wales, and *Cymdeithas yr Iaith*, the Welsh Language Society, campaigned to have Welsh recognised and used as an official language equal with English in all matters of state and local authority administration.[2] The Society saw itself as the radical, anti-establishment arm of Welsh nationalism, willing to take risks and to mobilise young people in defence of their threatened culture.[3] By sustaining a prolonged period of active pressure on the language front the Society reasoned they could force a change in government policy aiming to establish the co-equality of Welsh with English.[4] In July 1963', the Society announced an abstention from direct action in response to the establishment by Sir Keith Joseph, the Minister for Welsh Affairs, of a committee under the chairmanship of Sir David Hughes Parry to 'clarify the legal status of Welsh Language and to consider whether changes should be made in the law'. However, a vociferous minority called for a reappraisal of the total strategy of non-violent direct action and the Society was in danger of disintegrating. By 1971 the presence of over 100 Welsh defendants in jail for language-related offences had become an emotionally charged issue, as the Society had not convinced most of the target group of the legitimacy of their claims to speak as representatives for the Welsh language.

Fears for cultural survival were not assuaged by the 1971 census figures indicating that the Welsh-speaking proportion had fallen from 26.06 per cent in 1961 to 20.84 per cent in 1971. Many of the 431,245 Welsh speakers in the Welsh-speaking core areas were experiencing community decline and territorial fragmentation, and there was no regenerative policy to establish linguistic zones for administrative purposes.

Education has been the bedrock upon which the language movement has flourished by legitimising the role of Welsh. It has developed the value of bilingual skills within the fragmented bilingual economy and public sector labour market, and become the focus of a national project of identity reformulation. For many engaged in the language struggle, education was the principal focus and justification for their involvement, often in the face of a hostile and unsympathetic response from politicians, local authorities, fellow-professionals and many parents. For a growing minority the Welsh-medium educational infrastructure, from the nursery school level right through to the university sector, provided a series of distinctive, inter-locking socio-cultural networks which validated and reinforced developments at each level in the hierarchy. This was crucial in the cultivation of a sense of national purpose for professional bodies such as *Undeb Cenedlaethol Athrawon Cymru, Mudiad Ysgolion Meithrin*, and for pioneering local education authorities such as Flintshire, Glamorganshire, and since 1974, for Gwynedd Education Authority, which has had the most complete bilingual system of all local authorities.[5] Finally, as bilingual education has been both academically and socially successful, it has served as an additional marker of the country's distinctiveness within a British and international context. The school's role in reproducing Welsh language skills has increased following the reforms of the 1988 Education Act which insisted that Welsh be a core subject in the National Curriculum established alongside a National Assessment Programme. The granting of core status recognises the reality of bilingualism and the teaching of Welsh as a subject in all schools makes it more likely that all children will have experience (and for many some real competence) of the language as they enter adulthood, which also serves to reduce the latent tension which has long existed between fragments of the two language communities.

Beyond the educational sphere there remain the pillars of popular Welsh culture. Mass literacy and the development of a lively and innovative publishing sector has contributed greatly to the promotion of Welsh since the mid-nineteenth century. In 1977–79, as a result of the development of VHF wavebands, an English-medium Radio Wales and a predominantly Welsh-medium Radio Cymru service was launched. The latter provides some 127 hours per week, 90 of which are in Welsh.

Successful language campaigns heralded the introduction of a bilingual road fund licence disc, the adoption of bilingual road signs and public information signs.[6] In 1974, the Crawford Committee proposed a separate Welsh-medium television channel, as did the Conservative manifesto pledge of 1979. However, on taking office the new administration withdrew their commitment, preferring to improve the existing broadcasting arrangements. This policy change engendered the largest mass protests witnessed in postwar Wales, with a plethora of social movements, political parties, non-aligned interest groups all campaigning in tandem to force the government to honour its pledge. The focus of this campaign was the decision of Gwynfor Evans, on 5 May 1980, to fast to death unless the government announced the creation of a separate television service.[7] On the 17 September 1980 the government reversed its decision and *Sianel Pedwar Cymru* (S4C) was established on 1 November 1982, becoming a major boost to the promotion of Welsh through popular and varied Welsh-medium broadcasting. Some 30 of its 145 hours a week are transmitted in Welsh, mainly at peak time. The channel reaches a relatively high percentage of its target audience, although it is facing a rather unpredictable future with more confidence now than was true of the mid-1980s.

A statutory framework: The Welsh Language Act 1993

Legislation has been critical in authorising linguistic rights, and in establishing the infrastructure wherein such rights can be exercised without let or hindrance. Too often titular rights to certain services are held in abeyance, because of a lack of commitment to honour language choice rights at the point of local contact. Nevertheless Welsh social reform has been progressed in education, language rights and governance, by the Education Act of 1988, the Welsh Language Act of 1993 and the Government of Wales Act of 1998, which authorised the establishment of a National Assembly for Wales following elections in May 1999.

The Welsh Language Act 1993 is a unique piece of legislation. Among its key provisions are that it places a duty on the public sector providing services to the public in Wales to treat Welsh and English on an equal basis. It also inaugurated a new era in language policy and planning. Its chief policy instrument is the refashioned and strengthened Welsh Language Board, established on 21 December 1993, as a non-departmental statutory organisation. Initially funded by a grant from the Welsh Office, it is now funded mainly by the National Assembly Executive, which in the year ending 31 March 2001 totalled £6,498,000.[8] It has three main duties: 1) advising organisations which are preparing language schemes on the mechanism of operating the central principle of the Act, that the Welsh and English languages should be treated on a basis of equality; 2) advising those who provide services to the public in Wales on issues relevant to the Welsh language; 3) advising central government on issues relating to the Welsh language.

Since 1995 a total of 157 language schemes have been approved including all twenty-two local authorities. The Board is an Assembly Sponsored Public Body whose funds are voted by the Assembly and whose eleven members are appointed by the Assembly Secretary through open competition. Their responsibility is to provide direction to the Board and to guide and oversee its work. Although separate from the Civil Service, Board officials are public servants whose duty is to implement legislation. Despite its wide-ranging remit, the Board is a small organisation: at 31 March 2002 the Board employed 32 staff.

The Board has five core functions: 1) promoting and facilitating the use of the Welsh language; 2) advising on and influencing matters related to the Welsh language; 3) stimulating and overseeing the process of preparing and implementing language schemes; 4) distributing grants to promote and facilitate the use of Welsh; and 5) maintaining a strategic overview of Welsh-medium education. Though the Board's remit extending to cover anything to do with the Welsh language, direct responsibility for policy formulation and service delivery for the vast majority of Welsh language matters does not lie with the Board, but with other organisations. The Board acts as facilitator and advisor, working in co-operation and partnership with organisations and as the planning agency seeking to share its vision and mission with its partners.

In 1993 it set itself four priorities: 1) to increase the numbers of Welsh-speakers; 2) to provide more opportunities to use the language; 3) to change the habits of language use and encourage people to take advantage of the opportunities provided; and 4) to strengthen Welsh as a community language.[9] In its 'Strategy for the Welsh Language' (1999) the Board summarised recent achievements and current concerns in the following manner.

> The Welsh Language Act of 1993, the *mentrau iaith*, the spread of bilingual education at primary and secondary level, Welsh as a compulsory subject in the National Curriculum, the vitality of movements such as *Mudiad Ysgolion Meithrin, Urdd Gobaith Cymru*, local and national *eisteddfodau*, Welsh language schemes, increasing use of bilingualism and business and the economy are just a few of the many examples where language planning has successfully bucked the trend of downward shift.

During 1999–2000 a revised strategy was formulated as 'The Welsh Language: A Vision and Mission for 2000–2005' in which four areas of language planning are given priority. 1) Acquisition planning – producing new speakers of the language, through the school system and by teaching the language to adults. 2) Usage planning – increasing the opportunities to use the language through language schemes, running marketing campaigns to encourage people to take advantage of the opportunities. 3) Status planning or increasing the use of the language in domains such as information technology and the National Assembly for Wales. 4) Corpus planning – ensuring that standardised terms continue to be developed for new area and ensuring that clear Welsh and user-friendly forms of the language are used by public sector bodies.

The Government of Wales Act 1998

The high point in the struggle for recognition of Welsh as a national language was the establishment of the National Assembly for Wales in May 1999. The Assembly has operated from the beginning as a bilingual chamber for it must treat both languages equally (as far as is both appropriate in the circumstances and reasonably practicable) in the conduct of its business; that is *all* its business, whether public or not. This is a more far-reaching norm that previously encouraged under the Welsh Language Act.[10] The Labour government's unambiguous commitment in the White Paper 'A Voice for Wales' to give equal status to both languages has therefore been transferred to the Government of Wales Act and has been warmly welcomed by many agencies and political parties.[11] The Assembly's standing orders have also been devised so as to translate the principle of equal treatment into practice.[12]

A central issue in the normalisation of Welsh is the extent to which it can become a cross-cutting medium of governance and administration and not limited to its own Culture Committee, i.e. not become commodified and separated out as a 'problem area'. A second issue is the degree to which establishing a bilingual Assembly will influence the language-choice behaviour of the public.

If the Assembly can be widely seen as operating an effective bilingual policy, it could bring a great deal of benefit in normalising the language. The success will rest with the way in which the operations of the Assembly are conducted and conflicts between Welsh-speakers and non-Welsh-speakers, if not avoided, are at least mediated. The Assembly has set itself a primary aim of creating a bilingual Wales which will rest largely on the expertise and sensitivity of those in government. It can also directly influence related organisations by the manner in which it exercises its fundamental commitment to operating as a bilingual institution, including the comprehensive televising of key debates, selected committee meetings and the adoption of sophisticated telecommunication systems to disseminate information.

The bilingual operation of the National Assembly for Wales

Operational bilingualism was not a prominent feature of the former Welsh Office systems. Under the requirements of the Welsh Language Act 1993, the Welsh Office prepared a Welsh Language Scheme approved by the Welsh Language Board, but subsequent developments have demonstrated that this was essentially a patina of bilingualism, rather than an attempt to institutionalise Welsh as a language of work. This is significant because the Welsh Office was very much rooted in a monolithic English medium culture. The increasing expectations and pressure to work bilingually in the NAfW therefore came as a jolt to established working patterns and continues to be an issue of some concern in the absence of a clearly defined and resourced internal bilingual structure. Many civil servants have yet to adjust to the legitimacy of effective working through the medium of Welsh. One long-term implication within the devolution settlement is the possibility of establishing a distinct Civil Service for Wales, with all the attendant training requirements, including, of course, the option for the successful acquisition of Welsh as a second language. Currently, such provision is partial, fragmented and additional to statutory hours of work.

A central determinant of the operation of a bilingual chamber and committee structure is the behaviour of the Assembly Members. One implication for many AMs who consistently use Welsh is the perception that their contributions are under-reported by the media. Welsh language policy was initially entrusted to the Post-16 Education Committee, but after the creation of a coalition Cabinet it became the responsibility of a new Culture Committee. However, several AMs, the Welsh Language Board and commentators question why Welsh (or bilingualism) has not yet been made a crosscutting issue like Europe or Environment.

A key division of the NAfW is the Translation Unit, which is performing exceptionally well, even though it is understaffed. As at September 2000, it had a staff establishment of 51. However, recruiting high quality professional translators by only offering modest salaries was a continuing problem. The main strategic difficulty lay in convincing other elements of the NAfW that the role of the TU was to provide a translation service – not to be a one-stop shop for all matters linguistic. A second difficulty was that as the Assembly takes over an audit function for many agencies not previously subject to Welsh Office control, the translation needs of these agencies have been redirected to the Translation Unit. Currently, no strategy has been devised to prioritise and influence this exponential growth of demand for translation.

A third difficulty is the perception that Welsh language planning need constitute nothing more than an efficient translation service. For some heads of section, there is little understanding of the skill and time requirements involved in providing a statutory bilingual service, and thus a tendency to underestimate the degree of professionalism and in-service training required in the discharge of this function.

A fourth consideration is the development of a bilingual Document Management System as a way of providing greater efficiencies. The *Cofnod* is both organic and adapted from *Hansard* and thus suited to British parliamentary procedures. The *Cofnod* offers a complete transcription service of all full meetings. It aims to provide an accurate bilingual record within twenty-four hours. The record of plenary sessions takes two forms: 1) a working version for the Assembly Intranet within twenty-four hours; and 2) an official bilingual version for archive use within five working days. Having translated contributions in Welsh into English, the remainder of the twenty-four hour *Cofnod* is sent to external professionals who translate it from English into Welsh. According to a six-month study of the *Cofnod*, this produces an average of 19,211 words in English per meeting. The resultant proceedings are saved in HTML and PDF format, and mounted on a web server.

An abiding tension, not yet resolved, is that the Presiding Officer's responsibility is to serve all AMs equally. Whereas members of the Executive are increasingly frustrated that their urgent needs and special interests are not served preferentially by OPO personnel.

Considerations of language policy

The NAfW is responsible for developing its own internal language scheme and for devising a range of language policies to realise its aim of 'creating a bilingual Wales'. Recent research suggests that AMs welcome the positive and instructive relationship between the NAfW and the Welsh Language Board and that the Board should have more statutory powers to influence the socio-linguistic situation and anticipate keenly the NAfW's own review of the Welsh language.[13] AMs recognised that there were pressing issues that only a stronger legislative framework could countenance, e.g. the role of language in the workplace, in economic development and regional planning, in revitalising Welsh-speaking communities, in the judicial system, in health provision, and in retail and consumer affairs. The consensus was that this would be best achieved via amendments to existing legislation, although some expressed strong support for a new Welsh Language Act. Members welcomed the preparation of a new Welsh language scheme, within which bilingual conventions and practices could evolve. AMs use of Welsh in sessions is tempered by concerns over the cost implications of 'un-prioritised' translation work, and the time lag in the receipt of Welsh versions of official documentation (up to five days later than English for committee papers) is said to disadvantage members who choose to work in Welsh.

A positive indicator is the willingness of AMs to learn Welsh or to improve their existing Welsh language skills. To date, no central mechanism exists by which the linguistic skills of members and political staff, let alone civil servants, can be systematically improved. This is a major consideration if the Assembly wishes to be a more functional bilingual organisation and contribute effectively to social change. AMs and advisers also noted significant difference in the linguistic working culture of the NAfW Cardiff Bay and the dominant monolingual operation of its Cathays Park site. Consequently, Williams and Evans recommended that selected civil servants be released for extended periods of time in order to attend intensive Welsh language and language awareness courses. This is related to the training implications for the HE sector in Wales of operating a bilingual administration for there is a skills gap in the bilingual servicing of the NAfW requirements, especially in relation to legal affairs, IT and public administration.

There is an urgent need to supplement existing data required to determine bilingual policy as follows:

1 regular statistical monitoring which focuses on real language *use* in addition to competence;
2 the relationship between the Welsh Language Board and the Assembly's Statistical Directorate needs to be strengthened, in order to provide appropriate data for language policy and planning;
3 the collection of socio-economic data needs to include a wider variety of sociolinguistic indices;
4 the WLB, the WDA, the WTB and other agencies need to integrate their deliberations and policies so that they have a mutually beneficial impact in the field of community development and economic regeneration.[14]

National language policy is likely to focus on language planning in relation to education and public administration, equal rights and the socialisation of citizens within civil society. This involves, *inter alia*, issues such as interaction with the British state and its unwritten constitution, the European Convention on Human Rights, European Community language policies, the development of bilingual education, bilingual service provision in local government, health and social services. Second, economic policies and regional development initiatives which seek to stabilise predominantly Welsh-speaking communities, to create employment and to promote bilingual working opportunities. Third, consideration of the interests of Welsh language and culture as they are impacted upon by town and country/structure planning and improvements to the transport system.[15] In addition the pressing housing, property control and rural service issues highlighted by various bodies including *Jigso*, *Cymuned* and *Cymdeithas yr Iaith* are likely to be addressed directly.

The Assembly's recruiting policy and training programme could also impact on the public sector and especially local government. Currently there is an acknowledged shortage of competent accredited translators, experienced language tutors, and skilled bilingual administrators and technical specialists. The training infrastructure for a bilingual workforce is woefully inadequate. Consequently special attention should be paid to how the government's training agencies, such as ELWa, are resourcing or failing to resource the required training programmes for an increasingly sophisticated, bilingual economy. The skills gap in the workplace needs to be addressed urgently if the relationship between the Assembly and the rest of the public sector is to operate harmoniously.

The necessity to produce bilingual legislation will also have a direct impact on the development of a Welsh-language legal community to match that of the media community, as co-equality of language use becomes a situational norm in many domains. It is imperative, therefore, that both the university system and professional training of legal specialist take due regard of this trend and attend to the very real employment and training needs of the profession forthwith. In addition, strong positive messages on the societal value of bilingualism will not go unheeded within the private sector, which is itself in need of important structural initiatives such as 1) a powerful NAfW economic committee; 2) structural change and internal merging of key agencies to produce a more powerful and integrated Welsh Development Agency; 3) the bilingual structure and operation of the Assembly; 4) vigorous education, training and language policies; 5) pressure by the National Assembly on a range of agencies and quangos, including the Welsh Language Board, to review its own future, to engage in more medium-term holistic, language planning and community development programmes.

Central agencies, such as the National Assembly, the Welsh Development Agency and the Welsh Language Board and they have a critical role as legitimising institutions constructing new forms of partnership through their statutory obligations and pump-priming initiatives. Quite radical initiatives to strengthen the role of Welsh as both a community language and as a language of the workforce are underway. But the long-term infrastructural support and dynamism will be non-governmental, largely located within the private sector and grounded within local communities who have already exhibited a remarkable initiative in supporting regional economic enterprises. Political leadership and direction are crucial now to realise such initiatives as a self-sustaining process.

Language policy in Northern Ireland

The 1991 Census indicated that 142,000 people in Northern Ireland had some knowledge of the Irish language, the vast majority of whom came from the nationalist community where the language is taught in most Catholic secondary schools. Partly as a reaction to the Irish language movement, a campaign emerged in recent years for recognition of the Ulster Scots linguistic tradition.[16] Ulster Scots is recognised as a language for purposes of Part II of the Council of Europe *Charter on Regional or Minority Languages*. The North/South Co-operation (Implementation Bodies) *Northern Ireland Order* 1999 provides that Ulster Scots is to be understood as the variety of the Scots language traditionally found in Northern Ireland and Donegal and has established an Ulster Scots Agency.[17]

The Department of Culture, Arts and Leisure has lead responsibility for developing agreed language policies and guidance on language issues to other Departments within the Executive. Linguistic diversity is a relatively new policy area and has emerged from the Good Friday Agreement which commits the Government to:

> recognize the importance of respect, understanding and tolerance in relation to linguistic diversity, including in Northern Ireland, the Irish language, Ulster-Scots and the languages of the various ethnic minority communities, all of which are part of the cultural wealth of the island of Ireland.
>
> In the context of active consideration currently being given to the UK signing the Council of Europe Charter for Regional or Minority Languages, the British Government will in particular in relation to the Irish language, where appropriate and where people so desire it:

- take resolute action to promote the language;
- facilitate and encourage the use of the language in speech and writing in public and private life where there is appropriate demand;
- Seek to remove, where possible, restrictions which would discourage or work against the maintenance or development of the language.
- make provision for liaising with the Irish language community, representing their views to public authorities and investigating complaints;

- place a statutory duty on the Department of Education to encourage and facilitate Irish medium education in line with current provision for integrated education;
- explore urgently with the relevant British authorities, and in co-operation with the Irish broadcasting authorities, the scope for achieving more widespread availability of Teilifis na Gaeilge in Northern Ireland;
- seek more effective ways to encourage and provide financial support for Irish language film and television production in Northern Ireland; and
- Encourage the parties to secure agreement that this commitment will be sustained by a new Assembly in a way which takes account of the desires and sensitivities of the community.

The Linguistic Diversity Branch, which began work in February 1999, has a total of eight staff, but does not, as yet, have a grant making capacity.

The North/South Language Body, known in Irish as *An Foras Teanga* and in Ulster Scots as *Tha Boord o Leid*, was established by the North/South Co-operation (Implementation Bodies) Northern Ireland Order 1999 which came into operation at devolution. It has two separate agencies, *Foras na Gaeilge* and *Tha Boord o Ulster Scotch*. The NSLB has a duty of promoting the Irish language; facilitating and encouraging its use in speech and writing in public and private life in the South and, in the context of Part III of the *European Charter for Regional or Minority Languages*, in Northern Ireland where there is appropriate demand; advising both administrations, public bodies and other groups in the private and voluntary sectors; undertaking supportive projects, and grant-aiding bodies and groups as considered necessary; undertaking research, promotional campaigns, and public and media relations; developing terminology and dictionaries; supporting Irish-medium education and the teaching of Irish.

The NSLB has the following functions in relation to Ulster-Scots language and culture: Promotion of greater awareness and use of *Ullans* and of Ulster-Scots cultural issues, both within Northern Ireland and throughout the island.[18] The Language Body has 24 Board members, including the two joint chairpersons.

North/South Language Body corporate planning

The *Foras na Gaeilge* indicative programme of activities for the medium term is envisaged in terms of four main sectors: 1) development of planning and policies over a wide range of areas; 2) external funding of organisations and projects; 3) projects and partnerships of the Foras; 4) administration and personnel.

Tha Boord o Ulster Scotch released its *Heid Ploy* (Corporate Plan) on 2 January 2001 consisting of four themes at a cost of £1.45 million. They are: 1) supporting Ulster-Scots as a living language and promoting its use and development; 2) acting as a key contributor to the development of the Ulster-Scots culture; 3) establishing partnerships with the education and community sectors to promote the study of the Ulster-Scots language, culture and history; 4) developing the public's understanding of the Ulster-Scots language and culture. In the year prior to devolution (1999/2000) Government support in Northern Ireland for projects with an Irish language dimension grew to over £10 million (including £8 million for Irish medium education). In the same period funding for Ulster-Scots was £118,000.[19]

Council of Europe Charter for Regional or Minority Languages

On 4 June 1998 the UK government announced its intention to sign the Council of Europe *Charter for Regional or Minority Languages*. On 2 March 2000 the UK government signed the *Charter*, recognising Irish, Scottish Gaelic, Welsh, Scots and Ulster-Scots for Part II. It thereby committed itself to apply the general principles and objectives of recognition and non-discrimination. The Charter was ratified on 27 March 2001, and came into force on Monday, 2 July 2001.

Upon ratification, the UK government specified Irish, Welsh and Scottish Gaelic for Part III of the Charter – *Measures to Promote the Use of Regional or Minority Languages in Public Life etc*. The NI Executive is to ensure that the Charter is observed and implemented in Northern Ireland in respect of devolved issues and to inform the Foreign Secretary.

The Good Friday Agreement contains undertakings that the government would explore the scope for achieving more widespread availability of (TG4) *Teilifís na Gaeilge* in Northern Ireland, and seek more effective ways to encourage and provide support for Irish language film and television production in Northern Ireland. Similarly the *Education (Northern Ireland) Order* 1998 places a duty on the Department of Education for Northern Ireland to encourage and facilitate the development of Irish medium education. The Department is currently funding eleven Irish-medium schools (nine primaries and two secondary) with approximately

1,900 pupils. There are no current demands from within the school system for Ulster-Scots to be taught.

Language governance implications for Northern Ireland

In order for Irish, and to a lesser extent Ulster-Scots, to flourish as vehicles for the communication of ideas, skills and a pluralist culture, it is essential that new networks and a new set of institutions be established which enable the target language to be embraced by all in society should they so choose. Thus issues of the development of Irish-medium schools, attractive texts and resources, the training of teachers, the introduction of optional (or mandatory) Irish lessons in all state-funded schools need to be tackled afresh, with a great deal of respect for the existing institutional arrangements based within Roman Catholic networks. However, logic alone suggests that if Irish is always to be associated with Catholic cultural imperatives, it will not serve as a bridge or a platform upon which more cross-cutting networks can be established. Thus it is imperative that DENI reconsider the whole issues of language choice within the educational system, including the training of teachers and the location of resource centres. This is critical so that a free choice may be offered to every non-Irish-speaking citizen to benefit from a bilingual experience either for themselves in adult education or more probably for their children. In similar terms the exposure to elements of Ulster-Scots should be widened within the remit of the education authorities.

Community development experience in Wales suggests that individuals need direct government support to enable them to establish and maintain certain community networks that enhance the vibrancy of a bilingual heritage. This could take the form of language enterprise agencies, the creation of a more visible bilingual landscape through public signs, the development of resource centres, the adoption of stress-free teaching methods for adult learners, media developments and collaborative projects with colleagues in the Republic of Ireland, Scotland and Wales. Community research into patterns of Irish and Ulster Scots language use is needed to ascertain processes and problems. This would likely focus on youth activities and on the specification of the relationship between bilingualism and the economy so that employment prospects might be considered in tandem with socio-cultural considerations. Finally, it is imperative that the Northern Ireland Assembly and the civil service declare clear, consistent and realisable roles for all the constituent languages and prioritise and monitor its action plans and policies so that the interested public is convinced that pragmatic medium-term goals are being set.

The Republic of Ireland

One of the central features of the nineteenth-century Gaelic revival and the move towards independence achieved by the Treaty of 1921, was the need to distance and further differentiate Irish culture and values from British mores and interests. The three most prominent agencies for cultural liberation in the national struggle, were Catholicism, the land and the language.

In 1922 the newly independent state launched a comprehensive strategy for the restoration of Irish as a national language. Thus Irish speakers were given preference in public service positions such as *Gardai*, army officers, teachers and civil servants, thereby creating a new middle-class Irish-speaking population. The 1937 Constitution gave recognition to two languages, Irish and English, but declared Irish as the first official language. There followed a policy of incremental reform to establish State initiatives to promote the use of Irish, to stabilise *Gaeltacht* communities and to encourage a nation-wide system of voluntary language organisations, the most prominent of which is *Comhdhail Náisiunta Na Gaeilge*.

State support for agriculture did not stabilise the Irish-speaking communities and as a result of education and planning policies large numbers of *Gaeltacht* residents quit the predominantly Irish-speaking areas for employment opportunities in urban, anglicised locales. Thus the government committed itself to a two-pronged attack to arrest the decline of Irish. The first policy sought to define and defend the fragmented Irish-speaking areas, the *Gaeltachtai*. Hindley advances five lessons, which with hindsight might have made the Irish language policy less dependent upon ill-advised territorial language planning.[20] The implementation of government policy was characterised by:

1 Lack of policy precedent. There were no precedents in 1925 for any attempt to revive a national language, which had already become a minority tongue within its own national territory.
2 Lack of socio-spatial planning. There were no precedents, other than native reserves in the colonies, for demarcating minority language areas in order to preserve their cultural identity – except when as at Versailles the minority was a majority elsewhere.
3 Lack of census interpretation experience. There was little experience of the inadequacy of census enumeration of language ability as a guide to language use or genuine command.
4 Lack of conceptual awareness. There was no awareness of such concepts as 'critical mass' below which a language ability as a guide

to language could fall in numbers or proportions only at its extreme peril, nor of village and urban 'systems' command of Irish, at least one of which was essential for language survival.
5 Lack of theoretical sophistication in terms of policy options. There had been no conceptual exploration of the territorial or individual alternatives in language planning strategies, nor indeed had much need been felt for language planning in the English-speaking world to which all *Irish*-speaking scholars belonged.

Eoin Mac Néil was very conscious that one should not place an undue burden on the school system to bring about a revival. Nevertheless, as Minister of Education, he was to preside over the legislative steps which made such dependence possible and inevitable. Ó Gadhra phrases the dilemma thus:

> Central to this language restoration policy was the idea that it was possible to restore Irish through the schools – with little thought being given to matters like incentive, or the simple linguistic reality we now all accept i.e. teaching Irish even well in the class is NOT sufficient. You need motivation, you need planning; you need political support and moral support from leaders and role models. Above all you need to place an emphasis on chances to use the language you have learned, written and oral. Above all else, you have to convince the native Irish speakers of the value of their own heritage which they must be encouraged to hand on to their own children and indeed to everybody else who is interested.[21]

The challenge was not faced either then or now, despite a range of reforms undertaken to safeguard the Irish language:

1913 Irish became compulsory for matriculation to the National University.
1922 Irish was designated the 'national language' and competence in it became compulsory for entry to the civil service, police and army.
1926 The Official *Gaeltacht* was defined and demarcated.
1937 The status of Irish was reaffirmed in the Constitution.
1943 *Comhdháil Náisiúnta na Gaeilge* was funded as a co-ordinating agency for voluntary language organisations.

By the early 1960s the declining viability of the family farm sector, out-migration of the young and low levels of participation in tertiary education necessitated a change of economic policy. Instead of protectionist agricultural policies and a concentration on the internal market, Ireland developed the export market together with small and medium-sized enterprises. In this modernising context severe doubts were raised as to the linkage between educational success and competence in Irish. Consequently, in 1973 Irish ceased to be a compulsory examination subject at the conclusion of secondary education. Ó Riagáin demonstrates the painful disjunction between economic policy and language policy, because such socio-economic mobility as was available depended on inherited economic capital in the form of family land-holdings or small shops; the incentives for Irish built into the educational and government employment systems affected relatively few young people.[22]

The government continues its support for all-Irish schools but has weakened the rule that all secondary students should learn Irish and the Irish language requirement for second level teachers. Restructuring of the National University has also meant the abolition of Irish as a necessary requirement for university entry.

Top-down and bottom-up planning

The principal features of twentieth-century language policy and the need for a national action plan was spelled out in the late 1980s by *Board na Gaeilge*.[23] The strategic policy initiatives identified then are still valid now, albeit within the context of a healthier Irish economy. It was reported that only around 5 per cent of Irish citizens use Irish extensively in their homes, neighbourhood or at work, although a further 10 per cent of the population use Irish regularly if less extensively. Weak rates of language reproduction lead the authors of the report to suggest urgent remedial action along the following lines. The state should take the initiative in changing the operating context of Irish usage and in changing the popular consciousness about Irish identity. The state should recreate an ideological basis for Irish language loyalty and learning. To this end it advocated that *Board na Gaeilge* be given wider powers to counter the marginal position of Irish within government agencies, arguing that central government itself, through its discourse, sense of complacency and lack of leadership, was one of the key agencies militating against promotional measures in support of Irish.

Second, the report called for a popular cultural movement, both to resist provincialism and the downgrading of Irish, and also to act as a fulcrum for the re-creation of virile Irish-medium social networks. Third, the basic rights of Irish speakers in their dealings with state agencies needed much greater specification. While Article 8 of the *Bunreacht na hEireann* set out the constitutional standing of both official languages, there was little in the Irish system which set out the detailed practical legislative provisions. Calls for a revised Irish Language Act have led to the introduction of a Bill in April 2002. Infrastructural provisioning and planning, a key element for the realisation of any relatively free language choice in a multilingual society, were to include giving legal effect to the concept of the bilingual state; strengthening Irish in the public service; increasing the visibility and usage of Irish in the state-sponsored media and arresting the decline of Irish in the *Gaeltacht*.

The Department of the Gaeltacht, *Udaras na Gaeltachta* and the *Bord na Gaeilge* have been accused of failing to achieve a high degree of policy integration. In tackling the chief issues which remain namely: Irish language speakers outside the *Gaeltacht*; migration; language learning; traditional conceptions of the role of the Irish language in society and economy; television and the media occupying an important niche; the *T na G* television station; Irish as an economic resource; and the work of *Gaelscoileanna*.

Despite communal and government efforts, the task of revitalising Irish has proved greater than the resources and commitment hitherto shown. The underlying fault is an overoptimistic assessment of the capacity of state intervention to restore Irish as a national language without a concomitant investment in socio-economic planning to bring about the necessary conditions to regulate the market forces which encouraged widespread Anglicisation.

In 1991, some 1,095,830 persons (32 per cent of the population) were returned as Irish speakers in the Census of Population. National percentages mask wide regional and class variations. The designated Irish-speaking areas, the *Gaeltacht*, contain only 2.3 per cent of the state's population, but 45 per cent of all Irish-speaking families. Ireland, at the end of the twentieth century, had 260 voluntary Irish-medium playgroups serving 2,500 children; 120 Irish-medium primary schools, 26 post-primary schools serving some 22,000 children outside the *Gaeltacht*. Too little effort has been expended on the professional/vocational elements of Irish medium education, giving rise to fears over a general decline in standards of written Irish, particularly in relation to authenticity of expression in both public and private sector employment.

Elements of holistic language planning belatedly characterise the Irish experience. But for far too long it was assumed that dedicated language initiatives, based in part on goodwill and in part on a symbolic adherence to Irish as a token of national identity, would suffice. The reality, of course, is far more complex and we accept Ó Riagáin's view that language policies 'cannot be treated as an autonomous, independent factor' (p. 283). They must be related to trends and initiatives, grounded in the socio-economic context of everyday life, but always with the force of state legislative power and redress if public organisations and state institutions are to respect citizen language rights.

Once again we return to the centrality of legislation in legitimising new statutory norms as the hopes of Irish language planning today rest on the re-invigoration of the public sector through the passage of a new Irish Language Act. In 1998 *Comhdháil Náisiúnta na Gaeilge* argued that there is a need for a new Language Act so as to give practical effect to the existing language rights of citizens. It recommended that the new Act should: 'Define and set out the State's duties and obligations in respect of the Irish language and give effect to the rights of citizens in relation to that language.' It also advocates that the new Act will provide for:

1) Institutional arrangements concerning the implementation of the said rights and duties.
2) Amendments to existing legislation and Government schemes to ensure that they are in accordance with the status of Irish as the 'national language' and the 'first official language'.
3) Institutional arrangements to ensure that all legislation enacted in the future is in accordance with the status of Irish as the 'national language' and as the 'first official language'.
4) The establishment of structures that will be responsible for the execution and implementation of the Act and for ensuring that State services through Irish are freely available to Irish speakers and *Gaeltacht* communities.[24]

In April 2002 an Official Languages (Equality) Bill, 2002, was published comprised of five parts covering preliminary and general interpretations and regulations, the use of both languages in the House of *Oireachtas* and the administration of justice, the rights to deal with services from public bodies in the official languages, the establishment of an Official Languages Commissioner together with a final part relating to the role of the Ombudsman and issues of civil or criminal liability.[25] While it is too early to interpret its impact on the fortunes of the Irish language, but this latest initiative reflects a growing European-wide trend to deal with national and minority language rights in a far more systematic manner than hitherto.

Scotland

Unlike Welsh or Irish, Gaelic in Scotland cannot be considered as the national language, in part because of its demo-linguistic history being marginalised since the fourteenth century and the persistence of the Highland/Lowland divide. For non-Gaelic speaking Lowland Scots, there has historically been a sense that Gaelic had little to do with them, the language (unlike Welsh in Wales or Irish in Ireland) was not part of a patrimony, lost, imagined or orthewise. This ideological divide has been exacerbated by three centuries of Whig history and historicism, and the acceptance of what some call a 'teutonist' ideology. Thus, rather than being seen as a variant on language shift, it is more profitable to interpret this complex relationship as a form of ethnic redefinition.[26] Consequently this limits the extent to which devolution itself promises a *prima facie* improvement in the situation of Gaelic.

Until devolution, distinctly Scottish institutions such as a separate legal system, the Presbyterian/Calvinist national church, and the education system, with their attendant ideologies, have been crucial in reinforcing and carrying forward a national identity. Neither Gaelic nor Scots, will achieve salience in national politics, neither language received any mention in the Scotland Act 1998. Gaelic gets some provision in the Standing Orders of the Scottish Parliament (Scots gets none at all), and there have been some titular concessions to Gaelic, as in some signage at the Parliament, a Gaelic Officer, and the language is used in a number of functions.[27]

On 14 June 2002, the Scottish Executive Minister with responsibility for Gaelic, Michael Watson, signalled that his government was establishing a Gaelic Language Board and a small-unit of Gaelic-speaking civil servants within the Executive to deal with Gaelic matters.[28] Language activists, academic commentators and some politicians welcome this as a necessary but not a sufficient recognition of the need to implement a national policy on Gaelic. The next urgent step is the passing of a Gaelic Language Act as recommended by the Meek Report.[29] Scottish devolution gives a platform for the discussion of indigenous issues, although Gaelic, when seen from the majoritarian perspective, is a 'local' rather than a 'national' issue. When coupled with the 'rights' discourse which the Human Rights Act has ushered in and the new minorities discourse on 'multi-culturalism, citizenship and development' which the *European Charter on Regional and Minority Languages* may be able to advance, there are now some ideological bricks and mortar out of which a coherent Gaelic policy may be fashioned.[30] But time is running out for language transmission within fragile Gaelic communities and the progress in bilingual education does not offer a substitute for the organic reproduction of a total culture.

Let us turn for the remainder of the chapter to explore how the political-legal context can be further influenced so as to consider issues of language policy more effectively.

UK devolution, governance and democracy: unfinished business

> Parliament's more liberal and tolerant attitude towards the different nations of the UK is demonstrated by the devolution statutes. Its respect for the individual is demonstrated by its introduction of the Human Rights Act, the Freedom of Information Act and the Race Relations (Amendment) Act of last year. Together these represent a colossal change. We have a modern democracy based on involvement, openness, accessibility, scrutiny, accountability, privacy and respect. These are the essential elements of a modern democracy.[31]

David Williams reminds us how this devolved constitutional pattern came about initially through a White Paper,[32] a referendum held in September 1997, the Government of Wales Act of 1998 consisting of 159 sections and 18 schedules, the National Assembly for Wales (Transfer of Functions) Order (1999 S.I. 672), the Memorandum of Understanding and supplementary agreements between the United Kingdom Government, Scottish Ministers and the Cabinet of the National Assembly for Wales (Cm.4444 of October 1999), the National Assembly for Wales (Transfer of Functions) Order (2000 S.I. 253) which corrects a number of omissions and deficiencies in the first order of 1999 (see HL, Vol. 609, c488, 7 February 2000) and a variety of other related measures.[33]

Sherlock argues that much concerning the devolution arrangement for Wales was novel within a British context – decentralisation, proportional representation, a bilingual Assembly and an obligation to develop bilingual legislation together with the obligation to comply with the rights set out in the European Convention on Human Rights.[34]

> The fact that an issue of such constitutional significance as the transfer of the bulk of the Assembly's powers could be achieved by subordinate legislation is also noteworthy. Likewise the regulation of intergovernmental relations within the United Kingdom not by

legally binding instrument but by 'concordats' described as a form of 'pseudo-contract' by one academic[35] is of interest. (Sherlock, p. 59)

Devolution has also changed the pragmatic character of the British constitution in requiring a greater degree of categorisation and definition in both the implementation of policy and the exercise of governance.[36] Rawlings reminds us that previously internal processes of government are external consequent to the establishment of formal interrelationships between devolved administrations, and the subsequent awareness of the need for public accountability and scrutiny of these activities.[37] The Assembly's procedures and structures are detailed in the Standing Orders that in turn reflect the Government of Wales Act 1998. In its attempt to ensure a form of inclusive politics the Act contains requirements which avoid the excessive dominance of any one group or the arbitrary exclusion of another. The Act also makes certain requirements of the standing orders of the Assembly together with the demands of a 'full scrutiny' process.

Current arrangements are likely to be revised to remedy two flaws: the fact that the NAfW has no legislative powers or powers of taxation. For, unlike Scotland, Wales does not have direct revenue-raising powers, and unlike Scotland and Northern Ireland, the power to make primary legislation is not transferred. Equally significant, unlike Scotland and Northern Ireland, where all power is transferred except that which is expressly reserved, the NAfW may exercise only those powers expressly allocated to it under section 21 of the Act. The Act is in essence an enabling mechanism under which the Orders in Council may be made to transfer specific powers to the Assembly.[38] Williams argues that such legislative devolution is federalism without the courage of its convictions keeping Wales dependent upon Westminster and Whitehall. With regard to subordinate legislation and administrative action, the courts would be equipped with the normal powers of administrative law, important in many instances, but removed from authority to strike down primary or quasi-primary legislation.[39]

At first sight the eighteen subject areas in which the Assembly apparently has competence suggest an impressive array of domains in which all executive and subordinate lawmaking powers reside. However, rather than transferring powers to the Assembly by general area or subject heading, the preferred option has been to list powers section by section, sub-section by sub-section and to transfer the vast bulk of functions by an *Order in Council* of 1999.[40] The division of powers within the Assembly is rather different from Scottish and Northern Irish arrangements in that the latter two legislative bodies have an Executive, which Wales does not (although increasingly it acts as if it did). Thus while legislative and executive responsibilities are institutionally inscribed in Edinburgh and Belfast, the NAfW in Cardiff operates as a unitary 'body corporate'. In effect, the Assembly has an unitary status but operates quite clearly with a Cabinet system. The growth of concordats between various UK governments and departments and the Assembly Cabinet, rather than the whole Assembly, turns on their being such a separation. Thus, critically when sharing information, the UK government treats the Assembly Cabinet as a separate and distinct entity from the body corporate of which it is a part. This 'body corporate' status has important implications, not only for 'opposition' parties, but also for the position of the civil service within the Assembly. In contradistinction to Scotland and Northern Ireland where the legislative bodies have their own staff, which are quite distinct from the general civil service,[41] in Wales no separate administration was established. Structural tensions are occasioned by such arrangements, as for example regarding the availability of legal advice for AMs, which is independent of the advice given to the Assembly Cabinet.[42]

A second issue revolves around parity with other nations within the UK. The membership of the British-Irish Council provided for in the Northern Ireland Act 1998 comprises in the words of the Good Friday Agreement:[43] 'representatives of the British and Irish Governments, devolved institutions in Northern Ireland, Scotland and Wales, when established, and, if appropriate elsewhere in the United Kingdom, together with representatives of the Isle of Man and the Channel Islands.' In essence, the NAfW is the only body identified in the statement that does not have primary or quasi-primary legislative power.

There remains the West Lothian question. Currently Wales and Scotland are yoked together in most post-devolution discussion, yet whereas the Scottish White Paper of 1997 expressly envisaged that statutory provision for a minimum number of Scottish seats at Westminster would come to an end (4.5), the Welsh White Paper of 1997 expressly stated (3.37) that setting up the Assembly 'will not reduce Wales's representation in Parliament'. Williams avers that 'if Wales is indeed to lose its admittedly preferential position at Westminster after all, then the scheme of 1997 will have delivered a double whammy to the Principality in the form of no primary legislative power in Cardiff and reduced representation in London'.[44]

A fourth issue is the doubt surrounding the future role of the Secretary of State for Wales, who should remain accountable and answerable in the House of Commons on major issues related to Wales. The consensus is that the Secretary, as representative of Wales in the Cabinet, should field questions related to Wales, even if there is a division of view between the NAfW and Whitehall. A fifth issue is the contrast between the functionally clear and unambiguous Scottish scheme and the overly complicated and nuanced Welsh scheme. Williams argues that by nature the Welsh scheme of executive devolution involved not only a complex process of subordinate legislation, but also the inevitable particularity of the Orders transferring functions of the Welsh Office and other departments to the NAfW.

Commenting on the first end of year report Sherlock concludes that despite all the constraints the NAfW has achieved a great deal.

> With limited extra staffing resources, the staff of the Welsh Office, largely concerned with the implementation of policy, have become the servants of a new legislative body which aims to innovate and develop, rather than merely follow, policy. Almost overnight there is a legislative body within the United Kingdom which drafts and makes its legislation bilingually and which sets its budget with input from 'backbenchers'. In terms of many of its procedures, it must be the envy of the most 'modernising' Westminster parliamentarian, and its 'family-friendly hours' approach leaves House of Commons all-night sittings looking rather archaic. The percentage of women both in the Assembly and in the Cabinet[45] give a very favourable picture of intention to break new ground in the area of equal opportunities and it has remained well ahead of central Government in terms of freedom of information.

Clearly, the constitutional settlement will evolve; this has been recognised explicitly by a number of agencies and bodies, most notably the Royal Commission on the House of Lords in 2000.[46] Other commentators emphasise that devolution to Wales has brought many challenges as well as the opportunities, for the development of distinct law and policy. Not least of the challenges is that of establishing appropriate legal frameworks through Westminster legislation and Assembly subordinate legislation which would contribute to a body of Welsh law.

Finally both C. H. Williams and Roddick emphasise that devolution not only made the Welsh dimension of generic UK policy more salient but also that changes in the administration of the justice system have helped stimulate a greater sense of national identity in the practice of law. New institutional developments include, regular sittings of the Court of Appeal Civil Division and Criminal Division in Cardiff, the facility of issuing proceedings and having them heard in the Administrative Court in Wales, local sittings of the Employment Appeal Tribunal, the establishment of a Mercantile Court in Cardiff, the establishment of the Administrative Court of Wales, hearings in Wales rather than in London as was the normal practice of judicial review cases involving the National Assembly and all other public bodies in Wales. The appointment of a High Court Judge whose fluency in Welsh facilitates the conduct of trials bilingually or entirely in Welsh, according to the wishes of the parties, without translation is also significant. The Welsh civil society and economy are also being nourished by post-devolution developments, witness the recent establishment of three specialist legal associations, the Wales Public Law and Human Rights Association, the Welsh Personal Injuries Lawyers Association and the Wales Commercial Law Association. Cumulatively it is estimated that legal services in Wales generate around £250 million of GDP that is around 1 per cent of the total and set to grow as the NAfW enacts more bilingual legislation.

Conclusion

Any consideration of the relationship between language, law and politics as practical policy must deal with the following difficulties in implementing agreed plans:

1 Statutory obligation or goodwill only? There is a critical need for statutory obligation – goodwill is not enough if policy aims to provide a genuine choice of language service. This issue is a major stumbling block for Northern Ireland and in the search for 'secure status' for Gaelic in Scotland.
2 Holistic versus sectoral language planning. 'Joined-up thinking' within and between government departments and their partner agencies in the community is a *sine qua non* of new forms of horizontal governance. 'Holistic language planning' can so easily become 'sectoral language planning' and the radical cutting edge of innovative policy is lost.
3 Symbolic or practical language schemes? Agreed language schemes, whether at Assembly level or level of local authorities, can very often be symbols of good intent rather than genuine services at point of local demand/contact. There is a critical need to monitor the actual working of the schemes. Hence the need to tackle the twin issues of adequate resourcing of language schemes and target community implementation. Processes of empowerment, ownership, participation

and partnership are far easier to assume as given rather than work on as part of infra-structural development of language planning.
4 Institutional or individual language rights? In whom are basic rights vested? Individual citizens or institutions implementing an equal opportunities policy? Are notions of equality or equity tested in the courts in relation to language rights?
5 Public sector or plural sector approach? Initial language policy schemes are targeted at public sector institutions and educational domains. However, to be truly useful, language schemes should have a medium term aim of influencing language rights behaviour in most socio-economic contexts.
6 Top-down or bottom-up planning? How does the partnership between central and local agencies, vital community initiatives, the voluntary sector and the world of work, mobilise and reflect society's language-related energy to reinforce the central thrust of language schemes?
7 Tension between instrumentalists and analysts. In all cases of language revitalisation there is an acute tension between advocates of front-line services and language teaching requirements, and those who in addition recognise that sound planning requires accurate trend and impact analysis, together with an effective audit and monitoring function of language planning.
8 Priorities of language governance agencies. Are language governance agencies essentially a grant disbursement operation or also a genuine language planning and policy unit? How effectively will they cooperate at an UK and European level to press for structural reforms and international recognition of their role in delivering multilingual policies?
9 Internal reticence within the civil service. Usually the biggest stumbling block to the implementation of language schemes is the reticence of civil servants not directly concerned with LP schemes. Two temptations loom large: a) to view all language-related issues as being the special responsibility of an LDB/WLB only (the ghetto approach); and b) to refuse to accept the legitimacy of cross-cutting language issues within key functions of the local state, e.g. economic development, environment, health and social services (the head in the sand approach). Language awareness training coupled with firm political direction can overcome some, but not all of this reticence.

The development of a fully comprehensive bilingual society is a project in social engineering which will require investment, training, encouragement and crucially, political conviction and power to act. Having seized the opportunities which structural reforms of the British state have allowed, the next step is to promote bilingualism in as many avenues of daily life as is reasonable without ever losing sight of the political fact this is done under the consensual eye of the majority. But this presumes new forms of governance in which governments become catalytic, steering and sparking action rather than prohibiting change; community-owned, empowering rather than serving; and which are mission-driven, results-oriented and customer-focused. The bottom line is how well policy and practical politics safeguards the interests both of individual speakers and vital communities. And all of the argument presumes a continued will on behalf of individuals to fight for their rights and to demand of governments the freedoms to interact one with another in forms which we, as citizens, decide.

Acknowledgements

I am grateful to Robert Dunbar of Glasgow University for his insights, especially in relation to current developments in Scotland. Aspects of this work were supported by ESRC Grants no. R 000 22 2936 and L291 25 2007 R010W for which the author is grateful.

Notes

1 See W. T. R. Pryce and C. H. Williams, 'Sources and methods in the study of language areas: A case study of Wales', in Colin H. Williams (ed.), *Language in Geographic Context*, Multilingual Matters, Clevedon, 1988, pp. 167–237.
2 Since the Acts of Union of England and Wales, 1536 and 1542, Welsh had been proscribed as a language of officialdom and thus did not benefit from being institutionalised in the affairs of the state. On legislation before the Welsh Language Act of 1967, see D. B. Walters, 'The legal recognition and protection of pluralism', *Acta Juridica*, 1978, pp. 305–26.
3 For an authoritative account see C. Dafis, 'Cymdeithas yr Iaith Gymraeg', in M. Stephens (ed.), *The Welsh Language Today*, Gomer Press, Llandysul, 1973.
4 See C. H. Williams, 'Non-violence and the development of the Welsh Language Society, 1962–c. 1974', *Welsh History Review*, 8, 4, 1977, pp. 426–55; C. H. Williams (ed.), *National Separatism*, University of Wales Press; Cardiff, 1982, C. H. Williams, 'Christian witness and non-violent principles of nationalism', in Kristian Gerner et al. (eds.), *Stat, Nation, Konflikt*, Bra Böcker, Lund, 1966, pp. 343–93.
5 See G. Humphries, 'Polisi Iaith Awdurdod Addysg Gwynedd – Adolygu a gweithredu ym 1986', *Education for Development*, Vol. 10, No. 3, 1987, pp. 7–23. For an excellent overview see C. Baker, *Aspects of Bilingualism in Wales*, Multilingual Matters, Clevedon, 1985.
6 For an analysis of the first decade 1963–73, see Williams (1977), Table 2 and pp. 439–54.

7 See G. Evans, *Bywyd Cymro*, ed. Manon Rhys, Gwasg Gwynedd, Caernarfon, 1982, and in translation by Meic Stephens, *For the Sake of Wales*, Welsh Academic Press, Bridgend, 1996. Arguments for a separate channel are set out in G. Evans, *Byw Neu Farw? Y Frwydr dros yr Iaith a'r Sianel Deledu Gymraeg*, Plaid Cymru, Aberystwyth, 1980.
8 *Bwrdd yr Iaith Gymraeg, Adroddiad Blynyddol a Chyfrifon, 2000–01*, Bwrdd yr Iaith Gymraeg, Caerdydd, 2001. In 1998 notices had been issued to a further 59 bodies to prepare schemes and, during 2000–1, a further 23 language schemes were approved.
9 C. H. Williams, 'The Celtic world', in J. A. Fishman, (ed.), *Handbook of Language and Ethnic Identity*, Oxford, Oxford University Press, New York, 1999, pp. 267–85.
10 The central issue is how the Assembly operates as a bilingual institution. Basic guidelines were specified in the Government of Wales Bill (1997), clause 46. While the Welsh Language Act (1993) speaks of treating Welsh and English on a basis of equality in the conduct of public business, the Bill, in Clause 46, is less limited in its scope.
11 HMSO, *A Voice for Wales: The Government's Proposals for a Welsh Assembly*, HMSO, Cardiff, 1997.
12 The National Assembly Advisory Group (NAAG, 1998) outlined three principles regarding bilingual practice, namely that the Assembly should adopt and extend the Welsh Office's existing Welsh language scheme; that Members should be able to use English and Welsh in Assembly debates and committee meetings; and that members of the public should be able to use English and Welsh when communicating with the Assembly. NAAG National Assembly for Wales, Cardiff: *National Assembly Advisory Group Consultation Paper*, 1998.
13 For this report, see C. H. Williams and J. Evas (2001) at http://www.cymru.gov.uk/cynulliaddata/ 3AB9FCC30008CCBA00003DAF00000000.rt
14 C. H. Williams (ed.), *Language Re-vitalisation: Policy and planning in Wales*, University of Wales Press, Cardiff, 2001.
15 C. James, and C. H. Williams, 'Language and planning in Scotland and Wales', in H. Thomas and R. Macdonald (eds.), *Planning in Scotland and Wales*, The University of Wales Press, Cardiff, 1997, pp. 264–303.
16 There was no question on knowledge of Ulster-Scots in the *Census* held on 29 April 2001.
17 The Ulster-Scots Language Society estimates 100,000 speakers in Northern Ireland. For context see A. Mac Poilin (ed.), *The Irish Language in Northern Ireland*, Ultach Trust, Belfast, 1997, and M. Nic Craith, 'Irish speakers in Northern Ireland, and the Good Friday Agreement', *Journal of Multilingual and Multicultural Development*, vol. 20, 6, 1999, pp. 494–507.
18 The Irish Language Agency (*Foras na Gaeilge*) has its headquarters in Dublin (7 Merrion Square, Dublin 2), and a regional office in Belfast. The Ulster-Scots Agency (*Tha Boord o Ulster Scotch*) has its headquarters at Franklin House, 10–12 Brunswick Street, Belfast, BT2 7GE.
19 The funding available for the year 2000/1 was £667,000. Resources were made available for projects with a language dimension, which met the objective criteria of a range of mainstream programmes. In 2001/2 funding of £11.42 million was available of which the Irish Language Agency received £10.12

million and the Ulster-Scots Agency £1.3 million. (Northern Ireland provided £3.5 million of this.)
20 R. Hindley, *The Death of the Irish Language: A qualified obituary*, Routledge, London, 1990, and C. H. Williams (ed.), *Linguistic Minorities, Society and Territory*, Multilingual Matters, Clevedon, 1991 review the statistical evidence and political motivations which underlay the exaggeration of any contribution the *Gaeltacht* might have made to language revitalisation.
21 N. Ó Gadhra, 'The Irish *Gaeltacht* communities on the eve of the third millennium', paper presented to the Nineteenth Annual Celtic Colloquium, Harvard University, 30 April 1999, p. 7.
22 P. Ó Riagáin, *Language Policy and Social Reproduction: Ireland 1893–1993*, Oxford University Press, Oxford, 1997 demonstrates that government initiatives in economic, social and regional planning spheres, have more important effects on language patterns than do legislation or government language policies.
23 Board na Gailge, *The Irish Language in a Changing Society*, Board na Gaeilge, Dublin, 1988. See also P. O Flatharta, 'On the delivery mechanism of social and economic development of the *Gaeltacht*'. Paper presented at the ECNI International Seminar, Flensburg, ECMI, 18–20 June 1999. C. H. Williams, 'Language planning and regional development: Lessons from the Irish *Gaeltacht*', in C. H. Williams (ed.), *Language in Geographic Context*, Multilingual Matters, Clevedon, 1988, pp. 267–301.
24 Comhdáil Náisúnta na Gaeilge, *Towards a Language Act: A discussion document*. Comhdáil Náisúnta na Gaeilge, Dublin, 1998.
25 *Bille na dTeangacha Oifigiúla (Comhionannas)*, Official Languages (Equality) Bill, Dublin, 24 April 2002.
26 I owe this observation and other insights on Gaelic to Robert Dunbar of Glasgow University. Language issues have been, at best, a tiny footnote in Scottish devolution. Gaelic has not even developed a symbolic role in nationalist discourse, whereas institutions and ideologies have played the defining role in national self-definition. See R. Dunbar, 'Minority language rights regimes: An analytical framework, Scotland, and emerging European norms', in J. M. Kirk and P. Ó Baoill (eds.), *Linguistic Politics*, Queen's University, Belfast, 2001, pp. 231–54.
27 The first officer for Gaelic, Alec O' Henley, courageously resigned his position in May 2002 in protest at the lack of progress on the language front. For the use of *Gaelic* in the parliament see http://www.scottish.parliament.uk/.
28 The Task Force on *Gaelic* reported in September 2000. It led to the establishment of the Ministerial Advisory Group on *Gaelic* (MAGOG).
29 *A Fresh Start for Gaelic*, Report of the Ministerial Advisory Group on Gaelic, Edinburgh, 2002. See also the excellent papers by W. McLeod, 'Language planning as regional development?', *Scottish Affairs*, vol. 38, 2001, pp. 51–72; and A. MacCaluim and W. McLeod, *Re-vitalising Gaelic? A Critical Analysis of the Report of the Taskforce on Public Funding of Gaelic*, Department of Celtic and Scottish Studies, Edinburgh, 2001.
30 See R. Dunbar, 'Minority language rights under international law', *International and Comparative Law Quarterly*, Vol. 50, 1, 2001, 90–120. For the Charter, see Council of Europe, *European Charter for Regional or Minority Languages*, Council of Europe, Strasbourg, 1993.

31 W. Roddick, 'Creating legal Wales', *Agenda*, Spring 2002, p. 38.
32 A Voice for Wales, Llais dros Gymru, Cm. 3718 of July 1997.
33 D. Williams, 'Wales, the law and the constitution,' in *The Cambrian Law Review*, Vol. 31, 2000, p. 53.
34 See A. Sherlock, 'Born free, but everywhere in chains? A legal analysis of the first year of the National Assembly for Wales', *The Cambrian Law Review*, Vol. 31, 2000, pp. 59–72.
35 R. Rawlings, 'Concordats of the Constitution', 116 *Law Quarterly Review*, 2000, p. 257.
36 This information is from Sherlock (2000), who argues that whilst it was sufficient for an Act to give powers to the Secretary of State without specifying a particular department, Welsh devolution requires a disentangling of those powers which might have been exercisable by the Secretary of State for Wales from those devolving upon other ministers. See the NAfW (Transfer of Functions) Order 1999 (S. I. 1999/672).
37 R. Rawlings, as cited in Sherlock, p. 60, who also warns of the structural tension between the avowed transparency of the NAfW and pressures exercised by central government on the Assembly cabinet not to be unduly generous with 'backbenchers' when discussing central government policy and sensitive information. This point was discussed, says Sherlock, in the Assembly debate on the concordats, see *Assembly Record*, 7 October 1999. The concordats between UK governments and the administrations of the devolved legislatures indicate that a duty of confidentiality may arise in respect of shared information. *The Memorandum of Understanding and Supplementary Agreements* (Cm 4444, 1999).
38 Some sections of the Government of Wales Act confer powers directly on the Assembly; e.g. sections 27 and 28. Orders in Council may not remove powers from the NAfW without the latter's approval. See J. Jones, 'Making Welsh law', in J. Jones (ed.), *The Law Making Powers of the National Assembly: Conference report*,' Wales Law Journal/The Law Society, Cardiff, 2001, 40–53, and T. Jones, 'The subordinate law making powers of the National Assembly for Wales', in J. Jones (ed.), pp. 6–12.
39 Williams, p. 54 adds 'given that limitation it is surely surprising that a special judicial procedure, ultimately involving the Judicial Committee of the Privy Council has been provided for in the 1998 Act with regard to the so-called devolution issues.'
40 The National Assembly (Transfer of Function) Order 1999, (S.I. 1999/672).
41 Just as they do within the Houses of Parliament. In Wales, section 34 of the Act provides that civil servants are part of the home civil service. To ensure impartiality section 63(2) of the Act stipulates that it is for the Permanent Secretary (of the Civil Service) to organise the allocation of relevant functions among staff.
42 See D. Lambert, 'The Government of Wales Act: An act for laws to be ministered in Wales in like form as in this realm?' *Cambrian Law Review*, 30, 2000, 60–70.
43 *The Belfast Agreement – An Agreement Reached at the Multi-Party Talks on Northern Ireland*, Cm. 3883, 1998.
44 Williams, p. 55.
45 Twenty-five of the 60 Assembly members are women, while the Cabinet has a majority of women.

46 *A House for the Future (Westminster, 2000)* Cm.45334 had this to say (at 6.4): 'Our terms of reference require us to take a particular account of the present nature of the constitutional settlement, including the newly devolved institutions ... We were (also) conscious that devolution is a very recent and novel development. We cannot be sure how it will work out in practice, what problems and tensions may arise and what the political consequences will be ... It would certainly be rash to assume that the nature or content of devolved powers will not alter over time.' See Williams (p. 53). See also R. Rawlings (2001) 'Quasi-legislative devolution', in Jones (ed.).

6
Ethnicity and Education
Mal Leicester

Introduction

The law, in an indirect and cumbersome fashion, may, to some degree, reflect and shape public opinion. Certainly Dicey takes as his starting point, in considering law and public opinion in England during the nineteenth century,[1] the 'close dependence of legislation, and even of the absence of legislation, upon the varying currents of public opinion', though, as Mannheim points out,[2] it is not clear 'whose opinion Dicey had in mind', describing him as having a 'a paternalistic' concept of public opinion as 'little more than the views of a sharply limited clan of intellectuals whose writings directly influenced the minds of the nation's legislation'. In contrast, 'public opinion' in this chapter refers primarily to the attitudes and values of the general population, as well as, where relevant, the influential views of pressure groups, practitioners, policy-makers and government committees within the educational world.

Dicey's volume concerns itself with education in only one brief section (pp. 276–9) and only with reference to his contention that during the later part of the nineteenth century, legislation tended towards the equalisation of advantages among all classes. He describes the provision of 'free' and compulsory elementary education (with disapproval), thus:

> It means, in the first place, that A, who educates his children at his own expense, or has no children to educate, is compelled to pay for the education of the children of B, who, though, it may be, having the means to pay for it, prefers that the payment should come from the pocket of his neighbours. It tends, in the second place, as far as merely elementary education goes, to place the children of the rich

and of the poor, of the provident and the improvident, on something like an equal footing. (p. 278)

Of the seventeen papers in Ginsberg's *Law and Opinion in England in the 20th Century*,[3] dealing with the first half of the century, only one is about education.[4] Glass comments on how little Dicey had to say about the development of educational policy, though he points out that the rapid development of compulsory education began only in 1886, culminating in the Education Act of 1944. With a very different perspective from Dicey, Glass illuminates the way in which this growth in universal education benefited the middle class much more than it did the working class. Neither volume addresses the issue of ethnicity, cultural pluralism or race relations. It was only with the immigration, which began in the 1950s, of people from Britain's former colonies, or the 'New Commonwealth', that ethnicity became of significant public concern – sufficiently significant that in 1976 the Race Relations Act was passed, clearly indicating a need for anti-discrimination legislation. Although Glass (understandably therefore) considers social class without an 'ethnicity' dimension, what he does say (as we will see) has its contemporary resonance in the current under-representation of some minority ethnic groups in higher education, in the correlation between higher education and socioeconomic status and in the role of teachers and government committees in providing pressure for progressive educational developments. Glass concludes his paper with the need to 'combine diversity of educational provision with equality of educational opportunity, but so to combine them as to attain greater social unity within the education system, and thereby to help in the creation of a more closely knit society'.

Following Ginsberg, the chapters in the present collection focus on the second half of the twentieth century. Within this framework is explored the interaction of ethnicity and education, as well as the mutual influence of this conjunction on both public opinion and educational and race relations legislation. One assumption that underpins this chapter is that education, as state provision of such formal learning as is deemed to be worthwhile, does indeed both reflect and influence social attitudes and values. Since immigration to Britain from her former colonies took place at the beginning of the half-century with which we are concerned, and triggered educational, social and legal changes connected with minority ethnic groups, my exploration of ethnicity and education will take the influence of this immigration on education as a significant starting point and trace it through to the current decade. Finally, it is suggested that the educational arena (formal and non-formal, at both school and post-school levels) is dominated by the movement to lifelong learning. By way of conclusion, therefore, I will seek to work out the likely developments for the education of minority ethnic groups of this powerful, new and developing educational theory and practice.

Immigration and multicultural education

Postwar Britain faced a labour shortage and British employees turned to the countries of the New Commonwealth (i.e. those former colonies and dependent territories electing to remain in the Commonwealth after independence, such as the West Indies and the Indian subcontinent) to recruit labour for the, mostly, semi-skilled and unskilled job vacancies. The arrival of the ship *The Empire Windrush* in June 1948, bringing Jamaicans migrating to Britain for work, is often cited as the beginning of postwar black immigration. London Transport, British Hotels and the Restaurant Associations advertised in the West Indies for workers. The Health Service also undertook a wide recruitment campaign.

Patterns of migration were similar across several European countries in the 1950s and 1960s, with males arriving first, followed by women and children. Communities quickly established themselves in London and in the industrial towns of the Midlands and North. By the late 1950s, the number of people from the Caribbean, Pakistan, India, Bangladesh and Sri Lanka was estimated to be 0.5 per cent of the total population. (The 1991 Census reveals an ethnic minority population of 6 per cent.) People living in Britain's colonies and ex-colonies were granted British citizenship under the 1948 Nationality Act and were thus free to work and reside in Britain. They could vote and remain indefinitely. The majority of black children in Britain today were born here. As Cashmore points out:

> All the studies of the day supported the idea that Caribbean migrants regarded their UK citizenship with some pride and regarded themselves, in a genuine sense, as British.[5]

However, these invited British citizens were not accepted by the white British as equals. Racism contributed to socio-economic inequalities. Tensions soon surfaced in British society to the point of violent disturbances in Liverpool in 1948, Notting Hill in 1954 and Nottingham in the late 1950s. There is overwhelming evidence that migrants and their children experienced racial discrimination to the point of serious disadvantage in their lives.[6] A survey of race relations in Britain carried out during the 1960s stated: 'There is racial discrimination varying in extent from the massive to the substantial.'[7] Black people received less than a fair share of employment, good housing, health care and educational qualifications. For example, in 1983 it took four times as many interviews for young black people to obtain work as for equivalently qualified whites, and black youths received more custodial sentences than whites for the same offence. The image (given in the mass media) of the white person as more civilised, intelligent and law-abiding than the black person is a powerful and destructive colonial legacy. Black people have come to be seen, by some whites, as a 'problem'. Moreover, though both black and white people may be racially prejudiced, the power of the whites as the dominant social group sometimes transforms endemic prejudice into damaging discrimination.

In this climate of public opinion, the British government took steps to restrict entry with the Commonwealth Immigration Act of 1962. Over the following years further legislation made citizenship increasingly more difficult to obtain. The majority of arrivals since the early 1970s have been relatives of British citizens or refugees (including Hungarians, Ugandans, Chinese and Vietnamese).[8] Moreover, as I have indicated, the prevalence of racial discrimination produced the need for the Race Relations Acts of 1965, 1968 and 1976 which 'legislated in favour of good community and 'race' relations, and attacked racial discrimination' (ibid., p. 2).

The Race Relations Act of 1976 (which applies to the whole of Great Britain, but not Northern Ireland) makes discrimination, on grounds of race, unlawful. Neither pupils nor employees nor anyone else who come into contact with the education service should be subject to such discrimination. This covers recruitment, promotion, transfer, conditions of employment or dismissal, training and the provision of goods and services. Two kinds of discrimination are unlawful: direct and indirect. Direct racial discrimination consists of treating a person, on racial grounds, less favourably than others are, or would be, treated in the same circumstances. For example, refusing to employ someone because they are black. Segregating a person from others on racial grounds also counts as less favourable treatment. 'Racial ground' includes race, colour, nationality, citizenship, ethnic or national origins. Indirect racial discrimination consists of applying a requirement or condition which, *intentionally or not*, has a disproportionately adverse effect on a particular racial group and cannot be justified on non-racial grounds. For example, word-of-mouth recruitment may exclude black applicants for a job if the networks and circles of people passing on the information are all white. Or a requirement for a qualification (say English GCSE), where this is not relevant to the job, and tends to disqualify ethnic minority groups, would constitute indirect discrimination.

The biased assumption and prejudices of the wider society were reflected within education. Black pupils were also viewed as a 'problem' in British schools. As Mullard says, since the early 1960s, when the Commonwealth Immigrant Advisory Council recommended to the Home Secretary that special provision should be made for the education of 'immigrant' pupils, the multiracial education movement in Britain has tended to view black pupils as a problem. They were a problem because they were black; they were a problem because many, especially those from India and Pakistan, could neither speak nor write English well enough to take an effective part in, or benefit from, school education. Numerically, they allegedly posed an administrative problem that was expressed in terms of overcrowded inner-city schools and a political problem that was expressed in terms of the fear that 'the whole character and ethos of the school' would be radically altered.

Distinct historical perspectives and approaches can be identified in the education of pupils from minority ethnic groups. Mullard[9] classifies these as the assimilationist model, the integrationist model and cultural pluralism. Anti-racist education can now be added to this list. From the early 1960s the government stressed the need for assimilation of ethnic minorities into the 'host' culture. In Bristol, for example, in 1968, an English language teaching service was started, based at the Hannah Moore Primary School. At this stage, educators throughout Britain thought in terms of English for immigrant children. Their conception of their task was one of assimilating these immigrants into 'this' society. Assimilation, it was believed, would integrate black pupils into the education system and the 'race problem' would evaporate with future generations. The Department of Education and Science (DES) maintained that the function of education was a 'successful assimilation of immigrant children'.[10] Black culture and language were dismissed as inferior and being black was equated with low status. Integration and assimilation into the 'host' culture was deemed necessary for harmonious race relations. As Rex and Tomlinson point out, 'blacks were forced into accepting British culture along with their servitude'.[11]

A change of government in the mid-1960s resulted in Roy Jenkins, as Labour Home Secretary, declaring in a speech that integration was 'not the flattening process of assimilation but an equal opportunity accompanied by cultural diversity in an atmosphere of mutual tolerance' (1966).

The concept of cultural pluralism was established. A pamphlet issued by the DES entitled *Education for Immigrants* clearly revealed a shift in emphasis:

> Schools can demonstrate how people from different ethnic groups and cultural backgrounds can live together happily and successfully and can help to create the kind of cohesive, multicultural society on which the future of the country and possibly the world depends.[12]

In the early 1970s the existence of racial prejudice in schools was given recognition for the first time. Within a framework of cultural pluralism the introduction of multicultural education was advocated, particularly at the curriculum level. Some educators recognised the educational potential of cultural diversity and began to develop a multicultural curriculum. Children would learn to celebrate the richness of diversity rather than to fear that which is different. Again taking Bristol as an example, the Hannah Moore language service quickly grew and developed and, in 1977, the Multicultural Education Centre was established. Language work was to be part of the progamme, but not the whole. Multicultural education involves learning about a variety of cultural traditions, breaking down prejudice and stereotypes and promoting a positive self-image among black students. Staff were also to support schools in the development of a multicultural curriculum, funded through Section 11 of the 1966 Local Government Act (Home Office, 1966). Local education authorities, through this Act, were able to seek grant aid to meet up to three-quarters of the salary costs of teachers, and others, employed to meet the educational needs of certain children of 'New Commonwealth' origin, where these needs are 'different from or additional to' those of indigenous pupils. This Section 11 funding was to help provide for some of the educational needs of particular groups of children. Since these children were mainly living near the centres of large cities, it followed that 'Section 11' funded staff worked in the inner city multiracial schools.

For some teachers and educators multicultural education did not go far enough to solve the problems of racism in schools and society. The 1980s witnessed the introduction of a more radical approach: anti-racist education. An anti-racist approach challenges the power relationships in society which maintain and reproduce race and class inequalities. According to Troyna and Carrington:

> anti-racists have also stressed the need for democratisation of schooling and for changes in the formal curriculum to include explicit teaching against racism and other forms of injustice.[13]

Anti-racist education challenges two main forms of racism: inter-personal racism and institutional racism. Inter-personal racism refers to racism between individuals, while institutional racism is racism that is rooted in the practices, customs and culture of institutions. Educators and academics engaged in debate at this time about whether education should be multicultural or anti-racist. In my view[14] it was an unhelpful polarisation since we should seek for a multicultural and an anti-racist curriculum within anti-racist institutions – an 'anti-racist multicultural education'.

These historical developments reveal a widening of perspective. For example, we started with a concern for the special needs of minority ethnic group children. (And, of course, the language and other educational needs of these, as of all children, ought to be catered for.) Then came the recognition that some multicultural education issues are relevant to all children in all schools – issues such as those of racial bias in learning materials and of ethnocentricity in the curriculum. (Unfortunately these important educational needs were not covered by Section 11 funding.)

Similarly, at first, teachers tended to think of multicultural education as an extra subject, or as a bit of extra content in an existing subject (a project on India, in geography, for instance), whereas later, some teachers thought in terms of 'permeation'. Multicultural education is thus understood not as an 'additional bit', but as an aspect of education which should permeate the whole of school life and the child's total educational experience; and all the school staff should be involved, working as a team towards shared objectives. Thus multicultural education is seen to be concerned with the overall ethos, policies, attitudes and objectives of the school as a whole.

Interest in multicultural education gradually increased among teachers who work at pre-school and post-school stages (nursery teachers and adult education lecturers). Multicultural education issues were seen to be relevant before and after school. Although these developments have had implications for those concerned with teacher education, provision of both pre-service and of in-service training in multicultural education was inadequate and even where it was provided it has often been inappropriate. In the mid-1980s, these perceptions of multicultural education were greatly influenced by a major government document, the Swann Report, a comprehensive collection of information, analysis and recommendations relating to multicultural education.

The history of adult education is rather different. Adult education has not experienced such a clear historical progression of approaches and perspectives. Policies and practice since the 1960s have largely centred on compulsory schooling, perhaps because ethnic minorities were more visible in schools than in adult education classes. The participation of black people in adult education during the 1960s and 1970s was low. Following immigration to Britain the immediate concern of black people was to establish a home and find employment. Participating in adult education would have been a low priority. Over the past decade more black people have entered adult education, although the numbers still remain small. Much adult education provision may be perceived by black adults as being white and middle class, teaching a curriculum that is irrelevant to their needs.

Compulsory schooling for some black children can be a negative and alienating experience because of the racism they experience from teachers and other pupils. Like white working-class adults, such experiences of initial schooling as children may result in reluctance to re-enter education as adults.[15] Some institutions, however, have taken positive steps to initiate multicultural and anti-racist adult education. For example, black access courses have been introduced to facilitate the entry of black adults into higher education. Education, across the life-span, is part of the wider social picture which reflects general public prejudices. Black students meet with overt and covert prejudice in white staff and students. They find stereotyping in learning resources, an ethnocentric curriculum and racially discriminatory institutional policies, practices and management structures. Moreover widespread social prejudices are then reinforced, in the white majority, through this mis-educative process. As we have seen, in the 1970s and 1980s there was a movement to promote multicultural and anti-racist education. The 1985 government-sponsored Swann Report, *Education For All*, encouraged schools in their development of an anti-racist, multicultural education and, of course, individual post-school institutions and individual adult educators have taken anti-racist initiatives. But good practice is limited and patchy[16] arising from these specific individuals and initiatives, rather than characteristic of the system as a whole.

The Swann Report 1985

In 1979 the government established a committee, under the chairmanship of Anthony Rampton, to enquire into the educational needs and attainment of children from ethnic minority groups, and to make relevant recommendations. In June 1981 this committee published an interim report, *West Indian Children in Our Schools*. The final report, *Education for All* was published in March 1985. Thus this report, commonly known as The Swann Report after its chairman, started out as an inquiry into the education of minority group children, but, after the taking of much evidence from numerous groups and individuals, became concerned with *Education For All*. It had been recognised that the social and educational well-being of black children and adults is in large part determined by the attitudes and actions of the dominant white majority and their white-dominated institutions. The problem is not that of a black presence but that of white racism. Since prejudice is learned – the educational task must be to help all children to unlearn racial prejudice. The Swann Report claimed that such prejudices are perpetuated, via stereotyping, through the media **and** through education.

The report was long and expansive. The issues it covers include: the ideals of pluralism and education for all, analyses of prejudice and institutional racism, achievement, aspects of language education, religion and question of separate voluntary aided schools, and teacher education. The final chapter looks at 'other' ethnic minority groups. Three major aspects of multicultural education threaded through the report are language education, the need for a curriculum appropriate for all children and race relations. The Report's eight long chapters and various extensive appendices were read by few. Fortunately, the Runnymede Trust produced a concise and accurate summary which was read widely by teachers and student teachers. It was thus influential in encouraging the development of an anti-racist multicultural education.

One important aspect of the Swann Report was the recognition of the existence of 'institutional racism' which it defined as the way in which a range of long-established systems, practices and procedures in education and the wider society, which were originally devised to meet the needs of a relatively homogeneous society, may unintentionally work against minority groups by depriving them of opportunities open to the majority population. The significant point about this conception is that it draws attention to structures and processes within institutions that are harmful in their effect. It is *outcome* rather than *intention* that is important. And, obviously, not just any outcome justifies the description 'institutional racism', but outcomes which are harmful to members of a particular racial group or groups because they disadvantage these people *qua* members of those groups relative to members of some other racial group or groups. Practices that work against relative interests in this way may be seen as unfair. These harmful outcomes can arise through passive or active forms of behaviour – 'failing to take account of' or 'actively working against'. The Swann Report[17] gives two examples: arrangements for electing governors may fail to take account of the need for minority ethnic group representatives; and the provision of *separate* language schools for children whose first language is not English may actively work against their interests. (This is reminiscent of the Race Relations Act distinction between indirect and direct discrimination.) This important conception of discrimination against ethnic minorities through routine institutional practices had some influence on educational establishments and gained some recognition in other areas. It by no means gained a general recognition, however. At the end of the century we have seen the Metropolitan Police Service deny the institutional racism which the Stephen Lawrence enquiry has revealed.

The Education Reform Acts 1986 and 1988

The 1986 and 1988 Education Reform Acts introduced the most far-reaching and important educational legislation since 1944. Various parts of the legislation have come into force since 1986 with considerable impact on the management of schools and colleges, control of budgets and the school curriculum. The major changes include:

1 Control of school budgets to be handed over to governors of secondary schools and larger primaries. (Though an LEA 'formula' will control how much total budget each school will receive.)
2 Changes in the composition of school governing bodies.
3 A national curriculum with three compulsory subjects – English, mathematics and science – and seven foundation subjects.
4 Testing for all children at 7, 11, 14 and 16.
5 Religious education to be given special status equal to that of a foundation subject; and a compulsory daily act of collective worship which should be, in the main, Christian.
6 The ILEA to be abolished and education handed over to the Inner London boroughs.
7 A University Funding Council to replace the University Grants Committee.
8 Control of further and higher education college budgets to be devolved to governing bodies. Reform of the size and composition of the governing bodies.

These changes have produced a variety of responses and concerns but ALAOME (The Association of LEA Advisory Officers for Multicultural Education) was critical of an absence of recognition of ethnic diversity and its educational implications. In an editorial of a special issue of FORUM on ERA, the suggestion was made that the Act is hostile to a multicultural society and is deliberately retrogressive. The new National Curriculum can be narrowly instrumental, rigid and ethnocentric. The Act calls for national testing at 7, 11, 14 and 16 years which can label many children as failures. The decrease in the influence of the Local Education Authority has lost to the schools, much advisory experience in relation to multicultural education, and the subsequent Governor Training gave equal opportunities relatively little profile.

Post-school ERA also moves in an inegalitarian direction. Though much of the Act relates to schools (with considerable changes in local management), financial matters and curriculum, which will increase the likelihood of greater inequality between schools all adult education is indirectly effected by worsening school provision. Those who benefit most from schooling are also most likely to return. Increased inequality for minority ethnic groups in schools will tend to decrease their participation in adult education and reinforce existing disproportions.

The governing bodies of colleges of further education have increased powers. There are considerable changes in financial arrangements for colleges, which has lead to greater competitiveness and which are problematic for low-fee and part-time courses. The Act has also destabilised many existing mechanisms for offering learners access and progression through coherent local educational links, in that colleges and adult institutions work increasingly independently of one another and of the LEA. The new 'efficiency indicators' may work against outreach programmes and non-formal, community-based education, since outcomes are inevitably hard to quantify. However, there are some loopholes for anti-racist initiatives. With provision being more directly in the hands of each institution, this has lead some colleges to more consultation with local communities and greater flexibility and responsiveness to local interests and needs.

Culture and conflicts of value

Progress (and setbacks) in the development of an anti-racist multicultural education generated, from time to time, serious educational conflicts (e.g. The Honeyford affair) bringing educational affairs to the attention of the media and, therefore, to public attention. From time to time, too, conflicts of value have arisen in the wider society (e.g. the Rushdie affair) and been incorporated into education debates.

Cultural diversity, then, has given rise to serious conflicts of value in the real world while education, in the context of cultural diversity, inescapably raises relevant theoretical questions too. Are there universal values to underpin education in a culturally diverse society and through which conflicts of value can be resolved? In other words, are there at least some values which are important in any cultural tradition and which are, therefore, built into any conception of 'education', or are some or all values culturally specific? In the series *Education, Culture and Values*[18] this issue of universal values emerged more strongly than any other. It was directly addressed in some twenty chapters and implicit in many more.

One contributor, Graham Haydon,[19] explored the notion of diversity of values. He pointed out that the diversity of values which people hold can be seen as superficial variations on the surface of deeper, universal, rational values or as representing deep, irreconcilable differences. He argued that this contrast is overdrawn. Even as we promote common values, we must respect differences and even if there are no necessary common truths, we nevertheless, for pragmatic reasons, need to promote some common languages, some common way of living together. Teachers need to be able to judge when the commonalities matter and the differences are trivial and when, on the other hand, the differences are vital. To make these judgements, teachers need to understand both the diversity of values in their complexity and the kinds of attempts that have been made to find common ground. He concludes his chapter on the pessimistic note that, in late twentieth-century Britain, teacher training has barely recognised this educational task. All this raises further fascinating philosophical questions about whether such universal values merely happen to be shared by all cultural groups in a given society (or world) or whether such shared values are necessarily universal. If they are necessarily universal, from where does this necessity emerge? Does it emerge from our common human condition, our being a particular kind of being in a particular natural world, or does it emerge from the nature of value itself. For example, all values may be underpinned by some basic foundational value of set of values.

A second question that arises from the acceptance of universal values is the question of whether all values are universal or only some values. Stephen Lukes, for example, has distinguished between what he calls rational One criteria of rationality, necessarily used in any rational judgements and rational Two criteria, which are local and may influence the rational One criteria. Perhaps, similarly, there are value One and value Two categories of value and value judgements. If this is so, then the value One values could perhaps provide the basic underpinning worth for what we are to count as worthwhile learning, that is to say, as education. Perhaps, too, such universal values could at least provide a bridge from which the resolution of conflicts of value Two values could be attempted.

If there are no necessary or even merely universal values, then are conflicts of value irresolvable? Given the categorical nature of values, is negotiation through compromise possible? If so, what are the conditions for successful negotiation?

By the 1990s, these highly abstract issues were brought into the heart of the educational arena with a values audit by The Schools Curriculum and Assessment Authority (SCAA). Nick Tate,[20] the Chief Executive, explained how and why SCAA sought to discover whether there are any values that are common to everyone across society. In his view, that there are such values, even in a multicultural society, is obviously true, though he recognises that there may be differences in application and ordering of these values. The SCAA statement of values is subdivided into valuing the self, valuing relationships, valuing society and valuing the environment. Tate believed that this statement of values would restore teacher confidence, trigger national debate about standards, elicit support for schools' promotion of pupils' spiritual, moral, social and cultural development and offer structure and guidance in this. All this, he says, would be a defence against 'relativism' of values.

Glynn Phillips[21] responded to Tate's chapter with his own, 'Should moral educators abandon moral relativism?' He pointed out that Tate attacks the relativism of moral values but does not provide a substantive moral position about what values ought to be promoted in schools. Phillips, therefore, engages with Tate's case against moral relativism. In his discussion he demonstrates the incoherence of full-blooded relativism, but he also discusses Bernard Williams' less problematic version. To recognise that, as it happens, cultures have alternative belief systems, does not entail that they must all be equally valid, but might, nevertheless, suggest a principle of tolerance – which is that we should tolerate the cultural norms of conduct of other groups provided those cultural norms of conduct themselves accept the moral principle of toleration. Essentially, Phillips explores some different versions of moral judgement in terms of the kind of relativism that each entails. His chapter concludes by what could be seen as an endorsement of the importance of moral philosophy in teacher education.

Ethnicity, identity and citizenship

During the 1990s discourse about 'multicultural education' became less prevalent, though associated debates about minority education, about guarding against ethnocentricity in the curriculum, about equal educational opportunities for all groups and about universal values have permeated other educational fields. One 'field' which has seen a relatively recent increase in attention, and which has certainly incorporated the 'plural society' issue, is that of citizenship education.

Ken Fogelman, Director of the Centre for Citizenship Studies in Education, and Janet Edwards, his deputy, write that 'Citizenship Education is an aspect of the curriculum that has become increasingly prominent during the 1990s.' They point out that in 1990, the National Curriculum Council named Citizenship as one of five cross curriculum themes.[22] The aim of Citizenship Education was said to be 'to establish the importance of positive, participative citizenship and provide the motivation to join in' (NCC, 1990a, 5). Of course there are various conceptions of Citizenship Education. Thus John Rowe (Director of Curriculum Resources, The Citizenship Foundation) identified several cognitive, affective and experiential models in what he claims is a controversial subject.[23] Nevertheless, in the present Western world, including Britain, where we find multicultural societies in liberal democracies, it is not surprising that issues of values, pluralism and equal rights are part of the Citizenship Education agenda. At its most idealistic level, this discourse presents a vision of global citizenship. Thus Lynch[24] says:

> The imperative of the 1990s is to share internationally the values of democratic pluralism in a process which will reinforce global interdependence and active membership of a world society. For educators the challenge of the 1990s is to deliver not just education for citizenship of a pluralist democracy but education for active global democracy founded on universal values about the nature of human beings and their social behaviour.

Contrast this with the racism of more narrow conceptions of citizenship such of that of Norman Tebbitt in his widely reported proposal, in 1990, for a 'cricket test' to assess the acceptability of South Asians and Afro-Caribbeans as British citizens. Such neo-conservative constructions of national identity would undermine the position of black Britains and further marginalise the Scots, Welsh and Northern Irish. Modood has suggested that Americans tend to operate with more inclusive, pluralistic constructions.

> We have something to learn from the Americans, who have come to have a notion of hyphenated identity. They take pride not just in

their Americaness but in asserting that they are Irish-American, Black-American, African-American, Greek-American and so on.... 'British', by contrast, is virtually a quasi-ethnic terms, so it is not surprising that descriptions such as British Black or British Pakistani are at present little more than courtesy titles and carry little conviction.[25]

Although a liberal consensus would accept the ethnic diversity of British citizenship and the importance of values of justice and equality within citizenship education, the problem or question about universal values continues to emerge. There is a potential tension between any particular conception of the good life or human flourishing and advocating a democratic education for tolerance, reasonable dissent and respect for differences.

Various 'answers' are offered to such 'problems'. My own suggestion has been that education (moral education and citizenship education) should provide a forum for debate about resolving conflicts of value – both general debate (can we construct an agreed procedure?) and debate about particular disputes.[26] We should surely also seek to develop those qualities and values, in pupils, which will contribute to a just and harmonious pluralism. Moreover, a multicultural education in common schools will emphasise commonalties and common values, indeed will encourage some convergence of values, that is those values required for the effective functioning of a just and harmonious pluralist society. Such values should be exhibited in the micro society of the school itself.

Thus my final picture is that education could provide a forum for debate about resolving conflicts of value – both general debate (can we construct an agreed procedure?) and debate about particular disputes... Specifically moral education in pluralistic societies could be based on developing those qualities and values in pupils which will contribute to a just and harmonious pluralism. Thus an essential requirement is for an anti-racist dimension to moral education. The pupils, as developing moral agents, should develop a commitment to eliminate racism and to acquire knowledge and skills relevant to this... Moreover, if the pluralist society must, paradoxically, also impose liberal values, let its education at least seek to ensure that pupils do learn to respect the various cultural traditions and the equal rights of all citizens. It is my belief that a multicultural education for all children in common schools will encourage further convergence of values. Those values required for the effective functioning of a just and harmonious pluralist society should be exhibited in the micro society of the school itself. This 'should' is both a moral ought, deriving from liberal values, and a pragmatic must for effective moral education. Thus my final picture is of a just community school, serving the whole community and teaching anti-racist pluralist values through its very functioning. Such an institution would recognise the right of all cultural groups to have a voice in negotiating what, in practice, just and pluralist provision will be like.

Lifelong learning and the New Age

Before we go beyond the end of the twentieth century and consider likely developments in the coming decade, I want to summarise the key points of developments since the 1950s. First, we have seen that it was the immigration, at that time, of people from the New Commonwealth that triggered educational and legal changes. The endemic social prejudice and discrimination experienced by these new citizens, in tension with ideals about equality, gave rise to the race relations laws of 1976. The presence of black children in schools set in train the development (through developing notions of assimilation, integration, pluralism and anti-racism) of a multicultural anti-racist education, particularly in the inner city multiracial schools. The Swann Report of 1985 gave governmental recognition to the need for schools to consider any different or additional needs of ethnic minority children. (Funding was available through 'Section 11' of the 1966 Local Government Act (Home Office 1966).) Significantly, the report also recognised the need for all children to unlearn prejudice, and to develop attitudes and values appropriate to a just and harmonious multicultural Britain. But multicultural anti-racist education was always a site of contest – generating a range of responses from the extremely racist, through the misguided ethnocentric to the radically progressive. Black groups, meanwhile, continued to experience educational and economic disadvantage. Black students tend to be underrepresented in higher education, for example, and many black groups suffer high levels of unemployment and poor employment. Relatively recently, the Education Reform Acts of 1986 and 1988 moved the education system in a conservative and inegalitarian direction.

At the end of the century we reached a position such that public opinion, education policy and the law all reflected recognition that racial discrimination is wrong and must be opposed. All but the most extreme will pay 'lip service' at least, to the ideals of equality. Sadly, however, endemic prejudice remains entrenched, and discrimination, to the point of group disadvantage, is a social reality, as educational and social science research and home office surveys consistently reveal. Even as I write there are race riots in Oldham and Bradford, apparently triggered by the British National Party's presence and activities in these materially deprived, multiracial areas of Britain.[27] Clearly then, in terms of establishing a just, multicultural Britain in the new century, there is a long way to go. Education will need to play a part in that process, in terms of the race relations education of the general population, and in terms of more equal educational opportunities for black children and adults. The key question, therefore, is whether the current movement to lifelong learning is likely to promote or hinder such positive developments. 'Lifelong learning' is high on the educational policy agenda. The idea dominates discussions of higher, adult and vocational education and increasingly influences educational thinking of all kinds. In the past decade, national policy papers have been published by the shelf-load in Britain and Europe, with influential reports from the Organisation for Economic Co-operation and Development, the European Commission, the G8 group of governments from the eight largest economies, and from UNESCO. Economic issues are at the forefront of these documents, accompanied by a concern to widen participation in vocational education and training, but subsidiary themes concerned with the wider benefits of learning, such as personal development beyond schooling and political education and active citizenship are also commonly included.

Given the unprecedented rapidity of change in modern societies (information flow and the new technologies, the globalisation of trade, scientific and technological advances and applications) it is not surprising that there is a perceived need to invest in human capital to equip individuals and nations for new roles and economic competitiveness. Less predictable was the accompanying emphasis on the development of personal qualities for individuals living in such societies and on education's role in combatting social and regional inequalities. In several societies the discourse about lifelong learning seems to encourage a vocational emphasis on learning for economic prosperity, a social education for citizenship and a liberal recognition of the importance of individual choices and personal development. It is often linked with the notions of a learning organisation and of a learning society – a society so organised as to provide maximum learning opportunities for each of its members.

But do the various changes under the lifelong learning umbrella, such as the development of The University for Industry, the New Deal for Communities, Individual Learning Accounts genuinely provide greater equality of opportunity for all social groups? Several contributors to a recent collection[28] suggest that there are real opportunities for individuals but, despite the rhetoric of widening participation, a danger of continuing social exclusion for some groups. For example, McIlroy,[29] in speaking of the role of the trade unions in lifelong learning, points out that despite the much-vaunted increased role of the unions in training they lack the power, in general, to force opportunities for training on reluctant, recalcitrant employers so that their ability to do so in specific, favourable circumstances is likely to entrench the training divide between different groups of workers.

Similarly, Withnall[30] argues that the tendency to concentrate on employment-related education and training will exclude post-employment, older learners. Stuart[31] is concerned that the emphasis on narrow forms of assessment might penalise the disabled. Elsdon[32] questions that sufficient is in train to include and benefit learning in the voluntary sector, and most significantly in relation to the concerns of this paper, Malach[33] doubts that the information flow about new opportunities will reach into the ethnic minority communities, while Hannah[34] highlights the ways in which refugees are excluded from educational opportunities.

Conclusion

My own view is that lifelong learning may over-vocationalise school and adult education, to the detriment of liberal and political dimensions. However, alternatively it could represent an opportunity to more fully interrelate these elements. The personal can be political, the vocational can incorporate liberal dimensions and education for active citizens could develop vocationally relevant skills as well as promoting political awareness and personal qualities, and thus be a factor in achieving more and better multicultural, anti-racist education post-school. If such progressive post-school education is to occur, however, political will and resources are required. They will be needed to promote accessibility for all ethnic groups to learning opportunities across the life-span. In particular, we will need to see a more flexible system of higher education. We would need further progress in what Duke[35] has called the 'adultification' of education bringing:

- The practice of openness and flexibility towards all candidates seeking entry to degree courses without normal entry qualifications, including willingness to recognise prior, experiential and other non-academic learning, to devise appropriate means of considering particular individuals' potential, etc.
- Acceptance of some measures and forms of affirmative action and monitoring in respect of groups with low levels of participation in HE, particularly minority ethnic groups and, in some subjects, women.

- Rescheduling of teaching times during the working day, week and year to create opportunities for face-to-face teaching – learning for different groups (housewives, shift-workers and other occupational and social groups).
- Ensuring that teaching and learning venues are accessible to the physically disabled, and child-care facilities available for those with young children.
- Partnership with other providers (HE, OU, FE, industry, community agencies) to make university study available through collaborative provision, including 'franchising', validation and other forms of partnership.
- Use of study centres, outreach or open learning centres for those for whom the campus is too inaccessible, and appropriate mixes of mode, eg to include short residential periods on campus.
- Consideration of new routes and steps into regular and new degree programmes via extra-mural and other continuing education courses.

My own vision for the new century is that of 'a National Education Service'. Education would be free in the way that good health care is universally available, without charge, in a well-funded National Health Service. (There could be an equal distribution of points or vouchers to ensure that the maximum possible uptake remains within socially affordable limits.)[36]

But at a time when the present Labour government is moving to increasing privatisation of the public services, (including schools!) the chances of this kind of radical change are clearly very small.

Notes

1 A. V. Dicey, *Lectures on the Relation between Law and Opinion in England during the 19th Century*, 2nd edition, Macmillan, London, 1962.
2 H. Mannheim, 'Criminal law and penology', in M. Ginsberg (ed.), *Law and Opinion in England in the 20th Century*, Stevens and Sons, London, 1959, pp. 264–85.
3 M. Ginsberg (ed.), *Law and Opinion in England in the 20th Century*, Stevens and Sons London, 1959.
4 D. V. Glass, 'Education', in Ginsberg (ed.), pp. 319–46.
5 E. Cashmore, *Class, Race and Gender since the War*, Unwin Hyman, London, 1989.
6 F. Milburn and W. J. Morgan, 'Adult education for ethnic minorities', *European Manual of Continuing Education*, Luchterhand Verlag Neuwied, 1996, Section 50.30.140, pp. 1–7.
7 W. W. Daniel, *Racial Discrimination in Britain*, Penguin, Harmondsworth, 1968.

8 J. Wrench and G. Lee, *Skill Seekers: Black youth, apprenticeships and disadvantage*. National Youth Bureau, Leicester, 1983.
9 C. Mullard, 'Multi-racial education in Britain: From assimilation to cultural pluralism', *Race, Migration and Schooling* (ed. J. Tierney), Holt, Rinehart, Winston, London, 1982, pp. 72–88.
10 DES, *The Education of Immigrants*. Circular 7/65. HMSO, London, 1965.
11 J. Rex and J. Tomlinson, *Colonial Immigrants in a British City: Class analysis*, Routledge, Kegan and Paul, London, 1979.
12 DES, *Education for Immigrants*, HMSO, London, 1971.
13 B. Troyna and B. Carrington, *Education, Racism and Reform*, Routledge, London, 1990.
14 M. Leicester, *Multi-cultural Education: From theory to practice*, NFER, Nelson, Windsor, 1989.
15 E. Hopper and M. Osborn, *Adult Students: Education, selection and social control*, Frances Pinter, London, 1975.
16 M. Leicester, *Race for a Change in Continuing and Higher Education*, Falmer Press, London, 1993.
17 DES, *The Swann Report*, HMSO, London, 1985.
18 M. Leicester and C. and S. Modgills (eds.), *Education, Culture and Values* Vols. I–VI, Falmer Press, London, 1999.
19 G. Haydon, 'Understanding the diversity of diversity', *Education, Culture and Values* Vol. II, Falmer Press, London, 1999, pp. 3–11.
20 N. Tate, 'Society's voice', *Education, Culture and Values*, Vol. IV, Falmer Press, London, 1999, pp. 3–8.
21 G. Phillips, 'Should moral educators abandon moral relativism?', *Education, Culture and Values*, Vol. IV, Falmer Press, London, 1999, pp. 8–16.
22 K. Fogelman and J. Edwards, 'Citizenship education and cultural diversity', *Education, Culture and Values*, Vol. VI, Falmer Press, London, 1999, pp. 93–104.
23 J. Rowe, 'Values, pluralism, democracy and education for citizenship', *Education, Culture and Values*, Vol. VI, Falmer Press, London, 1999, pp. 194–204.
24 J. Lynch, *Education for Citizenship in a Multi-cultural Society*, Cassell, London, 1992.
25 T. Modood, 'On not being white in Britain: Discrimination, diversity and commonality', in *Ethics, Ethnicity and Education*, M. Leicester and M. Taylor (eds.), Kogan Page, London, 1992, pp. 72–88.
26 M. Leicester, 'Values, cultural conflict and education', in Leicester and Taylor (eds.), pp. 31–9.
27 On 11 September 2001 (after this paper was completed) a terrorist attack on New York destroyed the twin towers of the World Trade Center, with massive loss of life. As complex and dangerous events are unfolding, the situation is rendered even more complex and dangerous by endemic Islamaphobia in Britain and the USA and by entrenched ethnic/national prejudices on all sides. The injustice of global inequalities remains a factor and once more conflicts of value seem irresolvable. The liberal dilemma of dealing liberally but adequately with attacks on liberal values is sharp. Laws affecting civil liberties are being proposed by the British Home Secretary. Thus, in the opening year of the twenty-first century, the unfolding interaction of the law, public opinion and ethnicity has never been more important.

28 J. Field and M. Leicester (eds.), *Lifelong Learning: Education across the life-span*, Routledge/Falmer, London, 2000.
29 J. McIlroy, 'Lifelong learning: trade unions in search of a role', in ibid., pp. 300–13.
30 A. Withnall, 'Reflections on lifelong learning and the Third Age', in ibid., pp. 289–300.
31 M. Stuart, 'Inclusive learning for "active citizenship": Disability, learning difficulties and lifelong learning', in ibid., pp. 228–39.
32 K. Elsdon, 'Lifelong learning and voluntary organisations', in ibid., pp. 250–63.
33 A. Malach, 'Black and other ethnic minority communities' learning needs', in ibid., pp. 239–50.
34 J. Hannah, 'Education, training and adult refugees in the UK and Australia', in ibid., pp. 263–76.
35 C. Duke, 'Creating the accessible institution', in O. Fulton (ed.), *Access and Institutional Change*, Open University Press, Milton Keynes, 1989, pp. 163–79.
36 M. Leicester, 'A mature and multi-cultural adult education', *International Yearbook of Adult Education* (ed. K. Künzel), Bohlau Verlag, Koln, Weimar, Wien, 2001, pp. 143–60.

Part IV

The Death of the English Constitution?

7
Europe and its Impact on the United Kingdom

Daniel Wincott and Jim Buller

Introduction

How, if at all, is Dicey's legacy relevant to our understanding of the place of the United Kingdom in the European Union?[1] Isn't using Dicey as a lens through which to view these issues inherently anachronistic? Does it not run a severe risk of Anglocentrism (both in the light in which it casts other European states and in its vision of the Celtic nations within the UK)? The arguments implicit in these questions contain significant elements of truth. They are revealing – about UK 'European' politics, about the EU and indeed about Dicey and his legacy. Dicey is the font of the 'modern' public law tradition in England and hence of 'modern' English conceptions of sovereignty. Writing in the second half of the nineteenth century, Dicey witnessed a number of reforms which extended the franchise, leading commentators to take account of the importance of this new electorate in understanding the governmental system. For Dicey, this change posed a fundamental challenge to British constitutional theory. Whilst Bagehot and his followers had stressed the sovereignty of parliament as the essence of the British constitution, Dicey argued that behind Parliament lay a more fundamental source of power: the sovereignty of the people. According to Dicey, in the long term the English polity and its outputs would give effect to the will of this expanded electorate. In short, law and opinion were inherently linked. Yet, unlike many other Victorians, Dicey remained optimistic about the ability of the (English) polity and constitution to retain its genius in the face of change. Whilst Dicey was quick to point out that these conclusions applied to England only in the nineteenth century, they remained the 'official view' of British politics, certainly in the first half of the twentieth century.

In common with much seminal work, Dicey's 'originality' rests not so much on his rigour and coherence as on an ability to 'reconcile' the seemingly irreconcilable, to marry elements of the inherited view of law, politics and sovereignty with newly emerging legal or political forms and techniques. Dicey's analytical method set the tone for subsequent legal positivism and his optimism (at least until the end of his life) about the emergent political trends – such as the extension of the suffrage – stood in marked contrast to many of his Victorian predecessors and contemporaries. Yet Dicey's conception of law retained clear elements of an older vision, in which the moral character of judges was more important than the formal rules they were supposed to follow. Equally, his sanguine view of the extension of the suffrage and the sustained – perhaps increasing – influence of opinion on law in England depended on the practical benefits resulting from 'democracy tempered by snobbishness'.[2]

To sustain his confidence about the development of the English constitution Dicey had to reconcile both his views that legislation followed opinion and his notion of (parliamentary) sovereignty with the rule of law. In relation to sovereignty, the image of 'The Crown in (both Houses of) Parliament' was crucial. The *balance* between the elements of 'sovereignty' provided for the restraint of arbitrary and capricious use of state power. Equally important was the part played by common law, the common law mind and particularly the absence of a distinct body of administrative law. Dicey's ability to reconcile the influence of 'opinion' with the rule of law was partly based on his view that socialism and democracy were ultimately incompatible. For Dicey, socialism required rule by experts, who would know what was in the public interest better than the public itself. Ultimately, then, the rise of collectivism notwithstanding, democratic 'opinion' could not take a socialist trajectory and remain democratic.

The first point to make about UK European policy is that it has been largely detached from public opinion. Indeed, overall European integration has been an elite project throughout Europe, in most countries sustained by a no more than permissive consensus and sometimes faced by large sections of hostile public opinion. In a sense, then, in the UK and elsewhere, the EU opens a gap between public opinion and law/legislation, which may be impossible to bridge even in principle and that is perhaps a matter deliberate of political design. One of the main purposes of this chapter is to trace the 'absence' of public opinion as a driving force in UK European policy, even – perhaps especially – during the 1970s and the referendum on membership.

This account might seem (anachronistically) to use Dicey to sanction Euroscepticism. Closer analysis points in different directions. Two aspects of Dicey's complex legacy are particularly relevant here. While Dicey remained optimistic that (at least English) opinion would preserve – and perhaps bolster – the rule of law, the European Union institutionalises a different form of liberalism in which proper political (and economic) order are preserved by isolating key decisions from democracy and public opinion. Not just the Commission, but the European Central Bank – and indeed the broader character of the EU as a regulatory order – represent deliberate attempts to insulate public policy from democratic control. Moreover, while the original justification for the independence of EU institutions from political control was to protect them from nationalistic influence (with the partial exception of the Court of Justice), the rationale for the independence of the ECB from democratic/popular control is neoliberal. Few such neoliberals or individualists today have Dicey's confidence in public opinion.

Second, and in this light, the continuing influence of Dicey's understanding of sovereignty and the rule of law may help to account for the particular (and peculiar) character of English Euroscepticism. Let us be clear here. We are not necessarily suggesting that the UK is a peculiarly 'awkward' partner within the EU.[3] At the level of national policy, all states pursue national interests (as they perceive them) in their European strategies. Moreover, Eurosceptics and Europhobes make up a significant group in the domestic politics of most countries. Eurosceptics who see themselves as liberal, free trade internationalists are, however, rarer. Many countries (including the UK) have, or have had, socialist Eurosceptics. In Britain and the Nordic states, socialists developed a view of unimpeded popular sovereignty vested in formally unicameral legislatures and resented European institutions as much for the shackles they placed on popular sovereignty as for the economic liberalism of this 'rich man's club'. Elsewhere in Europe statism and nationalism often sustain the Eurosceptics of the Right – including some strands of Gaullism. While it would be wrong to ignore the (visceral) nationalism in much English Euroscepticism, their ability to blend it within their self-image as free trade liberals, as well as their celebration of the liberties of English people, is more striking.

There is plenty of literature written on British politics the 1960s and 1970s which argued that Dicey's work was now outdated as a way of understanding how the British constitution operated in practice. However, the picture is more complicated than this. Dicey may longer provide an accurate *description* of the contemporary workings of the British polity, perhaps particularly in an era of increasing European integration. But in another sense, it remains directly relevant as a *normative template* of how British politics ought to operate. The defence of this viewpoint now lies at the centre of a growing Eurosceptical discourse that increasingly sees the Union as undermining the legitimacy of the British State. Rather than sitting *above* politics, Dicey's legacy may better understood as being a crucial feature of the battle of political ideas *within* politics, certainly in relation to British European policy.

Because he felt able to reconcile his view of the influence of 'opinion' with the rule of law, for Dicey the influence of opinion on law could become England's great political achievement. Elsewhere, democracy could not be tempered by snobbishness, and the distinct form of administrative law – what might be called 'law for the state' – developed. Both for reasons of national character and the form of the state, 'opinion' could and would not be allowed to shape legislation. Thus the flipside of celebrating the political genius of England was the disdain with which Dicey viewed foreign – particularly French – law and politics. Dicey's scorn for 'continental' political and legal systems may be another element in his legacy for 'European politics' in the UK today. As well as a nostalgic vision of parliamentary sovereignty, confidence that such sovereignty is practically consistent with the liberties of Englishmen is matched by a sense that 'the continentals' are not truly at liberty in the wistful imaginations of right-wing English Eurosceptics.

Escaping the demands of democracy: entry into the European Union, 1945–79

As implied above, the creation and development of the EU in the 1950s and the 1960s posed real challenges to British constitutional theory and practice. The first issue was the principle of supra-nationalism on which the Union was founded. This principle partly had its origins in the so-called 'German question': how to constrain the resurgent power of western Germany as it completed its period of reconstruction after 1945. The response of France, Italy and the Benelux countries was to pool sovereignty voluntarily with the Germans and place limits of their freedom of action in the name of European peace and prosperity.

This agreement led to the formation of supranational institutions, which raised questions for the British tradition of governance. Member states agreed first to create a 'High Authority' and then a European Commission, which enjoyed the exclusive right to initiate policy in areas where the EU enjoyed competence. A new European Court of Justice was also set up to monitor and enforce the Treaty of Rome. As such, the ECJ appeared to be like any other international court, policing a mutually agreed treaty between 'contracting parties' (member states). However, the Court's early decision to take a broader, interpretative approach concerning its own powers resulted in what some lawyers have termed the 'constitutionalisation' of the EU. In the early days, landmark judgements included *Van Gend en Loos* (1963) which established the principle that EU law had 'direct effect' in national jurisdictions. A year later, *Costa* v *ENEL* established the supremacy of EU law over national legislation in cases where the two conflicted.[4]

The principle of supra-nationalism and the EU institutions to which it gave rise proved to be a central theme in Whitehall's opposition to this nascent regional organisation. It was certainly a major factor behind the Attlee government's decision not to participate in the European Coal and Steel Community. It did not help that the principle of supra-nationalism was non-negotiable when Schuman unveiled his plan to the British Cabinet.[5] But even if the principle had been negotiable, it seems unlikely that London's reaction would have been much different. Any loss of sovereignty over British coal and steel was always going to be disagreeable to a government that had just nationalised those industries. In the inimitable words of Herbert Morrison: 'the Durham miners will never wear it.'[6] Such concerns also played a role in the decision not to sign the Treaty of Rome in 1957. It should be noted that high up the list of objections was the danger that the Common Market was thought to pose to Britain's Commonwealth trading links. However, ministers were also concerned that membership would subject them to irresistible pressure to agree to more integration in the future. If nothing else, it was thought such a state of affairs would prove unacceptable the British public.[7]

If the institutional structure of the EU posed uncomfortable challenges to the British Constitution, as it was commonly understood, the actual decision to join appeared to further contradict Dicey's understanding of the policy-making process. Or rather, foreign policy was not an area where the relationship between opinion and legislative activity (as set out by Dicey) applied. Perhaps the first point to note is that Macmillan's bid for membership did not reflect a groundswell of opinion in England – or indeed the UK more generally. The British population at this time shared, rather, the famous 'permissive consensus' that characterised public attitudes to European integration in most member states. If there was a notable feature of public sentiment at all, it was the way that enthusiasm for Europe tended to vary in accordance with the perception of the fortunes of the governing party more generally. Indeed, one could go further and question whether the public had any opinion at all on the subject, in the sense that they consciously thought about the nature and consequences of EU membership. A common response to surveys at the time demonstrated an impression of confusion and bewilderment: 'a feeling that this issue, whilst it would profoundly affect people's futures, was out of their hands and could not really be put back there.'[8] Put bluntly, people cared about matters that had a more immediate impact on their lives, such as prices, incomes and employment. Europe was a matter on which they were happy for the political classes to provide a lead.[9]

If public opinion was a quiescent background force, opinion within the main political parties represented more of a constraint on decision-makers at this time. The obvious reason was that Europe was a question on which politicians of all colours were divided. Political antagonism over the European question cut across lines that traditionally divided the British party system – and perhaps also the cleavages around which it was organised. Indeed, the intensity of these splits appears to have grown as the period wore on, especially in the Labour Party. Issues that consistently excited activists included the following: (i) the effect of the nascent Common Agricultural Policy on the farming community (a particularly sensitive topic for Tory MPs in agricultural constituencies); (ii) the effect of the Common Market on Commonwealth trade; (iii) the compatibility between the Treaty of Rome and domestic attempts to conduct an independent socialist economic policy centred around nationalisation and planning (a pressing concern for the left of the Labour Party – which places the issue of the compatibility between socialism and democracy that was at the heart of Dicey's concerns in a rather different light); (iv) the ability to conduct an independent foreign policy in a bi-polar world of superpower rivalry; and (v), the effect of supranational Community institutions on the sovereignty of British parliament. In short, these were issues that impacted directly on concepts such as nation and self-government. Not surprisingly, the need to keep parties united was a permanent theme of much of British diplomacy in this area during this period.[10]

If this portrayal of the domestic political context contains some elements of plausibility, two questions immediately present themselves. First, why did British policy-makers decide to join the EU at all? Put another way, faced with a domestic situation that appeared to be less than conducive to or compatible with membership, it seems reasonable to assume that this decision was not taken lightly. Second, having taken this decision, how did British political leaders manage to implement it? In other words, how was this political elite able to create the necessary domestic autonomy to negotiate membership of this supranational organisation? The discussion below will briefly consider these questions.

As suggested, faced with the domestic political context detailed above, we can only assume that in pursuing membership, the party leaders faced a serious challenge during this period. In fact, when it took this decision the British political elite was gripped by an increasingly severe crisis of confidence in its ability to govern. In Britain, the 1960s and the 1970s represented an era where the initial trauma of relative decline crystallised into panic about the 'ungovernability' of society itself. The perception of a *relative* decline involved a reappraisal of other countries. By the 1960s few senior politicians still shared Dicey's Victorian confidence in the superiority of British political institutions. Equally, the notion of 'ungovernability' understood British democracy – and perhaps liberal democracy more generally – as fundamentally threatened by a revolution of rising expectations in what the public required from government. 'Opinion' was no longer thoughtful and self-disciplining; democracy produced demands that, in aggregate, were impossibly burdensome and mutually inconsistent. Liberalism needed protection from democracy and political elites had to protect themselves from pressure.[11]

Membership of the EU was supposed to 'take British politicians away from all of this'. As such, there was an economic and a political case. The former rested on one simple proposition: 'growth by association'. Supporters of this argument pointed out that, economically, the six members of the Community had consistently outperformed Britain during the postwar period. This superior performance was put down to the fact that all these countries enjoyed preferential access to an enlarged 'home market' of 170 million people. Exposed to this larger market, European firms had been able to take advantage of economies of scale, leading to lower unit costs and prices and higher standards of living. It followed logically that if only British industry could gain access to this 'dynamic' area, it too would enjoy the benefits of its European competitors. At times, Whitehall had to admit that the exact outcome of this policy could not be predicted: much would depend to a large extent on the way British industry responded to the challenge. But ministers were confident that 'in the round', membership could provide substantial long term economic benefits.[12]

The geopolitical case came down to a feeling of increased isolation and vulnerability in a world fast dividing into a number of regional blocs.

By the early 1960s, Whitehall had begun to worry about the growing weight of the Community. More particularly, de Gaulle's schemes to develop machinery for European Political Co-operation brought home the fact that not only was this supranational organisation here to stay, it had loftier ambitions. At the same time, a link was also made between membership and preserving the 'special' relationship with the US. London feared that as the EU grew in strength, Washington would increasingly turn to this regional block as its major partner in the free world, thus leaving Britain further isolated.[13]

Behind this rhetoric, cruder governing concerns were at work. Put bluntly, EU membership presented British political leaders with an opportunity to rebuild a semblance of autonomy, from the increasing number of intractable problems that were crowding in on them. It should be pointed out that this political class differed in their understanding of how this strategy would work out in practice. Some were hyper-optimists, hoping that the Common Market offered a painless means of *escape*; a panacea which would *automatically* take care of Britain's troubles. Others were more realistic. EU membership would not absolve policy-makers from making difficult decisions, particularly on economic policy. But Europe would provide a supporting instrument: a sort of external discipline or impersonal 'enforcer' of competitive forces, locking the British economy into a number of supply-side reforms which many commentators agreed were desperately needed. Ultimately, this external organisation offered a way of avoiding responsibility for awkward and difficult decisions of which, quite frankly, 'chaps' in Whitehall had made rather a mess when developing 'domestic' solutions.[14]

The question remains: how was this elite operation achieved against a domestic background of party divisions and a more general concern (at the Establishment level) about the compatibility of the Treaty of Rome with British constitutional practice. It is possible to detect a number of common methods of political management, which were brought into play at different times during this period. The first was a preference for constructing a tacit frontbench agreement not to politicise this awkward question as membership was sought. In other words, faced with the problem of leading coalitions of mutually antagonistic factions, party leaders on both sides of the House judged that the normal rules of adversarial party politics did not always automatically apply when it came to handling this issue. It should be noted that this technique was not initially adopted in the early 1960s. Indeed, Macmillan consciously avoided trying to build a consensus for his decision to apply for entry, believing this policy to be a vote winner at the next election. Moreover, it is not clear that Wilson sought cross-party support for Labour's second bid in 1967. However, Heath gave Wilson such support anyway in the face of opposition from within the Conservative rank and file. As Heath himself makes clear in his autobiography, Brendan Sewill, then director of the Conservative Research Department, argued that such a move would not be good party politics. The Tories would be deprived of their ability to attack Wilson's policy if it was unsuccessful, thus handing Labour 'another glorious failure'.[15]

Although it existed in a precarious state, this tactical agreement continued just long enough for the Heath Government to achieve membership in the early 1970s. Despite continued pressure from Labour's rank and file to commit the party to oppose membership in principle, Wilson worked hard in the early 1970s to keep open the option of staying in. His policy of deferring judgement until the exact details of membership were known gave Heath just enough space to negotiate a deal before the party came out in opposition to the terms in July 1971.[16] Even in the face of official Labour opposition, cross-party cooperation continued. Most spectacularly, 69 Labour MPs defied a three-line whip imposed by Wilson and crossed the floor of the House to support the passage of the accession Bill. Just as important were the subterranean contacts. Under pressure during subsequent parliamentary votes on specific aspects of membership, a then young Tory whip, Ken Clarke, was able to conclude a secret deal with John Roper. Under this deal, pro-European Labour MPs agreed to absent themselves from Westminster whenever the Conservative majority looked particularly thin.[17] In return, Conservative support for Wilson's renegotiated terms was crucial in getting this deal through Westminster in April 1975. Wilson could not count on support from within his own party. Of the 315 available MPs only 137 supported the leadership.

A second method of depoliticising this question and creating some semblance of elite autonomy was to avoid making membership a matter of principle during the negotiations. To make membership a matter of principle would run the risk of confronting a divided party membership with a stark choice, something that was likely to set off inter-party conflict. Instead, the age-old qualities of British pragmatism and empiricism came into their own. Initially, Macmillan took this method to the extreme. Throughout the first membership bid, at no time was the party formally confronted with the question: 'Shall Britain seek to become a member of the Common Market?' Instead the motion that was introduced into the House of Commons on 31 July 1961 merely recommended negotiations to see if satisfactory arrangements could be made to meet

British interests. For all political leaders that followed, everything hinged on 'the terms' to be achieved. At the same time, what 'the terms' meant in practice could be gradually watered down to accommodate the harsh realities of European diplomacy. What started out as 'special arrangements' for Britain's Commonwealth partners were gradually redefined to mean New Zealand dairy produce and Caribbean sugar. Similarly, concerns about the incompatibility of Labour's interventionist economic policies with the Treaty of Rome were forgotten, despite pleas from Tony Benn that he was increasingly constrained by Community regulations at the Department of Industry. As with many aspects of Britain's relations with Europe, the exception was Edward Heath. Learning from the perceived mistakes of the Macmillan period, he went for quick and early negotiations. The *acquis* was accepted in principle, leaving much of the haggling to centre on the transition arrangements for British industry and agriculture.

A third and final method of depoliticising the European question was to downplay the constitutional aspect of membership.[18] In other words, the governing classes preferred not to talk about the implications of joining this supranational organisation for Parliament – the main legislative organ responsible for reflecting opinion and channelling it through Whitehall. This is not to say that leaders were blind to these concerns. In the early 1960s, both Macmillan and Gaitskell launched investigations into this question. Macmillan was satisfied that, whilst there may be limits to parliament's powers, these were likely to be specific and largely confined to areas such as trade and industrial matters. The Labour enquiry, chaired by Wilson himself, was much more critical. It concluded that the political objectives of the EU were dangerously obscure and that the potential erosion of sovereignty was very serious. Interestingly, during the re-negotiation of membership in 1974–5, such concerns were dropped. Rather as Wilson argues in his memoirs, serious problems on this front had not yet arisen, so sovereignty was a non-issue.

Instead, during this period, British political leaders felt the need to bypass normal constitutional procedures temporarily in order to manage this difficult decision. In a Commons speech in January 1975, Wilson announced that a referendum would take place on the terms, which he, with Callaghan, had recently renegotiated. Moreover, the principle of collective Cabinet responsibility was to be relaxed when it came to the campaign. The idea of a referendum was initially promoted by the Eurosceptics, who hoped to appeal over the head of the party to the electoral at large, which was thought to share a similar viewpoint. However, Wilson became attracted to this constitutional device because he saw this exercise in popular sovereignty as a way of resolving the European issue one way or another and, therefore taking it out of party politics. Indeed, to this end, he insisted on making any referendum verdict binding, not consultative as Jenkins and other pro-Europeans advised. When the Labour government officially came out in favour of the renegotiated terms, public opinion shifted decisively behind this line, delivering a two-thirds majority for the pro-European campaign. For some commentators, this development confirmed that voters held no deep feelings on the subject of Europe and were quite happy to take their lead from the top.[19]

Disciplining the demands of democracy: the Europeanisation of British economic policy, 1979–87

A superficial survey of the British political landscape at the 1983 election appears to suggest that very little has changed after ten years of EU membership. At the domestic level, the old problems remained. The Holy Grail of non-inflationary growth remained elusive, despite the promises of the new monetarist faith. To be fair, inflation had been brought down to acceptable levels. But arguably, this had little to do with the conscious decision to monitor and control £M3 and, rather more to do with the unexpected surge of sterling on the back of another OPEC price hike in 1979. Accompanying this monetary squeeze were the problems of mass unemployment and social unrest. In the summer of 1981, race riots occurred in a number of cities throughout the country. The National Union of Mineworkers was about to embark on its year long (and often violent) strike. Even the president of the Confederation of British Industry threatened a 'bare-knuckled fight' with the government if they did not do something about this appalling state of affairs.

A similar picture could be portrayed in the area of Britain' relations with the EU. In 1979, the Conservative Party had swept into Downing Street promising a new era of constructive and co-operative European diplomacy, but had soon settled into the rut of prickly intransigence inhabited by all administrations before it.[20] When it came to the domestic management of the issue, it could be argued that matters had actually deteriorated. Any semblance of front-bench agreement not to disagree in public about Europe had evaporated. Disillusioned with its own record in office and under new leadership, the Labour Party was now campaigning on a policy of withdrawal, a policy stance that enjoyed substantial public support at the time.[21] Aligned with this was a new national strategy for invigorating the British economy through a programme of public ownership and tariff measures. With the counterbalancing elements of the Crown and the Upper Chamber increasingly weak, the left was able to conjoin the ideas of popular and parliamentary sovereignty much more fully than Dicey and his peers might have feared. Moreover, this notion of popular/parliamentary sovereignty seemed to hand the left instruments of power that in principle might be used to achieve political control over economic might. Had Labour been in a position to win an election at this stage, Dicey's hope that democracy would prevent socialism (understood as 'rule by experts') would have appeared somewhat forlorn.

At the same time, the politicisation of the European question brought with it problems of party management for Conservative leaders. Europe, like a number of other issues, fed into the broader split between the 'wets' and the 'dries', which was hardening at this time. The former group had always suspected that monetarism would exacerbate not solve Britain's problems. By 1983 they considered themselves vindicated and a demand for a more positive, constructive approach to Europe became part of a more general alternative prospectus they proposed to solve the party's governing problems. More significant in response to Labour's change of policy was perhaps the stirring of anti-EU feeling on the backbenches. At this time, the leadership faced a number of calls to negotiate substantial institutional reform of the EU, or go for associate status.[22] Indeed, this development became a matter of concern in Whitehall. Civil servants in the Foreign Office and the Cabinet Office began to worry that this anti-EU sentiment would fuel Thatcher's instinctive hostility to this organisation. This, in turn, could put the option of withdrawal back at the centre of British politics.[23]

In this context, the Thatcher government adopted an unconventional approach to handling the European issue. More particularly, ministers broke new ground in attempting to reform the EU in such a way that it complemented their domestic policy programme. This initiative was part of a much broader strategy to create an ideological hegemony through the institutionalisation of neoliberal economic values at the European level. If the approach was novel, the relationship between legislative change and popular attitudes remained the same. Whitehall set out its policy independently of public opinion, which as noted, remained sceptical at this time. Paradoxically, the effect of this reform would be further to detach and insulate key aspects decisions concerning key aspects of economic governance from societal pressure. Far from reflecting Dicey's confidence in the compatibility of democratic opinion with the rule of law and the liberties of the English, it was now the individualists that sought to separate law from opinion, placing it instead in the hands of insulated technocratic elites. Expertise, seen by Dicey as the fatal flaw of democratic socialism, was becoming the protector of liberal individualism.

The first evidence of this strategy occurred in 1984. At the Fontainebleau European Council in June, negotiators managed to agree acceptable revisions to the formula for calculating Britain's budgetary rebate. At the same meeting, the British presented a White Paper, 'Europe – the Future' which emphasised the importance of European solutions to Britain's domestic economic problems.[24] More particularly, the paper asserted that the way of addressing issues of growth, outdated industrial structures and high rates of unemployment was to work for the completion of the Single Market. Progress needed to be made on such things as the harmonisation of standards, more rapid and better coordinated customs procedures and the mutual recognition of professional qualifications. Lord Cockfield took up the relevant Commission portfolio from where he proceeded to produce a detailed programme and timetable calling for the reduction of all non-tariff barriers by December 1992.

At the Luxembourg European Council in December 1985, the Thatcher government negotiated the SEA, with Cockfield's Single Market project at its centre. Whilst generally held to be a triumph for the British at this time, it is important to note that ministers did not have it all their own way. The first concession was on the issue of the Act itself. Whitehall was keen to avoid a formal revision to the Treaty of Rome because of worries that other European governments would use the subsequent intergovernmental conference to insert a number of changes not wanted by the British. Furthermore, London campaigned against extensions both to qualified majority voting and the European Parliament's legislative powers in areas pertaining to the completion of the Single Market. Another issue of concern at this time was Thatcher's inability to stop the negotiations including a general commitment to Economic and Monetary Union (EMU) in the preamble of the Treaty. Finally, the matter settled last of all (indicating its contentious nature) was the insertion of Article 118a, which extended qualified majority voting to matters of health and safety.

If the Thatcher government realised it could institutionalise its free market strategy through this process of Europeanisation, it is worth noting in passing that similar considerations underpinned the attractiveness of ERM membership, although such a policy elicited more controversy within the Party. After the experience of the first term, it is not surprising that Howe and Lawson, as successive Chancellors, began to view exchange rate policy as a better method of controlling inflation. However, if this change of strategy was to have any chance of success, it was clear that ministers would have to find a way of minimising the exchange rate volatility experienced in the first half of the 1980s. For Lawson, this meant pegging sterling to another currency with a sound record on inflation and securing organised international support for this semi-fixed exchange rate. By 1985, Lawson, Howe and other Euro-enthusiasts saw the ERM, dominated by the Deutsche mark, as a suitable institutional mechanism for this policy.[25]

From a domestic point of view, this gradual Europeanisation of British economic policy had a number of beneficial effects at the domestic level. To begin with, it helped depoliticise the European question from a party political point of view. Or rather, Labour was decisively beaten in the battle for political argument hegemony in this area, to the point where it refrained from making the Community an issue during the second Thatcher administration. Indeed, Kinnock had signalled a reappraisal of Labour's policy of withdrawal as far back as 1984. He stated that, by the next general election, Britain would have experienced fifteen years of EU membership, a reality that would be reflected in Britain's economic and political relations overseas and could not be easily reversed. On the other hand, fresh from his negotiating success at Luxembourg, Howe (now Foreign Secretary) heralded the phenomenon of 'Euro-Thatcherism'. Under the Conservatives, Britain had demonstrated the sort of positive role it could play in European affairs by adopting a more cooperative and constructive diplomatic approach.[26] As a result, the *principle* of membership was no longer a contentious one in British politics and, the option of withdrawal not longer a serious theme in the public discourse on this question.

Second, the SEA had a beneficial effect on party management. Put simply, it was a policy that offered something to Conservatives of all persuasions, thus helping to relieve inter-party tensions on the issue. Right-wingers could stress the centrality of market forces as a future principle underpinning Community development.[27] Those on the left of the party could highlight the *communautaire* nature of the initiative. It helped that, at the time of ratification, the SEA was not perceived as a controversial measure in Britain. The Conservative leadership played up the completion of the Single Market and played down the institutional change that might be involved. Whilst no one could disagree that the harmonisation of professional qualifications or the liberalisation of insurance services was not important, it was dull, esoteric stuff. Put another way, the legislation to bring down the non-tariff barriers was a long way away from the theoretical and political debate between inter-governmentalists and federalists about the future of the EU, which was always likely to animate the divisions between the Europhile and Euro-phobe elements within the party.[28]

Finally, the more general governing advantages that this strategy conferred on the Conservative leadership should also be noted. Put crudely, it was hoped that the Europeanisation of economic policy would enhance the centre's autonomy from the domestic pressures it experienced in the first term. By linking the fortunes of British business to Cockfield's 1992 programme (and it should be noted, by tying the conduct of British monetary policy to the external discipline of the ERM), industrialists would be forced to adapt or fold in the face of these autonomous external pressures. Firms would be more likely to control their costs when confronted with increased European competition, especially when the possibility of exchange rate devaluation was ruled out. There could be no discretion, no *ad hoc* approaches and no special pleading. These policies were part of an international legal framework, enforceable through the ECJ. In short, international treaty changes were designed to insulate the Conservative governing elite further, whilst converting the public to the values of economic liberalism and the 'limited liability' governing philosophy that accompanied it.[29]

1987–97: External institutional dynamics and the re-politicisation of the European question in British politics

In the period after the Single European Act, the Thatcherite strategy of embedding neoliberal governance in insulated European institutions took an unexpected turn. An integrationist dynamic within the EU became established which the British governing elite found very difficult to contain. Whilst in some quarters, this pressure for European integration dissipated, in the face of public resistance across Europe in the 1990s, momentum remained relatively enduring, especially in the form of the developing plans for a single currency. The main source of this 'endurance' lay in the *related* nature of a number of external structural developments – both to each other and, just as importantly, to the existing properties of the EU *as interpreted and deployed by actors working within these European institutions*. To understand this argument, we must first begin by delineating this changing international context as experienced by Whitehall from the second half of the 1980s onwards.

By 1987, international financial forces were having an unsettling impact on the European Monetary System. More particularly, having been a source of instability because of its persistent strength in the first half of the 1980s, the managed devaluation of the dollar as a result of the Plaza Agreement in January 1986, exposed the Exchange Rate Mechanism (ERM) of that system to further tensions. The dollar's descent put sustained upward pressure on the Deutsche mark, which, in turn, dragged up other European currencies in the wake of its 'undertow'. Eventually, the French government let the franc fall through the floor of its ERM band as an indication of its displeasure at the asymmetrical nature of the policy.[30] A post-mortem on the crisis carried out in Paris concluded that only the construction of supranational institutions would effectively insulate French policy-makers from destabilising global pressures, while simultaneously diluting the power of the Bundesbank over European economic policy. By January 1988 Finance Minister Balladur had produced a speech calling for the 'monetary construction of Europe' and, more particularly for the establishment of a European Central Bank.[31]

If international financial pressures began the momentum towards greater integration, this development was compounded by geopolitical shifts in the international system in the late 1980s. In particular, two changes are worthy of note. First, the fall of the Berlin Wall and the collapse of communism in Eastern Europe raised important questions concerning the balance of power in Europe. Whilst the Cold War may have been a source of much tension in the West, its structures did have the advantage of providing an environment which helped diffuse concerns about renewed German power. The collapse of these structures in 1989 heralded the possibility of Germany loosening its ties with the EU and turning its attention eastwards. Second, the reunification of Germany did nothing to alleviate these fears. What most worried Bonn's European partners was the style in which this policy decision was made. It was announced in the form of a ten-point plan without any consultation. The response of most EU member states was one of uncertainty and anxiety. The German question had re-emerged as a strategic problem.[32]

Finally, these related structural shifts led to the recreation of a balance of power configuration at the EU level that which strengthened this integrationist dynamic. More particularly, this took the form of a Franco-German consensus (powerfully supported by the Commission) which argued for the strengthening of European integration as a response to this uncertain external environment. In policy terms, this axis was able to exploit the general commitment to re-start progress towards EMU in the preamble of the SEA, a move which annoyed London caught British negotiators by surprise. In doing so, the French, in particular, believed that they could exert decisive control over these nascent structures and thus be in a much better position to contain the increasing economic and political might of Germany. In return, Kohl got a commitment to work for political union at the Rome Summit of 1990.

The dynamic nature of this change was further entrenched by the behaviour of other actors at the EU level at this time. The Commission has been cited in passing, but deserves further comment in this context. As some authors have argued, Delors (as well as a small group of his advisers) was a 'purposeful opportunist' during this period.[33] Put another way, this group employed a conscious strategy of linking further integration in related policy areas 'cultivating' a process 'spillover'. We have noted above how the Commission used the preamble of the SEA to launch the single currency project. Similarly, not long after the SEA was ratified, Delors could be heard arguing that the Single Market needed to be accompanied by a social dimension, otherwise Europe's workforces may not remain committed to what they saw as an essentially capitalist European project. Once again, the appropriation of evolving treaty language proved to be crucial. Perhaps the best example of this technique was the Working Time Directive that sought to guarantee a maximum 48-hour week for all EU employees. Delors introduced this legislation under Article 118a of the SEA, which, as already noted, related to questions of health and safety. Although the Thatcher and Major governments vehemently disputed this interpretation, the advantage for Brussels lay in the fact that all legislation pertaining to this article was subject to qualified majority voting. As a result, the Commission could bypass any possibility of British resistance. In June 1993, the Commission's proposals passed into law and, as predicted, Whitehall challenged this decision by taking the Commission to the ECJ. In November 1996, the Court rejected British claims, with the effect of provoking a wave of criticism from Britain's Eurosceptics.[34]

It follows that, when accounting for this integrationist dynamic, the role of the ECJ is just as important as that of the Commission. Its judicial activism in the 1960s has already been noted. However, this body presided over a number of decisions in the 1990s that brought home the importance of these rulings to many British politicians. Take, for example, the *Factortame* case in 1991, which forced home the principle of the supremacy of Union law. In this judgement, the ECJ overturned the Merchant Shipping Act 1988 (Britain's attempt to respond to the problem of 'quota-hopping') arguing that this legislation was incompatible with EU treaty commitments ensuring the freedom of establishment and the freedom to provide services.[35] Alternatively, one could point to *Francovitch and Boniface* v *Italy* (1991), which related to the issue of state liability. In this case, the ECJ held that, in certain circumstances, EU individuals were entitled to sue governments for damages sustained as a result of a failure to implement EU directives within a prescribed period.[36] It was under this principle that Nicole Seymour-Smith and Laura Perez successfully challenged the UK's unfair dismissal laws in 1995,[37] a ruling which went on to open the way for all female employees in Britain sacked between 1985–91 to claim compensation.[38]

From a governing point of view, the impact of these external developments was nothing short of disastrous. At the end of the 1980s, the issue of the single currency and how to respond split the Conservative leadership and ultimately contributed to the downfall of a number of senior party figures including Ridley, Lawson, Howe and Thatcher herself. In the first half of the 1990s, these divisions spread to the party as a whole as Euroscepticism took hold within the rank and file. One could point to the persistent pattern of rebellion during the ratification of the Maastricht Treaty, which saw the leadership experience defeat on one vote and postpone others it thought it was going to lose. Alternatively, there was the spectacle of the 'whip-less wonders' voting against the government during the passage of the 1995 European Finance Bill.[39] Finally, party leaders decided during the 1997 election campaign to allow Members of Parliament to ignore official party policy on EMU, therefore giving them the freedom to include personal statements in their own campaign literature. External institutional dynamics had re-politicised the European question in British politics. The important question here is why and, what (if anything) these developments indicate about the legacy of Dicey?

A 'cottage industry' has now grown up on the subject of Conservative Euroscepticism.[40] Whilst it is impossible to do justice to that literature here, three arguments appear important in the context of the question above. The first maybe termed the 'Euro-ratchet' argument.[41] In plain English, this growth of scepticism reflected a feeling that the leadership's loss of control over the EU policy process in the 1980s, meant that Britain had become locked into the inexorable development of a European super-state in the 1990s. Of course, the Major leadership officially disputed this view. For example, the Maastricht Treaty represented 'game, set and match' for Britain, proof that she was back in control and that the federalist tide had been turned. Had not Major successfully campaigned to get the phrase 'federal vocation' replaced with 'ever closer union amongst the peoples of Europe' in the preamble of the

Treaty? Had not British negotiators worked to get a formal definition of subsidiarity inserted into Community law for the first time? Finally, in areas where progress could not be halted, did Britain not enjoy legally binding opt-outs, as in the case of the single currency and the Social Chapter?

Conservative Eurosceptics did not find these arguments convincing. At the heart of their concerns was what they saw as the *evolutionary* nature of the EU's treaty language. Since the SEA, a feeling had grown that law was being used as a mask for politics and that formal treaty amendments conferred valuable institutional resources on actors looking to further the integration process. In this sense, the Maastricht Treaty could only provide further possible 'political opportunity structures' for proponents of Europeanisation.[42] Take, for example, the concept of subsidiarity. First, Eurosceptics highlighted that it only applied to areas that did not fall within the exclusive competence of the EU. Unfortunately, whilst most commentators agreed that such power was extensive (especially in economic policy), the Maastricht Treaty did not contain a written statement of its limits. Of course, subsidiarity went on to state that in areas where the EU did not have exclusive competence, Brussels would take on additional responsibilities only if they could not be sufficiently achieved by member states. The second problem for the Eurosceptics was it was not clear who ultimately made such a decision.[43] It *was* clear that, in the likely event of disputes, final adjudication would take place at the ECJ. Some commentators have suggested that European judges have become increasingly uncomfortable about being drawn into the EU political process in this fashion. Eurosceptics, however, thought it reasonable to expect that those self-same judges would protect the integrity of the Union's institutions as and when they were called on to do so.[44] In short, subsidiarity hardly appeared to be an unambiguous guarantee of decentralisation.

Eurosceptics also pointed to the inability of the opts-out to insulate British politics from the integrationist pressure they felt they could not hold back. In this context, the Working Time Directive became a source of some controversy in British politics at this time. One of the few measures to be negotiated under the Social Chapter during this period, this ruling required all companies with operations in two or more EU countries to establish representative mechanisms through which employees could be informed and consulted over company strategy. Despite being legally exempt from this directive, in practice it was widely adopted in Britain. Furthermore, while UK multinationals were legally entitled to exclude British workers from these consultative arrangements, in practice the majority of these firms extended these arrangements to their British operations.[45] When New Labour achieved office in 1997, in ended Britain's opt-out in this area, it demonstrated how lacking in contention the issue of the Social Chapter had now become.

In essence, the main claim of the 'Euro-ratchet' argument is that the Major leadership was guilty of misunderstanding the structural processes underpinning integration. However, there was a second factor that helps explain the vehemence of this opposition as it developed. Rather than being foolish, Conservative leaders were accused of being disingenuous in the way they behaved at this time. Some Euro-sceptics now began to believe that Major was a closet Euro-enthusiast. Moreover, they also suspected he understood the Euro-ratchet argument, although from his position, it had certain benefits. For a leadership that felt heavily constrained in this area, the best way to ensure a continuity of policy was, perhaps, to maintain a public demeanour of scepticism; whilst not actively resisting Europeanisation and allowing this external process to take the strain by dragging Britain in backwards.[46] This became known as the 'Europeanisation by stealth' argument. Two incidents in particular were crucial to its development.

The first was the refusal of the Conservative leadership to use the Danish rejection of the Maastricht Treaty to call for the negotiation of a looser arrangement. Bill Cash was said to be 'thunderstruck' at Major's resolution to carry on with the Treaty,[47] while another prominent Eurosceptic remarked: 'it was this very moment we realized that Major was not one of us.'[48] The second was the failure of British negotiators to challenge the legal nature of that self-same treaty after the collapse of the ERM in 1993. Of particular relevance here was the decision of Britain's partners to replace the discredited 2.5 per cent bands with the broader 15 per cent fluctuation rates, despite the fact that, strictly speaking, a new IGC should have been called to negotiate this amendment. Allegations about Ken Clarke's behaviour during this crisis did not help. According to claims by two French journalists, the Chancellor of the Exchequer intervened at an ECOFIN meeting to plead for action to save the ERM.[49]

Third and finally, if Eurosceptics believed that a covert 'Europeanisation by stealth' strategy was taking place, the intensity of their opposition reflected the fact that they believed the consequences for the English governing tradition would be disastrous. By and large, Eurosceptics could support measures such as the SEA and the ERM in the 1980s. These policies entrenched a neoliberal economic philosophy which they not only believed to be ideologically correct, but also understood to have certain governing advantages for Conservative leaders in office. However, attempting to maintain one's freedom of manoeuvre from societal forces by intensifying these external constraints could go too far. In the 1990s, Europeanisation had developed into a process over which British politicians did not have full control. It could lock decision-makers into policies with uncomfortable domestic consequences. Black Wednesday represented a classic example of this. Membership of the single currency could potentially be much worse.

In short, while Dicey's writings may have lost their relevance in terms of explaining British political practice in the twenty-first century, his work remains an important *normative template* against which Eurosceptics judge contemporary statecraft. Most Eurosceptic MPs accept that they (and through them, the British public) have little real influence over the policy process. However, the important point is that Eurosceptics believe that the electorate itself thinks that popular sovereignty exists, or at least *ought to exist* in British politics. If Europeanisation leads to the legislative process becoming too detached from public opinion, resentment, discontent and even a crisis of legitimacy may result.[50] Ultimately, in this vision Europeanisation may produce a nationalistic and xenophobic backlash that undermines the supra-national foundations of the EU itself.[51] Chris Gill's apocalyptic contribution to the Maastricht debates perhaps best sums up this message:

> ... stripped of power to influence or decide matters of state, we shall have created the classic recipe for failure: responsibility resting with a body of people who do not have the authority to discharge that responsibility in full measure. This will result in public disillusionment with politicians and with people's capacity to obtain satisfaction through their elected representatives. In the fullness of time that disillusionment will turn to frustration and anger, which will lead ultimately to the rejection of established political leadership, traditional party loyalties and the whole body politic.[52]

Public opinion and the Blair government's policy towards the European Union

When New Labour won the 1997 general election, there was a general presumption that the Blair government would preside over a substantial change in Britain's relations with the EU. Ministers themselves fuelled such expectations. In a speech four days after Labour had attained office,

Doug Henderson made clear that one priorities of the new government would be to made a 'fresh start' in this policy area.[53] Moreover, this rhetoric was matched by concrete achievements. One could point to the encouragement and acceptance of measures to give greater coherence to the EU's common foreign and defence policy, especially the creation of a Rapid Reaction Force. More recently, Jack Straw's constructive contribution to the debate about the future of the EU could also be cited. For example, one could not imagine a member of the present Conservative front bench accepting proposals for an EU constitution, designed to set out the principles underlying this organisation as well as clarifying the division of competencies that exist between its supranational institutions and member states.[54]

However, despite this oratory and these constructive initiatives, it could be argued that the policy of the New Labour essentially represents a continuation of the hesitant, semi-detached approach of the Major government. Or rather, the familiar story of party splits and prevarication continues to remain in evidence on the most important issue facing Whitehall in this policy domain – the Euro. Blair is said to have become increasingly frustrated as Brown uses his stewardship over the five economic tests to frustrate attempts to construct a positive case for membership. At the same time, David Simon, former Minister for Europe and the Department of Trade and Industry has criticised Treasury spending on Euro preparations as 'paltry' compared with the money dispensed to inform businesses about the millennium bug.[55] Finally, it is now being increasingly asserted that Brown is unnecessarily prolonging his assessment of his Euro tests in order to postpone any decision to hold a referendum until after the next election, when he may have replaced Blair as prime minister.[56]

How might we explain this hesitant and somewhat schizophrenic approach? What role does public opinion play in understanding this behaviour? At first glance, it would appear that the trend of policy outlined above goes some way to establishing the relevance of Dicey as an accurate explanation of events. A number of commentators have located the origins of New Labour's uncertainty on the Euro, in public opinion's consistently sceptical stance towards membership.[57] As Evans has argued, throughout the first term, approximately two-thirds of the British electorate felt that Britain should keep the pound.[58] Moreover, this sceptical trend could also be detected among business opinion. In September 2000, a MORI survey discovered that 'hard-line' opposition to the single currency had increased by 23 per cent, whilst support for joining was down 14 per cent.[59]

However, on closer inspection, it could be argued that this prevarication over Euro membership was not solely or even primarily a result of pressure from below. Other factors point to the continuing relevance of elite autonomy and governing considerations in accounting for this non-decision. Perhaps the first point to note is a loss of faith within the Treasury in European solutions to Whitehall's continuing need for an image of governing competence.[60] The origins of this shift in attitude lay in the traumatic experience of 'Black Wednesday'. In response to Britain's ejection from the ERM, Lamont instigated a return to a more 'domestic' economic strategy which set an explicit target range for the rate of inflation and, pledged to use a mixture of monetary, fiscal and exchange rate policies to achieve that target.[61] However, the attraction of this domestic framework seems to have increased in the 1990s. Brown has entrenched this philosophy by granting operational independence to the Bank of England, whilst at the same time, developing a number of fiscal rules to enhance central control over public expenditure.[62] Indeed, it could be argued that these domestic policies have worked too well. The Blair government has presided over an economic record that has been judged very favourably as compared with the performance of the Euro-zone. The major problem facing pro-Euro campaigners at present, is how to justify membership of a single currency against the background of such a record.

This shift in philosophy appears to have been compounded by the Treasury's rather critical judgement of the arrangements governing the conduct of monetary policy in the Euro-zone. A common complaint is that the Stability and Growth Pact, designed at Maastricht to regulate the economic policies of member states, is too narrowly focused on monetary criteria. The Commission neglects to take into account the economic cycle as a whole when judging the budgetary performance of each government. At the same time, it also ignores the importance of public investment in contributing to long-term economic growth. Not surprisingly, these differing viewpoints have produced clashes between London and Brussels. During Labour's first term, Mario Monti, the Competition Commission held up Brown's Venture Capital Funds Scheme, fearing a breach with Single Market rules.[63] More recently, Brown's expansionary budget in 2001 was criticised for forecasting a budget deficit of 1 per cent of GDP by 2004. This figure did not breach the Maastricht criteria and Britain is not even a member of the single currency.[64]

To the extent that ministers have a policy at all on this issue, it adds up to what the media are now calling 'Euro-creep' (an alternative label for 'Europeanisation by stealth' strategy first identified by the Eurosceptics).

It should be stressed that the foundation of this strategy rests on the fact that the case for the single currency has been accepted in principle. There is no constitutional bar to this decision: any divisions that exist are largely about timing. At the same time, the Labour leadership hopes that as the holidaying public becomes increasingly familiar with the Euro, their attitudes will become less sceptical. Opinion will gradually be reformed through the impersonal, incremental yet automatic accretion of personal experience.[65] Behind this strategy is an understanding of opinion which is different, yet ultimately more persuasive than that of the Eurosceptics. Here, pro-Euro campaigners seize on poll findings suggesting that two-thirds of the electorate expect to be using the single currency by 2010.[66] In other words, aligned with present public scepticism is a resignation about the inevitability of Euro membership. If Europeanisation is destined to result in a legitimacy crisis in British politics, this picture suggests such an emergency is a long way off.

Conversely, in today's political climate, an explicit cross-party campaign in favour of the Euro may actually prove counterproductive. At a time when the political class is increasingly held in poor regard, to put it at the head of a coalition trying to 'educate' the public about the benefits of the single currency runs the risk of provoking further cynicism and hostility. It is true that a new cross-party body, 'Britain in Europe', has been set up for such a purpose, but this organisation is more notable for what it hasn't done. More particularly, Britain in Europe has been prevented from developing a specific pro-Euro discourse, finding itself confined to articulating the case for EU membership more generally.[67] At the same time, senior pro-European Conservatives such as Clarke and Heseltine have now (temporarily?) withdrawn their support, believing that Labour was trying to use this organisation to exploit divisions with the Tories.[68] The Treasury has tried to enlist the support of business to front a more limited campaign, but this strategy broke down when the CBI leadership found the issue to be too divisive for its membership.[69] Instead, ministers have been left hoping that a 'blitzkrieg' operation will be enough to rapidly turn around public opinion in any future referendum, as it was in 1975.[70]

Conclusion

We have developed two interlinked arguments in this chapter. First, we started with Dicey's interest in the relationship between collectivist and individualist tendencies in politics. We claim that Dicey's confidence that 'legislation' could and should follow 'opinion' is not generally shared by today's individualists. Whilst in power individualists have sought to insulate increasingly large areas of legislation from immediate democratic 'opinion'. Indeed, this tendency is widespread; it is found right across the political spectrum. In power, Conservative individualists have used 'Europe' as a site 'beyond politics', they have chosen to place significant external constraints on the options available in the domestic democratic political sphere. In doing so, they have gained some greater 'governing autonomy' within that sphere. The striking *absence of engagement* between English (and UK) 'opinion' and the European Union is key here.

Our second argument is that Dicey remains hugely important for understanding British European politics. While his *descriptive model* of the English polity is no longer plausible (if ever it was), Dicey remains important as a *normative template* of the 'legitimate' English (British) polity, at least for self-styled English individualists. His 'ability' to reconcile the changing balance of individualism and collectivism and 'legitimate' legislation with the rising tide of democratic opinion informs, we argue, the English Eurosceptic mentality. In this world-view, the striking success of the Thatcherite strategy of entrenching individualism at the European level, appears as a foolishly naïve failure. Their wistful appeal is to Dicey's 'democracy tempered by snobbishness' as the protector of a distinctively English individualist tradition against foreign traditions of administrative law.

Notes

1 Strictly speaking, one should refer to the European Coal and Steel Community (ECSC) from 1951 to 1957, the ECSC plus the European Economic Community (EEC) and the European Atomic Energy Community (EAEC or Euratom) from 1957 to 1967 and, the European Communities (or Community) from 1967 to 1993. The term 'European Union' became valid only after ratification of the Treaty on European Union at Maastricht. However, for purposes of simplicity, European Union will be used throughout this chapter, even for periods when it is technically incorrect.
2 A. V. Dicey, *Lectures on the Relation between Law and Public Opinion in England in the 19th Century*, Macmillan, London, 1905, p. 57.
3 See J. Buller, 'Britain as an awkward partner: Reassessing Britain's relations with the EU', *Politics*, 15(1), 1995, p. 33, and the follow-up debate in S. George, 'A reply to Buller', 15, 1995, *Politics*, p. 43 and S. Wilks, 'Britain and Europe: An awkward partner or an awkward State?', 16, 1996, *Politics*, p. 159.
4 R. Dehousse, *The European Court of Justice*, Macmillan, London, 1998.
5 J. W. Young, *Britain and European Unity: 1945–92*, Macmillan, London, 1993, p. 31 (hereinafter *Britain and European Unity*).

6 Cited in H. Young, *This Blessed Plot*, Macmillan, London, 1998, p. 64 (hereinafter *This Blessed Plot*).
7 Ibid., p. 92.
8 U. Kitzinger, *Diplomacy and Persuasion*, Thames and Hudson, London, 1973, p. 353.
9 See also J. Spence, 'Movements in the public mood: 1961–75', R. Jowell and G. Hoinville (eds.), *Britain into Europe: Public Opinion and the EEC, 1961–75*, Croom Helm, Beckenham, 1976.
10 See, for example, R. J. Lieber, *British Politics and European Unity*, University of California Press, Berkeley, 1970). pp. 138–42, 144–5; R. Bilski, 'The Common Market and the growing strength of Labour's left-wing', *Government and Opposition*, 12, 1977, p. 306
11 S. Brittan, 'The economic contradictions of democracy', *British Journal of Political Science*, 5, 1975; A. King, 'Overload: Problems of governing in the 1970s', *Political Studies*, 23, 1975.
12 Cmnd. 4715 The United Kingdom and the European Communities, HMSO, 1971.
13 M. Camps, *Britain and the European Community*, Oxford University Press, Oxford, 1963, pp. 274–83; E. Roll, *Crowded Hours*, Faber, London, 1985, p. 103.
14 J. Buller, *National Statecraft and European Integration: the Conservatives and the European Union, 1979–97*, Pinter, London, 2000, Chapter 2 (hereinafter *National Statecraft*).
15 E. Heath, *The Course of My Life*, Coronet, London, 1998, p. 358 (hereinafter *The Course of My Life*).
16 B. Donoughue, 'Harold Wilson and the re-negotiation of the EEC terms of membership, 1974–5: A witness account', in B. Brivati and H. Jones (eds.), *From Reconstruction to Integration: Britain and Europe Since 1945*, Leicester University Press, Leicester, 1993.
17 *The Poisoned Chalice*, BBC2, 16 October, 1995; *Britain and European Unity* p. 116; *The Course of My Life*, pp. 378–85.
18 Lord Beloff, *Britain and the European Union: Dialogue of the Deaf*, Macmillan, London, 1996.
19 D. Gowland and A. Turner, *Reluctant Europeans: Britain and European Integration*, Longman, Harlow, 2000, pp. 198–213.
20 S. George, *An Awkward Partner*, 2nd edition, Oxford University Press, Oxford, 1994, pp. 137–65.
21 J. Palmer, 'Britain and the EEC: The withdrawal option', *International Affairs* 58, 1982, pp. 638–47 (hereinafter 'Britain and the EEC'); J. Rasmussen, '"What kind of a vision is that?" British political attitudes towards the European Community during the Thatcher era', *British Journal of Political Science*, 27, 1997, pp. 111–18.
22 T. Taylor, 'Enough of this EEC socialism', *The Times*, 21 July 1982; see also D. Story and T. Taylor, *The Conservative Party and the Common Market*, Monday Club, London, 1982; D. Wood, 'An anti-EEC political portent', *The Times*; 27 April 1981, 'Britain and the EEC'; *The Times*, 25 March 1982; *The Times*, 11 November 1982, *The Times*, 20 March 1984.
23 For a more in depth discussion, see *National Statecraft*.
24 HMG 'Europe – the Future', *Journal of Common Market Studies*, 23, 1984, p. 73.

25 N. Lawson, *The View From Number Eleven*, Bantam, London, 1992.
26 *Hansard* Commons, vol. 63, 10 July 1984, col. 890; G. Howe, *Conflict of Loyalty*, Macmillan, London, 1994, p. 445; see also, G. Howe, *Conservatism in the Eighties*, Conservative Political Centre, London, 1982; and G. Howe, *The Conservative Revival of Britain*, Conservative Political Centre, London, 1988, p. 5.
27 T. Taylor, *Hansard*, Commons, vol. 63, 10 July 1984, cols. 934–40; see also the speeches of Michael Knowles and Sir Anthony Kershaw.
28 *National Statecraft*, p. 85.
29 *National Statecraft*, pp. 48–87.
30 H. Thompson, *The British Conservative Government and the European Exchange Rate Mechanism*, Pinter, London, 1996, pp. 73–4; J. Grahl, *After Maastricht: A Guide to European Monetary Union*, Lawrence and Wishart, London, 1997, pp. 71–2.
31 D. Gross and N. Thygesen, *European Monetary Integration*, 2nd edition, Longman, Harlow 1998, p. 396.
32 M. J. Baun, 'The Maastricht Treaty as high politics: Germany, France and European integration', *Political Science Quarterly*, 110, 1995–96, pp. 610–12.
33 L. Cram, 'Calling the tune without paying the piper? Social policy regulation: the role of the Commission in European Community social policy', *Policy and Politics*, 21, 1993; L. Cram, *Policy-making in the EU*, Routledge, London, 1997.
34 T. Bale and J. Buller, 'Casting doubt on the new consensus: Conservatives, Labour and the Social Chapter', *Review of Policy Issues* 2, 1996, p. 70 (hereinafter 'Casting Doubt').
35 D. Dinan, *Ever Closer Union?*, Macmillan, London, 1994, p. 299 (hereinafter *Ever Closer Union?*); R. Rice, 'Europe casts a long shadow over British domestic law', *Financial Times*, 3 August 1995 (hereinafter 'Long Shadow').
36 *Ever Closer Union?*, p. 303.
37 'Long Shadow'.
38 *Financial Times*, 1 August 1995.
39 K. Alderman, 'The passage of the European Communities (Finance) Act (1995) and its aftermath', *Parliamentary Affairs*, 10, 1996, pp. 1–20.
40 D. Baker, A. Gamble and S. Ludlam, 'Whips or scorpions? Conservative MPs and the Maastricht paving motion vote', *Parliamentary Affairs*, 46, 1993, pp. 151–66; D. Baker, A. Gamble and S. Ludlam, 'The parliamentary siege of Maastricht, 1993: Conservative divisions and British ratification', *Parliamentary Affairs*, 47, 1994, pp. 37–60; D. Baker, I. Fountain, A. Gamble and S. Ludlam, 'Backbench Conservative attitudes to Europe', *Political Quarterly*, 66, 1995, pp. 221–33; M. Sowemimo, 'The Conservative Party and European integration', *Party Politics*, p. 77–97.
41 J. Bulpitt, 'Conservative leaders and the "Euro-Ratchet": Five doses of scepticism', *Political Quarterly*, 63, 1992, pp. 258–75.
42 M. Thatcher, *The Path To Power*, HarperCollins, London, 1995, pp. 473; 496-7; N. Lamont, *In Office*, Little, Brown, New York, 1999, pp. 124–7 (hereinafter *In Office*); J. Redwood, *The Death of Britain? The UK's Constitutional Crisis*, Macmillan, London, 1999, pp. 30–1.
43 See, for example, Spearing in *Hansard* Commons vol. 201, 19 December, 1991, cols 495–6; Duncan-Smith, cols 354–5; Knapman, cols 395–6.

44 J. H. H. Weiler, 'Journey to an unknown destination: a retrospective and prospective view of the European Court of Justice in the arena of political integration', *Journal of Common Market Studies*, 31, 1993, pp. 417–46.
45 'Casting Doubt', p. 70.
46 for an interesting insight into this tactic, but in a different context, see J. Major, *The Autobiography*, HarperCollins, London, 1999, p. 120.
47 *The Poisoned Chalice*, BBC2 30 May 1996.
48 quoted in A. Seldon, *Major: A Political Life*, Weidenfeld and Nicolson, London, 1997, p. 294.
49 See E. Aeschimann and P. Riche, *La Guerre de Sept Ans*, quoted in the *Sunday Telegraph*, 22 October 1996.
50 See, for example, D. Heathcoat-Amory, 'A single European currency: Why the United Kingdom must say no', *The European Journal*, September 1996; J. Redwood, *Our Currency, Our Country: The Dangers of European Monetary Union*, Penguin, London, 1997; M. Portillo, *Democratic Values and the Currency: Occasional Paper 103*, Institute for Economic Affairs, 1998, pp. 17–18.
51 See, for example, Norman Tebbit in *Hansard* Commons, vol. 201, 18 December, 1991, cols. 326–7.
52 *Hansard* Commons, vol. 201, 18 December 1991, col. 415.
53 D. Henderson, 'Britain and the EU: A fresh start' (1997) 5 May speech to the EC IGC Working Group: http://www.fco.gov.uk/news/speech.asp.
54 J. Straw, 'Speech by the Foreign Secretary Jack Straw at the Hague', 21 February 2002: www.fco.gov.uk/news/speeches.
55 *Financial Times*, 21 November 2001.
56 S. Hall, 'What convergence really means', *Financial Times*, 5 July 2000; P. Stephens, 'A risky way to play it safe', *Financial Times*, 26 May 2000.
57 See, for example, H. Young, 'Ostrich time is over: It's the turn of the EMU', *Financial Times*, 16 September 1997; H. Young, 'Mr Blair speaks French: but has he learned the language of Europe?', *The Guardian*, 19 March 1998; H. Young, 'Blair needn't be afraid of the bully, Sooner or later he will call its bluff', *The Guardian*, 25 June 1998; P. Stephens, 'European muddle', *Financial Times*, 3 April 1998.
58 G. Evans, 'The Conservatives and Europe: waving or drowning?', in A. Park et al. (eds.), *British Social Attitudes: 18th Report*, Sage, London, 2001.
59 *Financial Times*, 26 September 2000.
60 This assertion needs to be qualified somewhat. It is not clear that Treasury officials were ever particularly enthusiastic about the Europeanisation strategy noted above.
61 *In Office*.
62 E. Balls, 'Open macroeconomics in an open economy', *Scottish Journal of Political Economy*, 45, 1998, pp. 113–31; D. Lipsey, *The Secret Treasury*, Viking, New York, 2000; for a critique of this strategy, see M. Portillo, 'Let wise economic counsels prevail', *Financial Times*, 23 May 2000; M. Portillo, 'Rigorous disciplines for hard times', *Financial Times*, 11 December 2000.
63 *Financial Times*, 6 February 2001.
64 *Financial Times*, 13 February 2001; 26 April 2001; 7 May 2001.
65 See, for example, *The Observer*, 25 November, 2001.

66 *Financial Times*, 9 October 2000; see also comments by Lord Marshall, *Financial Times*, 16 September 2000.
67 *Financial Times*, 16 September 2000.
68 *Financial Times*, 25 January 2000.
69 *Financial Times*, 31 January 2000; 28 May 2001.
70 *Financial Times*, 22 May 2000; 27 July 2000.

8
Dicey and the Celtic Nations: A Nightmare Come to Life?

Stephen Livingstone

Introduction

No issue preoccupied Dicey more during his life than the issue of devolution of power from Westminster to Scotland and Ireland (Wales was not considered), especially the question of whether Home Rule should be granted to Ireland. In his biography Cosgrove defends the emphasis on Dicey's engagement with the Irish question as being in accordance with the way Dicey himself apportioned his time, 'defence of the Union counted for more than his scholarly work'.[1] A central issue of British politics for most of his life, questions of the structure of the United Kingdom appeared largely to be settled in the year of his death with the coming into existence of the Irish Free State and Northern Ireland in 1922. For most of the next 70 years, bar the unsuccessful Scottish and Welsh devolution campaign of the early 1970s, and continuing doubts over the future of Northern Ireland from 1969, the issue slipped from prominence in British political debate. Ironically, some attribute this absence of territorial questions from British politics to the rise of collectivism Dicey elsewhere warned against.[2] Labour politicians in particular advocated the need for a strong, centralised, state to deliver universal benefits and public services.[3]

Yet right at the end of the twentieth century the issue reappeared with a vengeance as renewed campaigns successfully brought devolution to Scotland and Wales in 1998. Years of political negotiation with respect to Northern Ireland produced not just devolution, but also a whole new set of relationships with the Irish Republic and the creation of a British-Irish Council which brings together representatives of governments in Northern Ireland, Scotland, Wales and both the United Kingdom and Ireland.[4] Given that many commentators have observed that 'devolution is a process not an event',[5] it seems unlikely to be an issue that will disappear early in the twenty-first century.

In those Home Rule debates between 1886 and 1914 Dicey maintained a Unionist position, most extensively set out in his first work on the topic. *England's Case against Home Rule*.[6] However, unlike contemporary unionism, which tends to be advocated from *within* Scotland, Wales and especially Northern Ireland as to why these nations should remain within the United Kingdom, Dicey made clear that his concern was with the deleterious impact that Home Rule would have on England and on the structure of the United Kingdom as a whole. In his work on Ireland he did express the view that Home Rule would be bad for the Irish, especially Unionist supporters, largely because of a patronising doubt that the Irish would be able to ensure enforcement of the rule of law.[7] However, this was not his main concern and indeed he was quite prepared to consider separation of Ireland from Britain as a far better outcome for the United Kingdom as a whole than granting devolved powers to Ireland. This at least would allow the United Kingdom constitution to remain in force as it was for the remaining nations within that constitutional unit. Home Rule proposals, on the other hand, posed a significant threat to that constitutional order.

> The abolition of the House of Lords, the dis-establishment of the Church, the abolition of the monarchy, might leave the English constitution far less essentially changed than would the adoption of federalism even in that apparently moderate form in which it was presented by Mr Butt to the consideration of the English public.[8]

Many of Dicey's concerns as to the dangers of Home Rule for England now seem outdated and irrelevant, notably his concerns as to the dangers it posed for the survival of the empire, the military security of the United Kingdom and its economic prosperity. The empire has gone, an Ireland independent for 80 years has never offered itself as a base for hostile powers and the economic value of Scotland or Northern Ireland to England is probably less than it was in 1900. Moreover, devolution now occurs within the context of membership of the European Union, which already has removed power from Westminster and which in turn would independently impose constraints on the conduct of any devolved administrations, even if these were not also reflected in devolution legislation.[9]

However, some of Dicey's observations retain a contemporary value, especially as he focused less on the impact of devolution on the devolved nations themselves than on its implications for the constitution of the United Kingdom as a whole. Many commentators have observed that in the period leading up to the legislation of 1998 devolution was seen as a matter essentially *for* those living in Scotland, Wales and Northern Ireland. It was not viewed as matter for the United Kingdom as a whole and especially not as a matter that greatly concerned those living in England. Hence much less attention was given as to how to deal with the relationships between the new devolved institutions and those at the 'centre'. In particular little thought was given to what this 'centre' was and whether what were now effectively English institutions could double as 'national' institutions. Although these uncertainties have given rise to relatively few practical difficulties thus far, given a number of problems for the devolved administrations and the fact that the governments in London, Edinburgh and Cardiff are all drawn from the same political party, the potential is clearly there.[10] Dicey was alert to some of these problems and posed questions about whether such a new form of United Kingdom state could hold together which still seek contemporary answers. In this paper, after reviewing the form that the devolution arrangement has taken, I will seek to explore two of these. The first concerns whether the boost that devolution gives to expressions of Scottish, Welsh, Irish and perhaps eventually English identity requires a counterbalancing development of United Kingdom identity if the state is not to tear itself apart from within. The second looks at the arrangements, which have been put in place to deal with any conflicts between the centre and the devolved polities. In the end it may be the legitimacy of such arrangements and the way in which they operate which may decide whether Dicey's fears that home rule would be the beginning of the end for the United Kingdom are to come to pass.

The nature of the devolution arrangements

If Home Rule were to occur, Dicey foresaw a number of ways in which this might occur, none of which he professed himself happy with. The more acceptable was to give Ireland the status of a self-governing colony similar to Canada or Australia. This would leave the sovereignty of the United Kingdom Parliament untouched, but raised problems with regard to Irish representation in Westminster (the colonial model would suggest this should come to an end) and taxes (the model suggested Ireland would keep its own taxes but would lose the right to share in revenue raised in the rest of the United Kingdom and might indeed have to contribute towards reserved services). Neither, however, was likely to be satisfactory to Ireland as it would then have no influence over its defence and foreign policy, while also suffering a loss of income and vulnerability to tariff barriers. Gladstone wrestled, largely unsuccessfully, with both these problems in the various Home Rule Bills of the nineteenth century.[11] The more radical alternative was to move towards a federal United Kingdom. However, this posed significant problems of practicality (since England in size and resources would dominate the federation) as well as posing a clear threat to one of Dicey's central constitutional principles, the sovereignty of Parliament. In a properly federal system Parliament could not be sovereign, since the constitutional arrangements which allocated different powers to the different national territories would also delineate the scope of the Westminster Parliament's competence and hence take priority over it. Some other body, 'whether it be named Crown, Council or Court', would have to decide whether Parliament had acted within its powers or not.[12]

As it turned out, neither of these models was to be followed precisely, either in the case of Northern Ireland 1922–72, or in the devolution arrangements of 1998. Those arrangements though have resembled the self governing colony model more than the federal model. The approach taken to Northern Ireland devolution in 1922 has largely been followed in the late 1990s, though with significant modifications as regards the internal arrangements for constructing the legislative and executive bodies. In each case Westminster has devolved certain powers to the regional legislatures (in the case of Wales restricting these to secondary legislation) while reserving significant competence to itself as a national legislature. In theory, therefore, the sovereignty of Parliament is preserved as Westminster can at any time regain these powers and abolish the regional legislature, indeed it did so in respect of Northern Ireland in 1972. However, the nineteenth century colonial model was not followed through as regards taxation and representation. Apart from the Scottish Parliament's power to raise income tax by 3 per cent, devolution left the pre-existing financial arrangements unchanged. The devolved governments are funded by a block grant from central government, which is related to an estimate of their needs rather than the revenue they raise, much as the Scottish, Welsh and Northern Irish Offices were prior to devolution.[13] Nor did devolution lead to an immediate change in Scottish, Welsh and Northern Irish representation at Westminster, though a review of Scottish boundaries is currently taking place with a view of reducing the number of Scottish MPs.

Whereas the internal arrangements for the Northern Irish Parliament of 1922 largely mirrored Westminster (the party winning the most seats at an election had the exclusive right to form a government), with what are generally acknowledged to ultimately disastrous results,[14] the devolution arrangements of the 1990s provided for significant differences. In both Scotland and Wales the introduction of the Alternative Vote system dramatically reduced the chances of any one party winning an overall majority and has led to coalition governments in each jurisdiction. In Northern Ireland even more complex arrangements have been designed to ensure that all the major political parties have a share in executive power. While such arrangements have generally been welcomed as encouraging a more cooperative style of politics, they have also reduced the chance of any strongly nationalist political party gaining power in a devolved territory and using this to advance a claim for independence. This was clearly a fear of Dicey's and one of the reasons why he argued that Home Rule would not produce peace between England and Ireland. His fears that a strong nationalist party would be emboldened by the acquisition of some power and would use this rally support for even greater authority remain a concern for those anxious to preserve the Union. However, the way in which Scottish and Welsh devolution has been arranged reduces the chances that one political party alone will be able to achieve this. As to whether, in addition to this dramatic increase in local political representatives, devolution should also mean a reduction in representation at the national Parliament, Westminster largely ducked the issue and left representation unchanged, subject to the alterations for Scotland discussed earlier. Hence the anomaly remains that while English MPs may not vote on matters only affecting Scotland, MPs from north of the border remain entitled to vote on legislation which will only be implemented in England. However, the 'West Lothian question' did not give rise to any major problems in the devolution debates. It may be that, given the government's huge majorities in 1997 in all parts of Great Britain, few of the predominantly Labour Parliament perceived that there were likely to be many significant differences between English, Scottish and Welsh MPs when it came to issue of relevance only to England. While Northern Irish MPs did not belong to the governing party, they were perhaps seen as too few in number to be likely to have a significant influence.

On the surface, therefore, devolution has been achieved with a minimum of constitutional fuss. Indeed external observers have commented on how much even the reforming Labour administration of 1997 stressed the continuity of the new constitutional arrangements to as great or an even greater extent than the elements of change.[15] Dicey's fears that devolution would mean the end of parliamentary sovereignty appear to have gone unrealised as the new devolution arrangements have been smoothly fitted into the overall framework of Diceyian British constitutional principles. However, there are reasons to believe that all may not be as simple as it appears and that the form of the devolution arrangements has merely postponed rather than solved certain questions. These questions may reappear with a vengeance if a subsequent election were to produce significantly governments in different parts of the United Kingdom, a Conservative government in London, an SNP/Liberal Democrat coalition in Edinburgh and a Labour/Plaid Cymru coalition in Cardiff, for example. The first issue this might raise is whether Westminster could repeal the devolution statutes by a simple majority of all MPs. While in orthodox constitutional theory this remains possible, and as we have seen was actually done in the case of Northern Ireland in 1972, many commentators now believe that the holding of referendums prior to the enactment of the Scotland Act 1998 and Government of Wales Act 1998, has in effect limited Westminster's freedom without seeking further approval via another referendum. In Northern Ireland the position is even more complex as the devolution settlement is approved by a referendum and an international treaty between the United Kingdom and Ireland.

Even if Westminster were to stop short of repealing devolution or altering devolution legislation to significantly curb the powers of the devolved institutions there remains the risk of substantial conflict between governments of a different ideological complexion. A Conservative government in London may, for example, wish to aggressively pursue a privatisation policy that is strongly resisted in Edinburgh. Anxious to be able to convince foreign investors of business-friendly climate throughout the United Kingdom, Downing Street may then seek to use its financial or legal resources to pressurise the Scottish Executive into adopting a less hostile position. Such conflicts between central and regional government are the daily diet of most federal systems. Yet in these systems, as Dicey observed, constitutional arrangements have been agreed at the outset of the federation to resolve them within the framework of the federal union. In the United Kingdom, as we shall explore in more detail later in this chapter, the arrangements for dealing with such conflicts are few, lack formality and leave the ultimate power of decision with what are essentially English institutions. Looking forward to Irish Home Rule in a nineteenth-century Irish context, where he perceived a strong desire for greater independence from England, Dicey expressed concern as to whether Irish politicians and the Irish public would accept the resolution of disputes between England and

Ireland by essentially English institutions. Yet to reconfigure those institutions to introduce an element of parity would have a significant impact on the United Kingdom constitution as a whole. Arguably the devolution arrangements of the 1990s sought to provide for conflict resolution mechanisms essentially bolted onto existing institutions and processes. Whether this will be enough to deal with conflicts without endangering the legitimacy of such institutions remains to be seen.

Another way in which devolution may lead to a more significant rethink of current constitutional arrangements relates to issues of constitutional identification and symbolism. Prior to devolution there was little need to indicate, at least on a domestic rather than international level, what it meant to be a government or citizen of the United Kingdom. In respect to legal issues the role of the Crown covered a multitude of sins. Yet if devolution does, as many have suggested, lead to a greater identification of people with their 'national' institutions and civic space, there may be a need to delineate more sharply what is left over on a United Kingdom level.[16] This may be even more significant in England where, apart from the local government level, no clear distinction exists between institutions designed to deal with English issues and those designed to deal with United Kingdom issues. Once again, Dicey expressed a concern that the informal character of the United Kingdom constitution, its reliance on the concept of the rule of law to ensure the equality of citizens and the accountability of the state, might be sorely tested in the context of Home Rule. This might require a more formal statement of the nature, role and powers of the United Kingdom government and the meaning of United Kingdom citizenship. In most federal states a written constitution plays an important role in achieving this but once again the arrangements of the 1990s sought to achieve the decentralisation of power without this level of constitutional innovation. While not perhaps in the end as problematic as issues relating to the resolution of disputes, this issue of a failure to take seriously the issues of political identification on a micro- as well as a macro-level may pose problems for the outworking of the devolution settlement. It is to this, which we now turn.

Devolution and the issue of identity

Writing in respect of Ireland, Dicey expressed a clear concern that the introduction of federalism into the British constitution might lead to a transfer of citizens' loyalties and a consequent decline in allegiance to the United Kingdom. This, in turn, might itself endanger commitment to the maintenance of the union:

> National allegiance and local allegiance divide and perplex the feelings even of loyal citizens. Unless the national sentiment predominate, the federation will go to pieces at any of those crises when the interests or wishes of any of the States conflict with the interest or wishes of the Union.[17]

As with all of Dicey's arguments in respect of Home Rule, he noted this was not a matter of concern for those Irish or Scottish nationalists who did see Home Rule as a stepping stone to independence and who therefore welcomed the growth of Irish or Scottish, as opposed to 'British' identity. However, for those who espoused the cause of maintaining the Union yet favoured devolution he posed the question of whether creating political institutions which could become the primary focus of loyalty for people in Scotland, Wales or Ireland would inevitably dilute loyalty to the United Kingdom as a whole and further polarise any disputes which arose between the centre and the periphery.

This fear appears to be borne out by the early experience of devolution of power to Northern Ireland since the 1998 peace agreement. Issues of symbolism have bedevilled the establishment of new institutions such as the Assembly and the new police service.[18] Unionists have argued strongly that the symbols of such institutions should reflect the 'British' character of Northern Ireland, that the Union flag should be flown over government departments, for example. Nationalists have countered by stressing that the new arrangements at least dilute the exclusively British character of Northern Ireland, at most recognise its dual identity as British and Irish and hence that either both British and Irish flags or none should be flown. In the end compromises have largely been reached, in part through the intervention of the UK government, but the deeper issue remains unresolved. Although at its most intense in Northern Ireland, where a substantial section of the population wish to leave the United Kingdom and identify politically with another state, an aspiration which the Agreement recognises as valid when pursued through peaceful means, the issue is not one confined to there. Opinion polls in Scotland and, to a lesser extent, Wales have shown that people increasingly identify themselves as more Scottish or Welsh than British.[19] If political allegiances and commitment are increasingly to focus on the devolved institutions is there not the risk that these will eventually become the sole focus of political identity for those living outside England, draining the Union of the commitment which might sustain it. This potential development poses a challenge to those anxious to sustain the Union. The challenge is to find a way of sustaining and renewing identification with the United Kingdom as a whole as opposed to the constituent elements of it, to provide reasons for people in Scotland, Wales and Northern Ireland to continue to engage with the institutions of the Union as opposed to seeking to bypass or reject them. I would suggest that there are two ways in which such a development might take place. The first is to pursue a cultural focus and to seek to stress common notions of 'Britishness' throughout the different territories, which make up the United Kingdom. The second is to take a more institutional route and to develop the concept of citizenship of the United Kingdom. Neither need, or indeed is likely, to be pursued alone. Neither is without its problems.

The cultural route would be to stress the common elements of British identity, how people in England, Scotland, Wales and Northern Ireland share an overlapping history, language and literature. It would note the contributions of people from Scotland, Wales and Northern Ireland to the development of political, economic and cultural life throughout the United Kingdom.[20] It would point to common British cultural institutions, such as the BBC, which have been able to accommodate regional diversity while retaining an overall British character. Above all it might point to a history of movement of peoples between different parts of the United Kingdom for work or education, the relative absence of barriers to this movement and the consequent development of shared ideas and experiences.

Important and valid though this account is, the difficulty for efforts to develop a shared British identity alongside particular Scottish, Irish or Welsh identity is that it remains difficult to disentangle from an essentially conservative and backward looking vision of Britishness. Memories of empire are usually never too far away when discussions of the nature of Britishness take place and these maintain the association of Britain with imperialism, authoritarianism and ultimately racism. Recent controversy over whether and what recent immigrants to the United Kingdom should do to establish their 'Britishness' have only revived concerns that Britishness is ultimately a somewhat exclusive and narrow form of identity.[21] While efforts to distill the nature of 'Scottishness' or 'Welshness' may also ultimately produce a rather exclusive form of identity, which Scottish and Welsh Asians or Africans may find it difficult to relate to, at least the enterprise starts off without the negative historical baggage associated with Britishness. Above all there is the difficulty of disentangling Britishness from 'Englishness' especially as most of those from England, as opposed to Scotland, Wales or Ireland, do not generally recognise that there is a difference.[22] Even efforts to 'rebrand' Britishness as a more modern and forward looking identity, such as the 'Cool Britannia' fashion of the late 1990s, in the end seem to derive most of their images from England (especially London) and have difficulty incorporating other parts of the United Kingdom.[23] Moreover ideas of British identity must now compete with notions of 'European' or even 'global' identity, especially through the mass media, which people in Scotland, Wales or Ireland may now see themselves in terms of, then an exclusive national identity seems too provincial and there is a desire to identify with something bigger and more cosmopolitan. While even more amorphous than concepts of Britishness such European or global identity does appear more forward-looking and pluralistic.

Leaving aside issues of how a renewed sense of Britishness might be conveyed to people throughout the United Kingdom (through schools, the media?), and the dangers of backlash if this was perceived to be imposed in a top-down way, it is clearly problematic as to whether a cultural identification with Britishness alone can provide the glue which will keep the United Kingdom together. An alternative is to focus more on shared political institutions and the political concept of citizenship. Such an approach is familiar to people who live in federal systems, where their national citizenship gives them rights and duties over and above those they may enjoy as someone resident in a particular state or province. This may include certain rights, whether to political freedom or welfare entitlements, which exist at a national level and which strong national institutions will enforce when local polities threaten or deny them. The experience of the civil rights movement in the United States in the 1960s, which appealed to federal constitutional standards and federal institutions against the resistance of state authorities to grant equal rights to all citizens, readily springs to mind. Citizenship also grants political rights to participate effectively in larger political institutions, which may be able to address problems, such as those of defence or foreign policy, which are beyond the capacity of state or regional institutions. In the United Kingdom context the guaranteeing of certain individual rights by a United Kingdom government and institutions against restriction by regional authorities and the opportunity to participate effectively in UK-wide political institutions which address common problems, could be one way of reasserting the importance of the union for people living in the devolved territories.

If it is to be so, though, there is a considerable amount of work to be done at the United Kingdom level. Only recently, and shortly before the devolution legislation was introduced, did the United Kingdom develop a set of fundamental rights which it guaranteed to protect to all those within the territory. Even that provision, the Human Rights Act 1998, is a fairly limited charter of rights and the concept of what it means to be a citizen remains underdeveloped at a United Kingdom level.[24] There is little sense even of what nationally approved United Kingdom symbols are, as the Ulster Unionists discussed earlier have found to their frustration when seeking to assert their rights as 'British citizens'. Moreover, even those rights guarantees which are now legally established arguably find better protection in the devolved territories. Unlike Westminster, the Northern Irish and Scottish legislatures are prohibited from passing legislation inconsistent with the rights guaranteed in the Human Rights Act and in Northern Ireland the Human Rights Commission has been empowered by the Northern Ireland Act to consider the need for additional rights to be reflected in a specific Bill of Rights. Governments in Wales, Scotland and Northern Ireland have all declared their commitment to advance greater equality and social inclusion, suggesting that they see a need to develop a thicker concept of citizenship that that which is currently available on a United Kingdom level.

Moreover the continued opportunity to participate in larger, United Kingdom-wide institutions, such as Parliament, may also come to be seen as being of limited value. Just as nation states come to be seen as too big for the small political problems of the world so they have come to seem too small for the big ones.[25] Even national institutions may seem inadequate to deal with problems like the environment, transport or economic management. Instead people living in Scotland, Wales or Northern Ireland may feel that their need is to participate in European institutions more effectively. At the very least they may seek changes in how they are represented in the United Kingdom Parliament in order to have influence over those decisions taken at national level, for example, with regard to defence and foreign policy, which can impact on their own experience. This could involve something like reform of the second chamber of the legislature to ensure that greater recognition is given to the different geographical interests throughout the United Kingdom. However so far, in its moves beyond the removal of hereditary peers, the government has shown little interest in further reform of the House of Lords that might address these types of concerns. Again the suspicion remains that the type of constitutional reforms which are necessary to make the 'United Kingdom' aspects of the devolution arrangements attractive to all of its citizens go further than government is currently prepared to contemplate.

Overall, therefore, it remains doubtful as to whether Dicey's concerns that devolution would mean a diminution of identification with the United Kingdom can be assuaged. However, this does not necessarily mean that the break up of the United Kingdom is therefore preordained. From the start the unification of the United Kingdom, unlike that of Germany or Italy, for example, was more the product of political bargaining than of a desire to bring together a common people in one nation. Concerns about military security and access to markets played at least as significant a role as ideas of a shared identity. While some of these concerns may have been overtaken by events there remains a sense that most of the United Kingdom's citizens retain an instrumental attitude towards it and will be reluctant to bring the Union to an end unless it proves significantly disadvantageous to them and any alternatives appear both practical and beneficial. Northern Ireland, where nationalists do still cherish the desire to unite the Irish people in one country, remains an exception. What might change the position for people in Scotland and Wales is if they found their newly won autonomy being circumscribed by *diktat* from London. In other words, if significant conflict arose as to what was within the sphere of authority of the devolved institutions as opposed to being retained by Westminster and Whitehall. This brings us to the issue of how the devolution settlement to date envisages conflicts and puts in place mechanisms to resolve them. To this I now turn.

Resolving devolution conflicts

The possibility of conflict between the centre and the regions is built into any federal or quasi-federal system. Since such systems are invariably the result of compromise tensions may remain unresolved. Both the centre and the regions may subsequently seek to enlarge the scope of their power and authority, pushing the legal and political understandings, which underpin the system to its limits. In well managed federal systems this is a healthy tension and facilitates ongoing review of the effectiveness and legitimacy of the federal arrangements. However, there is always the risk that if the conflicts are not well managed they may precipitate the drive for secession. As has been seen earlier in this chapter the United Kingdom, even after 1998, is not a federation. Power is not divided between the centre and the regions but rather is devolved from Westminster to Scotland, Wales and Northern Ireland. In theory Westminster can at any time have it back or can legislate to resolve any conflict which has arisen.[26] However, if devolution is to have any real meaning this must remain a power of last resort. Too frequent use of the legislative power to override the decisions of devolved authorities or to circumscribe their competence will undermine their autonomy and almost certainly lead to disillusion with the devolution arrangements. Hence there is a need to find other ways of managing conflicts within the devolved conflict, ways which do not simply allow the centre to dictate the result but rather offer the devolved territories a fair opportunity to state their case and to prevail if they are acting within the confines of the devolution settlement.

Where are such conflicts likely to arise? The most obvious area is in relation to policy divergence, where a devolved administration pursues a different policy than that followed by the central government. In theory devolution is supposed to provide for this happening and arguably would be of limited value if it did not happen. Where it does occur, however, central government may find it inconvenient and may be tempted to force convergence. This may be because the actions of the devolved government contradict a UK-wide policy commitment or embarrass the United Kingdom government at the international level. If a Welsh National Assembly were, for example, to provide funding and a home for international NGOs hostile to US policy in the Middle East, or a Northern Irish executive to indicate that it would vigorously campaign against homosexuality (except where limited by human rights law), then the United Kingdom government might come under international pressure to intervene. Central government might also be concerned that the actions of a devolved administration would interfere with the execution of policy in areas reserved to it. Issues of nationality and immigration, for example, are among matters reserved to the United Kingdom parliament. However, while only the UK may decide who is admitted or granted asylum, issues relating to the provision of education and welfare services for asylum-seekers comes within the sphere of devolved powers. If Scottish or Welsh administrations were to take a policy decision to provide a very low or high level of such services to asylum-seekers, then the UK government might take the view that its asylum policy was being undermined.

A second area of potential conflict concerns policy in relation to Europe. The existence of the European Union has been an inspiration to nationalists throughout the United Kingdom. Noting how small nations such as Ireland have prospered through membership of the European Community and especially through European financial support, Scottish and Welsh nationalists have argued that independence within a European context should avert the risks of insularity and penury that some fear will be the consequence of separating from the United Kingdom. While this may overlook the fact that European financial resources are more likely to be needed in the east than the west over the next few decades, it is an idea which resonates powerfully with those seeking greater autonomy for different parts of the United Kingdom, especially as the European Union itself has sought to develop better relations with regions within the nation states which make up the Union. Even those within devolved administrations who do not favour separation have an interest in direct access to European institutions, especially as regards the distribution of European structural funds, which are allocated on a regional basis. However, foreign and EU relations remain within the sphere of powers reserved to Westminster, to be dealt with by UK government ministers and officials. Hence there is the risk that interests of the UK and regional governments might diverge with respect to Europe. For example, the UK government, concerned by the potential financial cost of expansion to the east, may seek to reduce support available under structural funds or the Common Agricultural Policy. However administrations in Scotland, Wales and Northern Ireland may be very happy to see these sustained or even increased.

A third area where there exists significant potential for conflict is in relation to finance. Ever since the ultimately unsuccessful devolution Bills of the late 1970s, budgets for administrations of different parts of the United Kingdom have been set under the 'Barnett Formula', named after the then Chief Secretary to the Treasury. This provides, essentially, that changes in the total level of spending available in Northern Ireland, Scotland and Wales are based on changes in the spending in England in 'comparable departments' through a formula related to the population of each of the different parts of the United Kingdom. Prior to devolution these budgets were then allocated as a total sum to the respective Secretaries of State, who then retained a discretion as to how to allocate resources *within* the territory, though constrained by UK wide commitments in certain areas, such as social security or public sector pay. Devolution essentially left this situation unchanged.[27] Issues as to what responsibility the devolved administration would have for raising taxes and contributing to the United Kingdom budget, which so exercised both Gladstone and Dicey, were therefore bypassed. The experience of Northern Ireland's devolved government in the 1920s, which began with an obligation to make an 'imperial contribution' which it soon found impossible to meet, seems to have contributed to a decision to reduce the devolved authorities scope for financial autonomy. Only the Scottish Parliament was granted, limited tax-raising powers and none of the devolved administrations was given significant powers to borrow money.[28] Hence while the devolved governments have discretion as to how they spend the cake available to them, they have little control over the size of this cake which may expand or contract depending on decisions of the central government. Against this limited financial autonomy however, may be set the fact hat most observers are of the opinion that the Barnett formula is relatively generous to Scotland, Wales and Northern Ireland since the needs assessment on which it is based is now over twenty years old. Arguably each of them have grown in the intervening period more quickly than the UK average and certainly more quickly than parts of England. Devolution may, therefore, give rise to two tensions relating to finance. The first concerns efforts by devolved governments to increase spending in a particular area, such as health or education, beyond the UK average. This may put the budget under strain and lead to pressure from the Treasury to reduce expenditure, in turn leading to claims that central government is inhibiting the policy autonomy of the devolved administrations. The second concerns potential demands from within England for a review of the Barnett formula, as it becomes increasingly transparent, and the transfer of greater resources to English regions.[29]

Overall, therefore, the devolution arrangements contain significant potential for conflict between the centre and the regions. The mechanisms for dealing with them have been characterised by a high level of informality and pragmatism characteristic of the British constitution. Rather than a written constitution there are a series of 'Concordats' to regulate the relationship between the devolved governments and the United Kingdom authorities. The principal agreement is the Memorandum of Understanding,[30] a multilateral agreement that sets out the basic principles to regulate relationships between the different governments of the United Kingdom. Below this there are a set of overarching supplementary concordats to seek to establish uniform arrangements in areas of government where coordination is thought to be especially desirable and a much larger series of bilateral concordats between the UK government departments and their territorial equivalents. One of the overarching concordats concerns co-ordination of EU policy issues, that emphasises respect for the particular interests of the devolved territories (including representation as part of the UK delegation at the Council of Ministers), but also the need always for a consistent UK line to be maintained in relations with the EU and for confidentiality as regards information shared. Overall, the concordats seek to find administrative means to prevent disputes arising and seek to bind the devolved governments into the policy of the United Kingdom government through a reliance of the former on the latter for information, which is shared but on the basis of confidentiality and an expectation of cooperation. Concordats stress continuity over change and have been described by as 'a reworking of the informal character of the British Constitution'.[31] Rawlings observes that 'whereas to the lawyer concordats appear low in the hierarchy of rules governing administration, the civil servant naturally sees things differently'.[32]

The main aim of concordats is obviously to prevent disputes arising, through seeking to produce cooperation and agreement in advance. However even this will not always succeed and there is also a need to provide means of resolving disputes once they have arisen. In some federations, this task is performed by a constitutional court. In others the court may share this role with some form of constitutional council. In the United Kingdom while a role for the courts exists, of which more later, a more significant body is the Joint Ministerial Council (JMC). Composed of Ministers of the UK government and ministers or Cabinet members of the devolved administrations the functions of the JMC, as described by the Memorandum of Agreement, are 'consultative' rather than 'executive'. It is described as reaching 'agreements' rather than 'decisions' in the expectation of cooperation by the devolved governments but without formally binding them. The JMC has no statutory basis and indeed its existence was disclosed to Parliament only in response to a request for inter-parliamentary liaison.[33] It meets in plenary at twice a year and on other occasions when called by either the UK government or by one of the devolved administrations.[34] Its composition may change depending on the issues under discussion but a UK minister always chairs it and the Cabinet Office is usually assigned the lead role in any administrative arrangements to take forward its discussions. From the start commentators have observed that the JMC arrangements appear designed to ensure that the centre retains control of inter-governmental relationships and that the likelihood of devolved administrations taking a different policy line is diminished.

As noted above though there does remain a role for the courts if efforts to resolve disputes informally have failed. The Scotland Act,

Northern Ireland Act and the Government of Wales Act provide for the reference of disputes as to the competence of the devolved legislatures and executives to the Judicial Committee of the Privy Council (JCPC) by the relevant law officers.[35] In addition, lower courts throughout the United Kingdom may refer devolution issues which have arisen in the course of proceedings before them to the JCPC or they can reach there by way of appeal from lower court decisions. The use of the JCPC as the final judicial authority to resolve devolution disputes reflects again the similarity of the devolution scheme to arrangements for dealing with the United Kingdom's relationships to its self-governing colonies. For many years it was the final court of appeal for questions relating to the interpretation of colonial constitutions and indeed it still performs this function for a small and diminishing number of Commonwealth countries.

How have these arrangements worked so far? In truth they have hardly been put to the test. The early years of devolution have been marked by a remarkable degree of policy convergence between Westminster and the devolved territories. There have been a few high-profile initiatives in Scotland, notably around tuition fees for higher education, banning of hunting and long-term care for the elderly, but these do not appear to have strayed too far from what was deemed acceptable in Whitehall nor, as yet, have they had significant financial consequences. Indeed all the devolved administrations have been more preoccupied with internal disputes in their first four years, including replacement of the First Secretary of the Welsh Assembly,[36] two changes in the First Minister of the Scottish Executive and the on-off establishment of the Northern Irish Executive. Establishing their authority and legitimacy with their own populations has absorbed more of the energies of the devolved administrations than flexing their muscles vis-à-vis London. At least in part because of this the centre remains very much in charge of intergovernmental relations. Indeed the formal elements of these have declined in use, with the JMC only meeting in plenary format once and even 'functional' committees of the JMC meeting fairly infrequently.[37] More work appears to have been transferred to meetings between officials who, with the exception of the Northern Ireland Civil Service, all remain part of a unified United Kingdom civil service. Scotland, Wales and Northern Ireland have all opened separate offices in Europe and ministers from the devolved administrations have attended Council of Ministers meetings, but always as part of the UK delegation and following an UK Foreign Office line. Westminster has been able to pass legislation for Scotland with little rancour to date.[38]

Few devolution cases, all from Scotland, have come before the courts and even these have concerned compatability with human rights requirements rather than the division of powers between Westminster and the devolved territories. In these the Privy Council has pursued a fairly conservative approach, rejecting challenges to decisions of the Scottish Executive and, in one case, legislation of the Scottish Parliament.[39]

Such harmony is no doubt due in large part to the fact that one political party is in power in London, Cardiff and Edinburgh, while such are the divisions between the parties in power in Belfast it is likely to be some time before they present a united front in dealing with Westminster. Although the replacement of Alun Michael by Rhodri Morgan as First Minister in Wales demonstrates that the national UK Labour Party cannot directly dictate to Labour administrations in the devolved territories, or at least cannot be seen to be doing so directly, it remains true that conflicts between the devolved governments and the centre can be managed though informal Labour Party channels. The involvement of Scottish members of the UK cabinet in power struggles within the Scottish Executive[40] also demonstrates the continuing ways in which devolution politics are integrated into United Kingdom political developments. Even with all this party induced concord however, there are straws in the wind of potential conflicts ahead. The Barnett formula is likely to come under increasing scrutiny, with MPs for Northern English constituencies already beginning to raise questions as to whether it remains a fair method for allocating resources.[41] The Scottish Executive signed the 'Flanders Declaration' of 2001, designed to secure a voice at the 2004 European Inter-governmental Conference (IGC) with a view to improving the position of 'constitutional regions' within Europe and it may well be that Wales and Northern Ireland will also prove more anxious to assert their autonomy within Europe over the next few years. How more likely is it that such tensions would sharpen with changes in government, either at Westminster or in the devolved territories. The next Scottish and Welsh elections in 2003 could see nationalists in power (presumably in some form of coalition) and a future UK general election could see the Conservative party returned to power through a recovery of its strength in England, though a similar revival in Scotland and Wales seems unlikely.

In such circumstances the essentially informal structures for managing conflicts between the centre and the devolved territories might come under much greater strain. The JMC and similar arrangements might prove unable to resolve disputes and it may be that the courts are called into action more frequently. Here another of Dicey's concerns surfaces.

The Home Rule scheme of 1886 also left it to the Privy Council to adjudicate on any conflicts resolving the powers of the English and Irish Parliaments. Yet Dicey wondered whether the decisions of what essentially remained an English institution would be accepted in Ireland. Although the Privy Council might hold Irish legislation to beyond the competence of the Irish Parliament he wondered if would be able to find people in Ireland to enforce its judgements.[42] Similar concerns may arise if the Judicial Committee of the Privy Council were to be frequently called into action to resolve disputes as to the scope of the devolved territories power. Although the make-up of the Privy Council in Scottish devolution cases thus far has always included two Scottish judges and there is the capacity to include a Northern Irish judge in cases from Northern Ireland (the position is less clear regarding Wales due to the absence of a separate Welsh legal system) it remains essentially an English court. Little thought was given at the time of the devolution statutes to the issue of whether these new arrangements required a new constitutional court to have the final word in deciding upon them.[43] If devolution disputes increase this question may be raised with growing intensity.

Conclusion

Dicey's central concern regarding Home Rule was that, far from reducing tension between England and Ireland, it would merely inflame it to the mutual disadvantage of both. Though he preferred maintenance of the status quo he felt that ending of the Union might be a better way forward than the introduction of a Home Rule regime which he felt was only likely to extend and prolong the agony. The initial years of devolution in the early twenty-first century have scarcely borne out fears that reducing the power of Westminster would increase disruption and discord. Instead, as has been observed earlier in this chapter, commentators have commented as much on continuity as change and how smoothly everything seems to have gone. Territorial issues no longer command the high standing they occupied in British politics in the mid 1990s. However, it has also been noted that devolution remains in its infancy and that the coincidence of one political party being in power throughout the United Kingdom may have resulted in certain tensions being merely masked rather than resolved.[44] As the devolution arrangements develop some of Dicey's concerns may resurface. In particular, it has been noted the devolution may further erode an already weak and contested sense of what it means to be 'British' and increase the need for union to be defended on instrumental and practical grounds as opposed to a shared sense of identity. This in turn will put under greater stress the essentially informal mechanisms for resolving disputes between different parts of the United Kingdom, an informalism which relies to a large extent on a sense of shared concerns and purposes.

How might this challenge be faced? One approach would be to take further the notion that the United Kingdom is evolving into a fully federal state and to facilitate this through a written constitution that would address the formal relationships.[45] However, this might raise many questions which the United Kingdom government is currently unwilling to address. These would include the status and role of the monarchy, representation for the devolved territories in Parliament, the need for a constitutional court and the status of the English regions.[46] Above all it might raise questions regarding the relationship to any new European Constitution, whether it involves entrenching partition in Ireland and whether such a federation is possible given that England would remain overwhelmingly the dominant partner. An alternative is to seek to build on the United Kingdom's character as a 'Union State' brought about by voluntary agreement of peoples who nevertheless wished to retain separate cultures and institutions.[47] One might then seek to make use of institutions which permit the continuance of formal dialogue of the different nations as to what is required to maintain and develop the union in contemporary circumstances. The British-Irish Council, established under the Belfast Agreement but largely moribund since, is one such institution. European institutions could also play a role in developing such a constitutional pluralism that seeks to recognise difference in the British Isles, but also acknowledges areas where acting jointly is to the benefit of all. In sum while Dicey's fears of devolution have as yet proved groundless, he did raise some significant questions as to how it should be realised. Over a hundred years later they are still searching for answers.

Notes

1 R. Cosgrove, *The Rule of Law: Albert Venn Dicey, Victorian Jurist*, Macmillan, London, 1980, p. xiii.
2 Notably in *Lectures on the Relation between Law and Public Opinion in England during the 19th Century*, Macmillan, London, 1905.
3 See V. Bogdanor, *Devolution in the United Kingdom*, Oxford University Press, Oxford, 1999, pp. 166–70 for discussion of the opposition of Labour politicians, many of them from Scotland and Wales, to any form of devolution lest it dilute collective wage bargaining and universal public service delivery.
4 Plus representatives of the Isle of Man and the Channel Islands.

214 Stephen Livingstone

5 See, for example, R. Hazell, 'The shape of things to come: What will the UK Constitution look like in the early 21st century', in R. Hazell (ed.), *Constitutional Futures: A History of the Next Ten Years*, Oxford University Press, Oxford, 1999, pp. 7, 8, quoting former Welsh Secretary Ron Davies.
6 A. V. Dicey, *England's Case Against Home Rule*, John Murray, London, 1886 (hereinafter *England's Case*).
7 See *England's Case* at p. 259.
8 See *England's Case* at p. 168.
9 For example, section 29(2)(d) of the Scotland Act 1998 prohibits the Scottish Parliament from passing legislation incompatible with Convention rights or Community law. A similar provision exists in the Northern Ireland Act 1998.
10 See R. Hazell, 'Introduction', in R. Hazell (ed.), *The State and the Nation: The First Year of Devolution in the United Kingdom*, Imprint Academic, 2000, p. 1.
11 See Bogdanor, n.3, pp. 29–42.
12 *England's Case*, p. 172.
13 For a discussion of the financial arrangements, see R. Hazell and R. Cornes, 'Financial devolution: The centre retains control', in Hazell (ed.), *Constitutional Futures*, Oxford University Press, Oxford, 1999, p. 196.
14 See C. McCrudden, 'Northern Ireland' in D. Oliver and J. Jowell (eds.), *The Changing Constitution*, 3rd edition, Oxford University Press, Oxford, 1994.
15 See, for example, B. Selway, 'The Constitution of the United Kingdom: A long distance perspective', *Common Law World Review*, 30, 2001, 3; S. O'Connor, 'Altered states: federalism and devolution at the "Real" turn of the millennium', *Cambridge LJ*, 60, 2001, p. 493.
16 On the role of devolution in leading to local elites identifying more with regional rather than United Kingdom institutions, see M. Evans, 'The new constitutionalism and the impact of spill-over', *Public Policy and Administration*, 15, 2000, p. 5.
17 Dicey, *England's Case*, p. 179.
18 See, generally, R. Wilford and R. Wilson, 'A bare-knuckle ride: Northern Ireland', in Hazell (ed.), p. 79.
19 See J. Curtice, 'Hopes dashed and fears assuaged? What the public makes of it so far', in A. Tench (ed.), *The State of the Nations 2001: The Second Year of Devolution in the United Kingdom*, Imprint Academic, 2001, pp. 236–40.
20 Beginning from the early years of the Union, when Irish and Scottish politicians played an important role in the development of Westminster parliamentary politics, see L. Colley, *Britons: Forging the Nation 1707–1837*, Yale University Press, New Haven, 1992.
21 See Y. Alibhai-Brown, *True Colours: Public Attitudes to Multiculturalism and the Role of the Government*, Institute of Public Policy Research, 1999.
22 See D. Miller, *Citizenship and National Identity*, Polity, Cambridge, 2000, p. 137.
23 For one example, see M. Leonard, *Britain, TM: Renewing our Identity*, Demos, London, 1997.
24 See A. Dummett, 'Citizenship and national identity', in R. Hazell (ed.), *Constitutional Futures*, Oxford University Press, Oxford, 1999, p. 213.
25 See, generally, D. Held, *Democracy and the Global Order*, Polity, Cambridge, 1995.
26 For example, section 28(7) of the Scotland Act 1998 provides that the Act does not affect the power of the United Kingdom Parliament to make laws for Scotland.

27 See R. Hazell and R. Cornes, 'Financing devolution: The centre retains control', in R. Hazell (ed.), *Constitutional Futures*, Oxford University Press, Oxford, 1999, p. 196.
28 Bogdanor (1999, p. 239) calculates that it would only allow the Scottish Parliament to raise £450 million extra as against a total Scottish budget of £14.6 billion.
29 In the early stages of the London Mayoral election Ken Livingstone argued that £2 billion of Scotland's money should be diverted to London, see Bogdanor n.3 at p. 248.
30 Cm 4444 (1999), subsequently revised and reissued Cm 4806 (2000).
31 R. Rawlings, 'Concordats of the Constitution', *Law Quarterly Review*, 116, 2000, pp. 257, 279.
32 Ibid., at p. 280.
33 'Federalism by stealth', *The Economist*, 24 October 1998, p. 40.
34 Hazell notes that in the first year of devolution all meetings were called by the UK government, see R. Hazell, 'Inter-governmental relations: Whitehall rules OK?' in Hazell (ed.) 2000, p. 150.
35 In Wales the Assembly itself exercises this function. For a discussion of devolution issues and their adjudication see N. Burrows, *Devolution*, Sweet and Maxwell, London, 2000, Chapter 6.
36 Subsequently styled First Minister.
37 See A. Tench, 'Inter-governmental relations a year on: Whitehall still rules OK?', in A. Tench (ed.), *The State of the Nations 2001*, pp. 153, 154–5.
38 See R. Masterman and R. Hazell 'Devolution and Westminster', in ibid., pp. 197, 203.
39 See A. O'Neill, 'Judicial politics and the Judicial Committee: The devolution jurisprudence of the Privy Council', *Modern Law Review*, 64, 2001; B. Winetrobe, 'Scottish devolved legislation and the courts', *Public Law*, 31, 2002.
40 See J. Mitchell, 'Scotland: maturing devolution', in A. Tench (ed.), pp. 45, 53–4.
41 See D. Bell and A. Christie, 'Finance – The Barnett Formula: Nobody's child', in ibid., p. 135.
42 Dicey, *England's Case*, at p. 259.
43 See A. Le Seur, 'What future for the Judicial Committee of the Privy Council', Constitution Unit, 2001.
44 See, further, J. Pierre and G. Stoker, 'Towards multi-level governance', in P. Duleavy, A. Gamble, I. Holliday and G. Peele (eds.), *Developments in British Politics 6*, Macmillan, London, 2000, pp. 29, 39–44.
45 On the prospects for this, see R. Brazier, 'How near is a written Constitution?', *Northern Ireland Legal Quarterly*, 52, 2001, p. 1.
46 Which so far have have not been as vocal in pushing for new institutions as some predicted at the time of initial devolution to Scotland and Wales.
47 See N. Walker, 'Beyond the unitary conception of the United Kingdom Constitution', *Public Law*, 2000, 384, N. MacCormick, *Questioning Sovereignty: Law, State and Nation in the European Commonwealth*, Oxford University Press, Oxford, 1999, Chapter 12, and more generally J. Tully, *Strange Multiplicity: Constitutionalism in an Age of Diversity*, Cambridge University Press, Cambridge, 1995.

Index

Abortion Bill, 93
Adam Smith Institute, 22
America (USA), 1–2, 49–51 *passim*,
 154, 172, 180, 203, 206
An Foras Teanga, 121
Anglocentrism, 165–6
Army Bureau of Current Affairs
 (ABCA), 19
Auld, J, 95–6

Bagehot, W., 165
Balfour, A. J., 21
Balladur, E., 180
Balliol College, Oxford, 1
Barnett Formula, 207–8
Beer, Samuel, 37, 40
Bell, Daniel, 36
Benelux Countries, 168
Benn, Tony, 174
Bentham, Jeremy, 9–10
Berlin Wall, 28, 180
Beveridge, William, 5
 Report, 20
Blair, Tony, 23, 26, 46–7, 186–7
Blunkett, David, 47–8
Bogdanor, Vernon, 40, 42
Boyce, D. G., 9–11
Brains Trust, 18
British Broadcasting Company
 (BBC), 202
British Empire, 24, 27
British–Irish Council, 213
British National Party, 157
Brogan, D. W., 15
 Weil Lectures (1959), 15
Brown, G., 186–7
Brown, Louise, 84
Burke, Edmund, 11, 34
Butler, R. A., 20
Butt, I., 195

Callaghan, James, 74
Campbell, Sir Colin, xii–xiv, 6

Carrington, B., 146
Cash, Bill, 184
Cashmore, E., 143
Catholic Church, 120, 123–4
Centre for Citizenship Studies in
 Education, 154
Chamberlain, Joseph, 10
Chernobyl disaster, 90
Church of England, 110, 195
Churchill, Winston, 19
Citizenship Foundation, 154
Clarke, Ken, 184, 188
Cockett, Richard, 22
Cockfield, Lord, 177
Cofnod, 117
Cole, G. D. H., 17–18
Collectivism, 5, 9, 32 *passim*, 188–9
Collini, Stefan, 4
Comhdhail Naisiunta Na Gaeilge,
 124–6, 128
Common Agricultural Policy, 170,
 174, 207
Commonwealth Immigration Act
 (1962), 27, 44, 144
Commonwealth Trade, 170
Confederation of British Industry
 (CBI), 188
Conservative Party, 37–8, 43, 175–6
 Heath Government, 173–4
 Major Government, 25, 42, 44–5,
  181–2, 184–6
 Thatcher Government, 22, 25,
  42–5, 175–9 *passim*, 179,
  181–2, 189
Cosgrove, R., 194
Costa v *Enel*, 169
Court of Appeal, 63–4, 94, 133–4
Court of Equity, 60–1
Crawford Committee, 112
Cromwell, Oliver, 19
Cymdeithas yr Iaith, 111, 119
Cymru Fydd, 110
Cymuned, 119

218 *Index*

Delors, J., 181
Denning, Lord, 63–4, 70–1
Department of Education in Northern Ireland (DENI), 123
Department of Education and Science (DES), 145–6
Department of Industry, 174
Deregulation, 42
Devolution, 3, 24–6, 113–15, 130–1, 194–213 *passim*
Dicey, Albert Venn, 1–5 *passim*, 9–13 *passim*, 32–41 *passim*, 44–53 *passim*, 59–61 *passim*, 70, 77, 84–5, 109, 141–2, 165–71 *passim*, 176–7, 188, 194–200 *passim*, 205, 211–13 *passim*
Dickens, Charles, 10
Dickinson, Lowes, 17
Disability Discrimination Act (1996), 39
Divorce Reform Act (1969), 65
Donor Insemination (DI), 91, 94
Duke, C., 158
Dunbar, Robert, 136
Dunleavy, Patrick, 43

Economic Affairs, Institute of, 22
Education Act (1944), 20–1, 142, 150
Education, multicultural, 145–59 *passim*
Education Reform Acts (1986, 1988), 112–13, 150–1, 156
Edwardian period, 12
Edwards, Janet, 154
Eekelaar, J., 76–7
Eisteddfodau, 114
Elsdon, K., 158
English Law Commission 75
European Central Bank, 167, 180
European Charter for Regional or Minority Languages, 120–2, 129
European Coal and Steel Community, 169
European Common Market, 4, 169–70, 172–3
European Community Language Policies, 118

European Convention on Human Rights, 118, 130
European Economic Community, 3, 5
European Finance Bill (1995), 182
European Union, 25–7, 47, 93–5, 100, 157, 170–6 *passim*, 186, 189, 195, 206–9, 213
  Courts of Justice, 167–9, 179, 181, 183
  Economic and Monetary Union, 177–85 *passim*, 187
  Human Rights Commission, 24
  Single Market, 177–9, 181, 184
  Social Chapter, 183–4
European Volunteer Workers Scheme, 27
Evans, G., 118
Evans, Gwynfor, 112

Fabian Society, 17
Factorame Case, 181
First World War, 16–17, 19
Flanders Declaration (2001), 211
Fogelman, Ken, 154
Foras na Gaeilge, 121
Foresight Programme, 47
Forster, E. M., 17
FORUM, 150
France, 2, 9, 13, 167–8, 180–1
Francovitch and Boniface v *Italy*, 182
Freedom of Information Act, 24, 130

G8, 157
Gaelic revival, 124–5, 129, 134
Gaelscioleanna, 127
Gaitskell, H., 174
Gallie, Ernest, 35
Gamble, Andrew, 46
Gaulle, General de, 167, 172
Germany (Federal Republic), 13, 15, 28, 180, 205
  Turkish *gastarbeiter*, 27
Gill, Chris, 185
Ginsberg, Morris, 1, 5, 32–3, 35–6, 142
Gissing v *Gissing*, 62–3
Gladstone, W. E., 197, 208
Glass, D. V., 142
Glendon, M. A., 70

Gollancz, Victor, 18
Good Friday Agreement, 120, 122, 132
Government of Wales Act (1998), 113, 115, 130, 199, 210
Graham, C., 42
Gramsci, Antonio, 18
Grierson, John, 19

Habermas, Jürgen, 104
Hale, B., 74
Hammersmith Hospital, 89
Hannah, J., 158
Hansard, 117
Hargreaves, Ken, 88
Harvard Law School, 1
Haydon, Graham, 152
Hayek, Friedrich von, 22, 44
Heath, Edward, 173–4
Henderson, Doug, 186
Heseltine, M., 188
Hindley, R., 127
HM Inspectors, 13
Hobbes, Thomas, 11
Hobhouse, L. T., 12
Hobsbawm, E. J., 36
Hoffman, Lord, 67
Honeyford Affair, 151
Howe, G., 177–8, 182
Hughes Parry, Sir David, 111
Human Fertilisation and Embryology Act (HFEA) (1990), 89, 91, 93, 98, 100–1
Human Rights Act (1998), 3, 24, 93, 129–30, 204
Hume, David, 11
Huxley, Aldous, 99

Immigration, 23, 26–8, 44, 143–59 *passim*
Immigration Advisory Council, 145
In vitro fertilisation (IVF), 84, 88–9, 93
Individual Learning Accounts, 157
Individualism, 9, 32–53 *passim*, 167, 177, 188–9
Inland Revenue Commissioners, 1
International Monetary Fund, 40
Ireland, Northern, 4, 14, 26, 109–10, 144, 154, 205
Assembly, 24, 109, 120–1, 123, 131, 134, 194, 197, 199, 201–4, 206, 209, 212
Law Reform Advisory Committee, 72–5
Ireland, Republic of (Eire), 26, 109–10, 123, 194, 207
Constitution (1937), 124
Irish Home Rule, 4–5, 26, 194–7 *passim*, 200–1, 212
Italy, 15, 168, 205

Japan, 15
Jenkins, Roy, 145, 175
Jigso, 119
Joseph, Sir Keith, 5, 111
Joseph Rowntree Foundation, 48

Kahn-Freund, Otto, 36, 75
Keynes, John Maynard, 5, 20, 22, 38
King, David, 98
Kinnock, Neil, 178
Kohl, H., 181

Labour Party, 22, 34, 38, 49, 170, 175, 178, 211
Attlee Government, 12, 169
Clause 4, 46
New Labour, 20, 22–3, 26, 28, 45–9 *passim*, 52, 184–8 *passim*, 198
Wilson Government, 48, 173
Laissez faire, 9, 15, 28, 34, 36–7
Lamont, N., 187
Lane, Allen, 19
Law Commission, 74–5
Report, 70–1
Lawrence, Stephen, 150
Lawson, N., 177–8, 182
League of Nations, 17
Left Book Club, 18–19, 22
Lewis, J., 74
Lewis, Saunders, 100
Liberal Democratic Party, 199
Liberal Government (1885), 10
LIFE, 88
Lloyd, Dennis, 14
Lloyd George, David, 26
Local Government Act (1966), 146, 156

Locke, John, 11
London Women's Clinic, 94
Lukes, Stephen, 152
Lynch, J, 154

Maastricht Treaty, 182–3, 185, 187
Mackay, Lord, 92–3
Macmillan, H., 169, 172–4
MacNeil, Eoin, 125
Maine, Sir Henry, 4
Major, John, 22, 25, 42, 44, 182, 184, 186
Malach, A., 158
Mannheim, Herman, 12–13, 141
Mansbridge, Alfred, 17
Married Woman's Property Act (1882), 60, 63
Marshall, Alfred, 17
Marshall, T. H., 10, 21
Martineau, Harriet, 10
Marxist view of the state, 14, 18
Masterson Case, 100
Matrimonial and Family Proceedings Act (1884), 67
Matrimonial Causes Act (1973), 65
Matrimonial Proceedings and Property Act (1970), 65–7
McIlroy, J., 157–8
Meek Report, 12
Mentrau iaith, 114
Merchant Shipping Act (1988), 181
Metropolitan Police Service, 150
Michael, Alun, 211
Mill, John Stuart, 10–11
Ministry of Reconstruction, 17, 20
Modood, T., 154
Monti, Mario, 187
Moran, Michael, 44
Morgan, Rhodri, 211
Morrison, Herbert, 169
Mudiad Ysgolion Meithrin, 112, 114
Mullard, C., 145

Nash, Adam, 101
National Assessment Programme, 112
National Centre for Social Research, 76
National Council of Labour Colleges (NCLC), 18
National Curriculum, 13, 28–9, 112, 114, 150–1, 153–4
National Economic Development Council, 38
National Health Service, 42, 93, 95, 143, 159
National Institute for Clinical Excellence (NICE), 95
National Union of Mineworkers, 174
Nationality Act (1948), 143
Neave, M., 73
New Deal for Communities, 157
Nicholls, Lord, 68–70
Norfolk, Duke of, 98
Northern Ireland Act (1998), 132, 204, 210
Northern Ireland Law Reform Advisory Committee, 72–5 *passim*

Oakeshott, M., 12, 16
Official Languages (Equality) Bill (2002), 127–8
Ó'Gadhra, N., 125
OPEC, 175
Organisation for Economic Co-operation and Development, 157
O'Riagain, R., 126, 128
Ormrod, LJ, 67–8
Orwell, George, 19

Paine, Tom, 11
Parliament, British, 2–3 *passim*, 12, 15, 24, 28, 32–3, 62–4, 88–9, 92–3, 130–2, 165–6, 170, 173, 176, 181, 183, 186, 194, 196–213 *passim*
Peel, Sir Robert, 11
Penguin Books, 19
Perez, Laura, 182
Pettitt v *Pettitt*, 62
Phillips, Glynn, 153
Piglowski v *Piglowski*, 67
Plaid Genedlaethol Cymru, 110–11, 199
Plaza Agreement (1986), 180
Plebs' League, 18
Powell, Enoch, 5, 12, 88
Pre-implantation Genetic Diagnosis (PGD), 85, 97–103 *passim*
Presbyterian Church, 129

Preston v *Preston*, 68
Privatisation, 42–4 *passim*
Progress Educational Trust, 89
Prosser, T., 42

Race Relations Acts (1965, 1968), 144
Race Relations Act (1976), 39, 142, 144, 156
Race Relations Amendment Act (2001), 130
Radio Wales, 112
Rampton, Anthony, 148
Rawlings, R., 131, 209
Rawls, John, 23
Rentoul, John, 44–5
Representation of the People Act (1949), 12
Rex, J., 145
Ridley, N., 182
Roberts, Ben, 12, 36
Roddick, W., 133
Roper, John, 173
Rose, Jonathan, 18
Rousseau, J. J., 35
Rowe, John, 154
Runnymede Trust, 149
Rushdie Affair, 151
Ruskin College, Oxford, 18
Russell Report, 12
Russia, 15, 19

Schiemann, J., 93
School Governor Training, 151
Schools Curriculum and Amendment Authority (SCAA), 153
Schuman, R., 169
Scotland, 109, 154
   Act of Union (1707), 25
   Home Rule, 24–6, 194–201 *passim*, 202–6 *passim* 212
   National Parliament, 24–5, 109, 131, 134, 209–11 *passim*
Scotland Act (1998), 129, 199, 209–10
Scottish National Party, 199
Scruton, Roger, 28
Second World War, 12, 18–19
Sewill, Brendan, 173
Sex Discrimination Act (1975), 39, 74
Seymour-Smith, Nicole, 182

Sheffield Area Health Authority, 95–6
Shelley, Mary, 99
Sherlock, A, 131, 133
Sianel Pedwar Cymru (SC4), 112
Simon, David, 186
Social Exclusion Unit, 48
Social Science Research Council, 48
Socialism, 9–10, 28, 45, 166
Society for the Protection of the Unborn Child (SPUC), 88
Spanish Civil War, 19
Stagflation, 40
Strategy for the Welsh Language (1999), 114
Straw, Jack, 186
Stuart, M., 158
Swann Report, 147–50, 156

T na G, 127
Tan y Llyn Episode, 110
Tate, Nick, 153
Tawney, R. H., 5, 12, 17, 20, 36
Taylor, A. J. P., 24
Tebbitt, Norman, 154
Teilifis na Gaeilge, 121–2, 127
Tha Boord O Leid, 121–2, 135
Thatcher, Margaret, 12, 22, 41–3, 44–5, 52, 176, 178–9, 181–2, 189
Third Way agenda, 22, 28, 46, 48
Thompson, E. P., 5
Times, The 19, 91
Titmuss, R., 36
Tomlinson, J., 145
Toryism, Old, 9
Treaty of Rome (1957), 169–70, 172, 174, 177
Troyna, B., 146

Udaras na Gaellachta, 127
Ulster, 26
Ulster Scots, 120–3
Ulster Unionists, 204
Unborn Children (Protection) Bill (1985), 88
Undeb Cenedlaethol Athrawon Cymru, 112
UNESCO, 157
Union of Democratic Control (UDC), 16–17

University for Industry, 157
Urdd Gobaith Cymru, 110, 114

Valentine, Lewis, 110
Van Genden Loos (1963), 169
Vinerian Professor of Law, Oxford, 1

Wachtel v *Wachtel*, 71
Wales, 24–5, 109–10, 154
  Act of Union (1536), 111
  Administrative Court, 133–4
  Home Rule, 24–6, 194–8 *passim*, 201–6 *passim*
  National Assembly, 24–5, 109, 113–19 *passim*, 131–4 *passim*, 206–12 *passim*
  Owain Glyndwr, 25
Wales Commercial Law Association, 134
Wales Public Law and Human Rights Association, 134
Warnock Committee, 88
  Report, 88
Watson, Michael, 129
Weatherill, Bernard, 28
Wednesbury, Judicial Review, 95–6
Welsh Courts Act, 110–11
Welsh Development Agency, 119
Welsh Language Act (1993), 113–15, 117
Welsh Language Board, 133–9 *passim*, 135
Welsh Language Society, 111
Welsh Personal Injuries Lawyers Association, 134
White v *White*, 68–9, 72
Williams, Bernard, 153
Williams, C. H., 118, 133
Williams, David, 130–3 *passim*
Williams, D. J., 110
Williams, Raymond, 5, 12, 24
Williamson, P. J., 139
Willmott, L., 74
Wilshire, David, 91
Wilson, Harold, 48, 173–4
Winstanley, Gerrard, 11
Winston, Professor Robert, 89
Withnall, A., 158
Workers' Educational Association (WEA), 17–18
World Trade Center bombing (2001), 49–50 *passim*

Yeaxlees, Rev. Basil, 17
Youdan, T. G., 62–3
Young, Iris Marion, 87

Zuckerman, A. A. S., 75